The Lunatic Lover

The Lunatic Lover

*And Other Plays by French Women
of the 17th and 18th Centuries*

Edited by Perry Gethner

HEINEMANN
Portsmouth, NH

Heinemann
A division of Reed Elsevier Inc.
361 Hanover Street   Portsmouth, NH 03801–3912
Offices and agents throughout the world

Acquisitions Editor: Lisa Barnett
Production Editor: Renée M. Pinard
Text Designer: Tom Allen/Pear Graphic Design
Cover Designer: Julie Hahn

Library of Congress Cataloging-in-Publication Data
The lunatic lover : And other plays by French women of the 17th & 18th
centuries / edited by Perry Gethner.
        p.   cm.
    Includes bibliographical references.
    ISBN 0-435-08637-5
    1. French drama—Women Authors. 2. French drama—17th century.
3. French drama—18th century. 4. Women—Drama. I. Gethner,
Perry.
PQ1215.L86   1994
842'.40809287—dc20   93-47317
                                                                              CIP

Printed in the United States of America on acid-free paper.
99 98 97 96 95 94 EB 1 2 3 4 5 6

CONTENTS

ACKNOWLEDGMENTS

I would like to thank the many colleagues and friends who read the manuscript in its early stages and provided useful comments and suggestions, especially Paul Epstein, John Howland, Helga Harriman, Jeanne Wray, Florence and Emmett Pybus, and Anne Labow. I also wish to thank the many colleagues who encouraged me to persevere during the long gestation of this project, especially Gabrielle Verdier, Henriette Goldwyn, Tilde Sankovitch, Bruce Morrissette, and Marie-Odile Sweetser. Most of all, I wish to express gratitude to Deb Dillow, Candy Bailey, Fadi Joueidi, Loah Bennett, and Fran Mihura, for their invaluable assistance in preparing the manuscript. Finally, I wish to thank the Dean of the College of Arts and Sciences at Oklahoma State University for a Dean's Incentive Grant that helped fund the early stages of my research.

INTRODUCTION

The present anthology aims to make available to the modern reader six examples of the best work by French women playwrights of the seventeenth and eighteenth centuries. Few people are even aware that women engaged in such activity in that period, yet it was precisely that period when they first achieved serious recognition. The works have long since gone out of print; the last previous edition of any of these plays was in 1821. Moreover, only one was ever translated into English, and that occurred in 1752. Thus, this volume should help fill a major gap in the history of French women writers and shed some new light on our knowledge of French drama of the classical period. In the interests of keeping the anthology from becoming overly long, I have limited myself to six works, although there are a number of other plays which I would consider worthy of being reedited. I have preceded each play with a biographical sketch of the author, a statement of the play's significance, a performance history, and, where appropriate, a discussion of the sources. Additional explanatory notes are placed at the end of the volume.[1]

The Plays and Their Authors

The six plays included in this anthology display the high quality that women playwrights were able to achieve, as well as showing the diversity of their output. There is hardly a type of drama which they did not cultivate during the period from 1650 to 1750, and the present collection, consisting of a farce, a comedy-ballet, a tragicomedy, two tragedies, and a melodrama, does not exhaust the variety. More importantly, all six of the plays reprinted here possess genuine literary merit, and all are sufficiently stageworthy to be candidates for revival by student groups today (although several plays would require judicious cutting). Even if one objects that none of them is a forgotten masterpiece, worthy of being ranked with the works of France's greatest classical playwrights, Corneille, Racine, and Molière, this is hardly a damaging admission. How many plays by other men deserve that exalted status?

In addition to the fact that these six plays make enjoyable reading, there are valid historical reasons for presenting them to the twentieth-century reader. Only a handful of scholars seem to be aware that there were women producing plays in the sixteenth, seventeenth, and eighteenth centuries, and that, despite the obstacles, the more gifted of them got their works publicly performed and sometimes managed to win high praise for their efforts. What this demonstrates is that the most prestigious branch of French literature, at the height of its glory, was actively cultivated by women, whose work was viewed as comparable to that of male writers. Even more surprisingly, the archives of the Comédie-Française reveal that in the period from 1680 to 1900, France's leading theatrical company rarely went for more than a decade without a play by a woman in its repertoire.[2] It is also significant that plays by Bernard and Graffigny were included in eighteenth-century anthologies of French drama, on an equal footing with the works of male writers.

The six authors included here are most likely representative of women playwrights of the period. Although we possess no specific information about their education, they all managed to acquire enough general literary background to present their works to a cultivated audience. Two of the women, La Roche-Guilhen and Bernard, came from Protestant families, where it seems that parents were more inclined to give their daughters a solid base of instruction at home. The fact that Pascal, Desjardins, La Roche-Guilhen, and Bernard all began their literary activity by age twenty-five suggests that they had received an early exposure to letters. Their families were either from the lower ranks of the nobility (La Roche-Guilhen and Graffigny) or from well-connected bourgeois circles (Pascal, Desjardins, Bernard). Four of them never married; those who did were productive either before their marriages (Desjardins) or after (Graffigny), but not during. None of them had children in the house during the period of their literary careers. Perhaps the most significant link between their biographies is that all six of them apparently wrote as a way of earning their livings but found that drama inevitably proved to be an inadequate source of income. Pascal turned to religious poetry for her livelihood, while all the others tried their hands at fiction. At least four of them achieved considerable success with their novels, judging from such indications as the number of reeditions and translations; in the case of both Desjardins and La Roche-Guilhen, unscrupulous editors took advantage of their celebrity by falsely attributing to them the work of other writers. All of them published under their own names; in fact, not one of the women playwrights during this period tried to hide her identity behind a male pen name.

It is probably not a coincidence that the four playwrights who had full-length works staged in Paris received guidance from well-known male mentors. Of course, the practice was neither new nor limited to women. By the middle of the century it was not uncommon for established playwrights to take aspiring young men under their wings. For example, Pierre Corneille sponsored Edme Boursault (who later became the mentor of Marie-Anne Barbier); La Grange-Chancel (to whose work Barbier devoted a critical essay) was a protégé of Jean Racine. Rarely, if ever, were male writers criticized for soliciting help or for receiving guidance from an older master. In the case of women writers, not only was male assistance of this nature singled out for condemnation; detractors did not hesitate to fabricate charges of plagiarism or ghost writing that everyone at the time knew to be false. All six of the women playwrights represented here found their literary reputations attacked at some point in their careers. Nevertheless, although such slanders and condemnations must have been terribly painful, the women writers did garner very substantial public recognition in their own time. Catherine Bernard, to cite but one example, won several prestigious poetry competitions and was elected to membership in an Italian literary academy. The gazettes of the period tended to be supportive of women writers and printed favorable notices about many of their works. Even if some early historians of French drama, such as the brothers Parfaict, found no merit whatsoever in the plays of the women included here, there were others, including Joseph Laporte, who waxed rhapsodic in their praise. And it is ironically appropriate that in at least one case a well-established woman playwright (Graffigny) took aspiring male writers under her wing.

In addition, the memory of these female writers did not vanish upon their deaths. Leaving aside the special problem of works first published posthumously, five of our authors had works reprinted after their deaths. Moreover, in the case of the most esteemed women (Desjardins and Graffigny), editions of their collected works appeared as late as six decades afterward.

The issue of women playwrights turning to literary mentors for guidance relates to the larger matter of literary taste. In a school of drama where both writers and audiences accepted a rigid set of rules as binding and where everyone was familiar with the plays of the great masters, there was necessarily a double expectation from new plays: they had to conform to the demands of the tradition, and at the same time they had to offer something fresh that would entertain the public. Even though most critics during the period would have been shocked by the notion that literary taste changes over time, those with a more practical approach to the theatre (actors and playwrights) must have realized that changes, however slight, were really occurring. Women who earned their living by writing had to be especially sensitive to popular taste, since their financial success depended on giving audiences what they wanted. The literary mentor could provide encouragement and ensure that the play conformed to the official rules. Still, when it came to breathing new life into the traditional molds and gauging the audience's desires, each individual playwright was on her own.

Thus, among the authors in the current anthology, we find limited, but significant, novelties in genre and thematic material. Pascal was among the first professional writers to rehabilitate the one-act farce; Desjardins contributed to the development of a more sophisticated type of comedy set at court; La Roche-Guilhen attempted to transplant the French comedy-ballet into England; Graffigny helped create the *drame* as an intermediate genre between tragedy and comedy. Bernard and Barbier, working within the prescribed limits of French tragedy, aimed to introduce more acceptable models of female heroism.

Yet, despite their concern for innovation, the playwrights were extremely cautious about airing what we would call feminist ideas. Their dissatisfaction with the role of women in society and with a host of male prejudices against the "weaker" sex will occasionally surface in their prose, including the prefaces to their plays, but only in rare instances are those concerns made explicit in the plays themselves. French audiences would not tolerate too radical a departure from conventional views in the theatre, as they showed most notably in their hostile reaction to Marie-Anne Du Boccage's tragedy *Les Amazones* (1749). Even though only one of the three Amazon leaders argues for the superiority of the female sex and for the continued exclusion of males from their midst, critics and spectators condemned the play, and even cast members tried to sabotage it. While one can sometimes detect hints of the authors' personal views between the lines, it is undeniable that freedom of expression (for both sexes) was far more restricted in drama than in other literary forms.

Why did the major breakthrough of women playwrights occur in the seventeenth century? The codification of an officially recognized dramatic theory was undeniably a factor in making the composition of plays more accessible to women. By spelling out the dramaturgical rules and aesthetic principles of theatre in easy-to-read French, as opposed to erudite Latin treatises, and by claiming that the rules themselves were derivable from common sense, and not merely from Aristotle or Horace, the theorists were making it easier for people without formal education to appreciate French plays and to discuss them intelligently. The official endorsement of the view that the French possessed a special and superior school of dramatists gradually produced a reevaluation of the relative merits of French drama versus the Greek and Latin, with the modern French writers deemed more worthy of study and imitation by aspiring young authors. This development, needless to say, culminated in the celebrated Quarrel of the Ancients and the Moderns, and it is hardly a coincidence that the champions of the Modern cause (Perrault, Fontenelle, Donneau de Visé) were also strong supporters of women's ability as intellectuals and of specific women writers. In addition, the Moderns felt that women had made a positive contribution to French letters as a whole by insisting on a higher level of refinement and delicacy, both in style and content, the lack of which could be viewed as a blemish in writers of antiquity.

The emergence of the salons as a focal point of intellectual life in the capital plays an equally significant role in the formation of women playwrights.[3] Not only did the salon constitute a kind of free university by allowing informal contact between women and male writers, helping the former to fill in gaps in their education, but it also directly involved women in the production of literary works. They listened to readings of works in progress, noted the comments of learned male acquaintances, were asked their opinions, and were sometimes instrumental in getting new plays accepted for performance and in ensuring their successes (which could include participation in cabals organized either to applaud or to hiss a play). In certain cases, members of a salon would put pressure upon a gifted but reticent lady to take up her pen, as was the case with Graffigny. The admission of women to predominantly male literary societies, both in Italy and in France, provided additional legitimacy and prestige to their activity. Even the French Academy, which delayed admitting women until the 1970's, made women eligible to enter its poetry competitions by the end of the seventeenth century.

Arguably the most important factor was the sense, shared by French intellectuals of all varieties, that France had a unique and valuable literary patrimony, and that adding to the collection of national literary treasures was practically a patriotic duty. By the beginning of the eighteenth century virtually all writers, both male and female, were convinced that France was the cultural capital of Europe and reigned supreme in the sphere of drama. Serious women writers believed themselves to be an integral part of the tradition and felt they had the right to cultivate the same genres and themes as their male counterparts. Despite the prejudice which they encountered and which they occasionally dared to denounce, they must have felt reasonably confident that their efforts could gain proper recognition.

While the factors just mentioned help to explain why women writers turned their attention to the stage, there were also socio-economic considerations at work. An influx of women, especially single women, needed to support themselves and were finding it increasingly possible to do so by writing. (The same would apply, for example, to women painters, who also became more numerous and more recognized in the eighteenth century.) While the theatre was not an especially lucrative area of literary activity, it could provide name recognition almost overnight and, in the case of a critical success, confer enormous prestige. In almost every case, the solution to financial worries lay in novels, rather than plays, but getting a play staged could be the first step toward a profitable literary career. We should also consider the larger questions of the increasing power exerted by the middle class, with a concomitant effect on literary taste; of the greater difficulties women faced in trying to enter the labor force in the sixteenth and seventeenth centuries; and of the greater concern with women's education (although the establishment of schools for girls was very slow in coming), but a detailed discussion is not possible within the scope of this introduction.

In the final analysis, the story we have sketched here is more than a little-known historical curiosity. It shows that women succeeded in making their presence felt in the most highly esteemed branch of literary activity, and that the male establishment was forced to take them seriously, to read and comment on their work, and to include them in theoretical treatises, histories of drama, and anthologies. The emergence of women playwrights in the seventeenth and eighteenth centuries can justifiably be called one of the early successes in the gradual process of emancipation.

Note on the Texts and Translations

For three of the plays there is only one previous edition. In these cases I have followed the text of that edition, correcting the obvious errors. In fact, two of the authors (Bernard and La Roche-Guilhen) clearly never had the opportunity to oversee the publication of their works. For the other three plays, which have been printed more than once, I have collated all the editions that appeared during the authors' lifetimes. In doing so I turned up no significant variants, confirming my hypothesis that not one of those playwrights revised her work once it had gone to press. Indeed, the first editions tend to be more accurate than the later ones, suggesting that the authors may not have overseen the subsequent editions, or even have been consulted about them (as is probably the case for those published in Holland).

The present translations are intended to be as accurate and as readable as possible, and, I hope, stageworthy. I have followed the common practice of rendering the rhyming couplets of French alexandrines in blank verse. My iambic pentameter is not perfectly regular, but it takes no greater liberties with prosody than can be found in English tragedies of the Restoration period. In the interludes of *All-Wondrous* and in the poems read within *The Favorite Minister,* I have tried to convey the sense of a different meter and rhyme scheme without following those of the original to the letter. I have generally opted for a flowing, conversational style, and have tried to avoid stilted or self-consciously poetic language. The pronouns "thou" and "thee" have been reserved for prayers and solemn invocations. I make no claims to be a poet; if I have succeeded in making these plays enjoyable for the English-speaking reader, I have achieved my goal.

The inconsistency in my translation of proper names is deliberate. In the tragedies I have used the English equivalents for the names of historical characters, except for the hero of *Laodamia.* Gelo, the Latin nominative form of his name, sounds just like "Jello" in English. For the non-historical characters, I decided to use whichever form of the name sounded better when the English text was read out loud, even if this meant mixing French forms like Sostrate and English forms like Phaedra within the same play. In the other plays I likewise used the principle of euphony in choosing whether or not to Anglicize the names. The hero of *All-Wondrous* presented the special case of an invented name that refers to the character's main attribute (like Foppington, Witwoud, Wishfort, and countless others in English drama of the same period): leaving him as Rare-en-tout would have been inappropriate.

I have added stage directions in a few instances when I felt that the stage action was not sufficiently clear to the reader.

Françoise Pascal

The Lunatic Lover
(L'Amoureux Extravagant)

The Author

The first French woman writer to have a play publicly staged by a professional company is the logical choice to begin this anthology. Françoise Pascal was born in Lyons in 1632, the daughter of a customs commissioner. She received a better than usual education, perhaps because of her family's connections to the local magistrature and to the Archbishop. By the age of fifteen she was exchanging verses with the influential court poet, Benserade. Between 1657 and 1664 she published six plays (three short farces and three full-length tragicomedies), along with some shorter poems. Even though she was extremely proud of her native city (she often referred to herself in print as "young woman of Lyons" and dedicated her first play to the city fathers), she left Lyons permanently around 1667, for reasons unknown, and settled in the capital. There she supported herself by painting portraits, and perhaps by giving drawing and music lessons, as well. Avoiding the salons, she preferred to frequent ecclesiastical circles. During the final portion of her life she published only a few volumes of religious poetry, including two collections of Christmas hymns designed to be sung to popular tunes of the day. In 1698 she was mentioned in a catalogue of famous living ladies, so she still must have been alive at that date. There is no record of her death.[4]

It is difficult to form a clear picture of Françoise Pascal from such scanty biographical material. For a single woman to be living alone in Paris during this period, supporting herself by her artistic talents, was quite unusual. She obviously possessed great determination and tenacity in pursuing a literary career, despite the special obstacles confronting a woman writer. She never used a pseudonym or tried to disguise her sex. Moreover, she openly objected to the view that women did not need education, even claiming (in a satirical poem entitled "La Belle Stupide") that a

3

woman who cannot converse intelligently does not deserve to be called beautiful, regardless of her physical appearance.

In the prefaces to several of her plays, starting with the very first one, *Agathonphile*, she denies the charge that she had a male collaborator and insists that her works are entirely her own. Her exaggerated protestations of modesty were probably intended to mollify her critics and to reinforce her claim to sole authorship. Could her decisions to stop writing for the stage and to leave Lyons have been the result of squabbles with envious male writers or local publishers? Might she have felt frustrated by unsuccessful attempts to have her plays staged? We shall probably never know.

The fact that Pascal cultivated a greater than usual number of dramatic forms demonstrates her ability to gauge the tastes of her public. If she began her dramatic career with a loosely constructed play about Christian martyrs, it is probably because she knew that such plays had been enjoying a revival of interest during the fifteen years preceding and because she grasped the usefulness of borrowing both title and plot from a highly successful novel by Jean-Pierre Camus. Her second attempt, *Endymion*, capitalized on the vogue for mythological plays with elaborate stage machinery that persisted in Paris until the operas of Lully came to supplant such works in the 1670s. But her shrewdest choice was to cultivate the one-act farce.

In 1657 the brief comedy was just beginning to regain respectability in literary circles. Ever since the middle of the sixteenth century, the word *farce*, linked to the dramatic heritage of the Middle Ages, was relegated to use as a pejorative term. The term *comedy* was henceforth reserved for five-act plays with highly complicated plots often derived from Italian or Spanish sources. It is clear, however, that the views of litterati did not fully succeed in reshaping the taste of theatre audiences. For much of the seventeenth century there was an Italian *commedia dell'arte* troupe based in Paris, not to mention a popular trio of actors from the farce tradition who played regularly at the Hôtel de Bourgogne theatre in Paris during the early decades of the century. Yet it was not until around 1650 that respectable playwrights began to compose and publish brief comic plays, and Pascal was among the very first to do so. Nevertheless, since she felt she could not label her plays either comedies or farces, she resorted to the term "comic play." By 1664 Pascal felt sufficiently vindicated by the increasing popularity of such plays to write to her dedicatee, "the little comic plays are today not only the entertainments of the court, but that of all the provinces of France, where they are performed, and you yourself view them with favor."[5] Within two decades the comic afterpiece had become entrenched as an indispensable component of French dramatic performances.

The Play

Significance

The plays of Françoise Pascal mark a critical new direction for women playwrights in France. Up until this point, the women who wrote plays seemed to have viewed their work as an essentially literary exercise, paying little attention to questions of stageworthiness or to the demands of public taste. For Françoise Pascal, who almost certainly met Molière during his stay in Lyons and who succeeded in getting at least two of her plays publicly staged, theatricality was a paramount consideration.

The overriding concern for stageworthiness explains some of the structural imperfections in *The Lunatic Lover*. A reader, although not a spectator, is likely to wonder what, if any, were the obstacles hindering the union of Cloris and Tyrsis or that of Amaranthe and Cleandre. There is passing mention of Amaranthe's father and of Tyrsis' jealousy, but all this is quickly forgotten in the play's abrupt denouement, arranged in a mere three and one-half lines! Why does Pascal depart from the tradition that makes the servant lovers the valet and maid of the two people who will wed each other at the end of the play? Are we to suppose that Cliton will leave the service of Cleandre, or that Dorinde will leave that of Cloris? Is shortage of money the main barrier to the union of Cliton and Dorinde? If so, should we suppose that the stratagem revolving around the alleged abduction and death of Cloris was planned well in advance of the play's opening? Why has Philon failed to realize that Cloris loves another, and why has she never before told him of her lack of interest in him? Why does Philon, who obviously knows his mythology, show such shocking ignorance of French prosody? Why are the roles of Tyrsis and Amaranthe, who logically should be important characters, reduced to a bare eight lines each?

Given the respectable level of craftsmanship Pascal displayed in her *Endymion*, published the same year, we cannot blame these problems on the author's incompetence or on the fact that she lived in the provinces. In reducing the plot of what could have been written as a three- or five-act traditional comedy to 350 lines, Pascal has deliberately curtailed the standard love intrigues of the conventional characters in order to leave ample room for the amusing antics of the lunatic lover and the two wily servants. Even if the result is more a series of practical jokes played on the title character than a skillfully contrived plot, the frenzied pace of the action sweeps us along and keeps the flaws from becoming too apparent.

Although seventeenth-century farces, like their precursors in the late Middle Ages, often emphasized slapstick and ribald humor, Pascal chose in this play to follow the model of refined and decorous comedy of which Pierre Corneille had been the leading exponent in the previous generation. Like Corneille, she presents elegant, well-to-do young people whose language and manners resemble those of the court. The men appear to be their own masters, free to marry as they choose and in control of their fortunes. The servants share their masters' refined speech and fascination with poetry. Vulgarity and physical humor are absent. Even the names of the characters, some of which ultimately derive from the pastoral literature of antiquity, are mostly to be found in Corneille's comedies. It is also possible that the play's title is an act of homage to Corneille, whose comedy *La Place Royale* bore the subtitle *The Lunatic Lover* in the original edition of 1637, although the title characters of the two plays have virtually nothing in common. However, for her last farce, *Le Vieillard amoureux* (*The Old Man in Love*), Pascal would turn away from the Cornelian model and write a work of pure slapstick. Might this be an indication that her earlier farces were not well received?

The theme of the mad poet who, by living too much in the world of his imagination, proves unable to cope with reality, was hardly new. However, the facts that Philon is not a professional poet or pedant and that he is wealthy enough to be the target of Cliton's swindle make him somewhat unusual. His "mad scene," in which he imagines a descent into Hades, is also drawn from well-worn convention; it is possible that Corneille's first play, *Mélite*, provided the direct inspiration. It might be significant that unlike the heroines of Molière's *Les Précieuses ridicules*, produced only two years later, the character whose mind has been unhinged by literature is a male.

Performance History

What little we know about the staging of Françoise Pascal's plays comes from the author's own statements. We know that her fifth play, *Sésostris*, was publicly performed in Lyons prior to its publication in 1661, and the dedication of her last play, *Le Vieillard amoureux*, gives the impression that it too was acted in that city, probably in 1662. (Pascal's use of the name Philipin for the comic valet suggests that she hoped to get her farce accepted by the Hôtel de Bourgogne troupe in Paris, since this was also the stage name of their leading comic actor. It is now believed that the Hôtel de Bourgogne did indeed mount Pascal's play in 1663, the year preceding its publication.)[6]

There is no obvious reason why *The Lunatic Lover* could not have been staged; it only requires a cast of seven and a minimal set. But there are a number of reasons to believe that it was not. Unlike *The Old Man in Love*, which was printed in a slim volume by itself, *The Lunatic Lover* and another one-act farce, *L'Amoureuse vaine et ridicule* (*The Vain and Ridiculous Lady Lover*), were published as part of a collection of short poems entitled *Diverses Poésies*. Moreover, the dedication, which is the only one of her play dedications where the addressee's name is reduced to initials, mentions the poems but not the plays, even though she refers to his willingness to look favorably upon "small works." Would Pascal have failed to refer to the two plays in the dedication if they had been performed, successfully or not? Again, why did she not insist on placing the farces at the beginning of the volume, if the reading public of Lyons knew the plays from performance and was eagerly awaiting their appearance in print? In fact, it was a common practice, especially in the 1630s, for authors to append a collection of their poems to the first edition of a successful play.

Another reason to doubt that the play was ever staged in its author's lifetime is the entry about Pascal in the *Grand Dictionnaire historique des Précieuses*, which she apparently wrote herself. She states, "at the games of the Circus [presumably the Roman amphitheatre in Lyons] there was performed a play which she composed, and which was found very beautiful."[7] The play in question was obviously *Sésostris*, yet five of her six plays were already published when she wrote these lines.

The first known staging of *The Lunatic Lover* occurred on March 24 and 26, 1985, in a student production that I directed (in French) in Stillwater, Oklahoma.

The Lunatic Lover

(L'Amoureux Extravagant)
Comic Play

Françoise Pascal

Actors[8]

CLEANDRE, in love with Amaranthe.

TYRSIS, in love with Cloris.

PHILON, lunatic lover.

AMARANTHE.

CLORIS.

DORINDE, maid of Cloris.

CLITON, valet of Cleandre.

The scene is a city street (in Lyons).

.　.　.　.　.

To Monsieur de L********[9]

SIR,

I do not fear to make a public admission that there are charms against which no defense is possible, and as the beauties of the mind are of that nature, I glory in admiring them in all persons who possess them. I indeed foresaw, SIR, that you would be surprised by my plan to offer some poems to you; but I was unable to prevent myself, and I could not properly use these flowers of Parnassus except by crowning the altars that are starting to be raised to your great talent in learned circles. It is true that I did not resolve without repugnance to present to you merely some strophic poems and sonnets, which deserve neither your esteem nor your perusal. Yet, SIR, I believed that minds which, like yours, are of the first rank, were not like those haughty plants which turn only toward the sun and seek only its light. You do not thus despise what is below you, and you sometimes condescend to look upon minor works with kindness. It is from that thought that I derived the boldness of presenting this work to you and to declare myself

SIR,
Your most humble servant
F. PASCAL.

Enter Cleandre and Cliton.

CLITON: Yes, you are lost, for love attracts you so.

CLEANDRE: Cliton, stop teasing. Go seek Amaranthe,
Give her this letter and act skillfully
So no one sees you.

CLITON: Sir, you need not fear.

5 Place full reliance on a faithful servant.
For you and your belov'd I'll keep things secret.

Exit Cleandre.

My word, my master's mad, since he's in love.
Unhappy he will surely be forever.
Before, his only care was eating well,

10 But Cupid is today the god he worships.
He loves this tyrant who disturbs his peace.

PHILON (*enters, unseen by Cliton*): Gods! what makes him to
speak so wrongfully
Of this god of love?

CLITON: The sanest intellect
Loses all sense as soon as love directs it.

15 PHILON: What's this? I'll have to thrash this insolent man.
(*to Cliton*) You dare to criticize love, you despise it!
Traitor, what drove you to discuss its flames?

CLITON: I was just saying love tyrannizes minds.
As soon as mortals have felt its attack,

20 Despite their pretty wit, they pass for fools.

PHILON: Then I'm one, knave?

CLITON: My word, that look of yours
Shows me I know the prototype of fools.

PHILON: Insolent one, what do you dare reply?

CLITON: That you're quite sensible.

PHILON: Unless you lie,

25 You must admit it, lowly, ignorant soul,
You who can't recognize a master of

Parnassus,[10] favored by the gods, whose genius
And beauteous verse the universe admires.

CLITON: So he's a poet, too, to top things off.

30   He's a perfect fool. My God! He merits pity.
Daydream your fill, great rhymer of this age!

Exit.

PHILON: Yes, let my work today break forth in public.
Here let's produce some verses to the glory
Of the sweet lady who reigns in my thoughts.

35   Ah, charming Cloris, mistress of my heart!
I adore you still, despite your cruelty.
But midst the raptures that have seized my soul,
Let's shine forth, my love, through our poetry.

He goes to meditate at a corner of the stage
and starts writing.

"O fair Star of my heart!"

Enter Dorinde; she and Philon don't see one another.

DORINDE: Lovers, my word,

40   Are in their blindness often quite a bore.
My mistress used to live in innocence,
But Cupid holds her now under his spell.
Once girls were the sole company she liked;
All other friends seemed odious to her.

45   Unfortunately, the beaux at last beguiled her.
Such is the sad state love has brought her to.

PHILON (*writing in a corner of the stage*): "Wonder of mortals!"

DORINDE: Ever since the day
This girl discovered what love is, I must
Incessantly be running to deliver

50   Her love-notes.

Enter Cliton.

CLITON: May the Lord accompany you
With your love-notes!

DORINDE: Cliton, where have you come from?

CLITON: I'm coming from a house where I was expected.
Don't try to guess: it is fair Amaranthe.
DORINDE: Even if the matter were much weightier,
55   I would not breathe a word.
CLITON: Can you keep secrets?
Can you be mum for long?
DORINDE: I can indeed,
Better perhaps than any girl on earth.
I can keep still.
CLITON: Just like a thunderbolt?
You wouldn't be a female.
PHILON (*still writing*):   That's no good.
60   I must erase it.
CLITON: Don't hide things from me.
What is your errand now?
DORINDE: You curious man!
To bear the missives of a girl in love.
CLITON: Accursed be love!
DORINDE: Don't curse it so. Just now
I was railing at it, but, Cliton . . .
CLITON: But yet,
65   You rail no longer. Isn't that your drift?
Just listen to me.
DORINDE: No, I'm in a hurry.
CLITON: I really, truly love you.
DORINDE: You're just joking.
You aren't clever enough.
CLITON: Dorinde, I'm serious.
DORINDE: I see my mistress. Bye now.
                    Exit.
PHILON (*still writing*):   "Youthful wonder."
70   CLITON: I'll follow you. Wait up.
                    Exit.
PHILON (*writing*):   "You have no equal."

Enter Cloris.

CLORIS: O God, how long that girl takes to return.
I can't imagine what is keeping her.
But isn't that the lunatic I see?
It's he. Let's get away.

PHILON (*seeing her*): Stop, dear beloved!
75   O blazing torch, do not eclipse yourself!
And I will show you something beautiful.

CLORIS: What will you show me?

PHILON: Verses in your praise,
Where I rank your beauty far above the angels.
I call your two eyes peerless luminaries,
80   And in a word I say that they are suns.

CLORIS: What an obnoxious man!

PHILON: Observe the style.

Enter Dorinde.

DORINDE: Madam, I'm back.

Dorinde and Cloris whisper.

CLORIS: How clever you have been!

PHILON: Inhuman maid! She doesn't want to listen.

DORINDE: See where he comes.

PHILON: Ah! I am being mistreated.

Enter Tyrsis.

85 TYRSIS: Dear Cloris, finally . . .

CLORIS: Don't speak that way.
Come hear the poems of this eminent man.

TYRSIS: And for whom are they written?

PHILON: Don't you worry:
They're written for Cloris.

Enter Cleandre and Cliton.

TYRSIS: Get out of here.
What? You're intending to bewitch my loved one
90   With your fine verses?

PHILON: Does her lovely eye,
Which wounds me, wound you also?

CLEANDRE: What's your quarrel?
Tyrsis, isn't it true that you are jealous
Of this erudite man?
TYRSIS: Surely I am.
But he has written poems; let's all hear them.
95   PHILON (*reading his work*): "O fair star of my heart, fair eyes,
Fair hands, fair mouth, fair waist, fair bosom I prize."[11]
CLITON: What's your opinion, gentlemen, of this poem?
Just see how love has put him in a frenzy.
My word, these lines have more than thirty feet,
100   And yet all of these feet are badly crippled.
PHILON: How dare you open your unlettered mouth?
You play the scholar, and you're just an ass.
CLITON: An ass, sir? 'Sblood and zounds! Were it not for
The present company, I'd take revenge
105   For this cruel insult, without much exertion.
Allow me, sir . . .
CLEANDRE: Cliton, you must behave.
But, sir, continue.
PHILON: Wait, insolent creature.
This sonnet is quite excellent. Just listen.
Observe the beauty of my learned genius,
110   And be enraptured, like the others here.
"Fair teeth, tresses most fine,
Adoring you is my design."
CLITON: This poem, I believe, lacks even six lines.
I never saw poetic vein like this.
115   Do not be angry if I tell you plainly,
You never knew what the term "Sonnet" means.
He jumps from eyes to hands, from hands to mouth,
From mouth to arms.
PHILON: This rogue's alarming me.
CLITON: From arms to bosom, and from them to hair,
120   And from hair to teeth.
PHILON: Moron, will you be still?

CLEANDRE: Keep reading, sir. Your verses are amazing.

TYRSIS: I must admit, they are incomparable.

CLITON (*whispering to the company*): While he has his eyes buried
    in the paper,
  Let's sneak away from him.

TYRSIS: What a great suggestion!

125 PHILON: My writing's jumbled; I can hardly read it.

CLORIS: If I don't leave here, I will faint from laughter.

           Exeunt Cleandre, Cloris, and Tyrsis;
      Cliton and Dorinde hide in a corner of the stage;
             Philon notices none of this.

PHILON (*reading*): "Proud and severe beauty,
  Will you never gracious be?"
  Heavens! They've left! Cloris has disappeared.

130 CLITON (*whispers to Dorinde*): We must alarm him.

PHILON: Ah! I'm all confused.

DORINDE (*pretending to reenter*): Sir!

PHILON: What's the matter? What misfortune grieves you?

Cliton (*pretending to reenter*): O God! Was ever such cruel won-
    der seen?

PHILON: Speak more distinctly.

CLITON: O supreme misfortune!
  Four or five robbers just now fell upon us
135   And kidnapped Cloris.

PHILON: O most fatal news!
  Shall I behold my fair one nevermore?
  Let's stab these insolent fellows to the heart;
  Let's go at once undo their violent crimes.

                  Exit.

DORINDE: But what's your plan? What do you aim to do?

140 CLITON: I'll tell you briefly what this mystery means.
  They say this madman is quite well-to-do;
  In fact, he owns great wealth, and furthermore,
  He manages it badly.

DORINDE: So you aim
To get some of that wealth?
CLITON: Indeed, I want
145 To trap him with my ruses. Let's tell him only
That his loved one has died during her abduction.
I'm off at once to notify my master,
And I'll reveal to you in full ere long
The plan that I've devised.
DORINDE: Then I'll go, too.
150 CLITON: Yes, certainly, you have to leave this place.
Or better not; let's hide. He's coming back,
Beside himself with rage.
Reenter Philon.
PHILON: Horrid violence!
I ran in vain after these ravishers.
They think they'll gain possession of my love,
155 But by the gods, Cupid and Mount Parnassus
I swear they'll die by my hand ere day's end.
CLITON: Go cry out now that Cloris is no more,
And I will take my leave.
Exit.
PHILON *(still talking to himself)*: I'll strike them down . . .
DORINDE: Ah, weep, Philon! During her kidnapping
160 Cloris has just expired from fear and grief.
PHILON: What are you saying, poor woman? Ah! I don't
Believe it.
DORINDE: Sir, it's certain. Her death was seen.
PHILON: What, odious death, then have you dared to take
This beauty rare at such a tender age?
165 Come, let's make haste and go down into Hades
To liberate her who inspires my verse.
Let's make Pluto and Proserpina tremble.
Let's overthrow that rebel troop with one blow.
No, you shan't have her; she belonged to me.

170   I want to frighten you by my approach.
       Yes, I'll demolish Charon's ferry-boat.
       I'll make those insolent three Fates take flight.
       I'll shake all Hades with my dreadful cries.
       DORINDE: What? You want to go among those shades of dark-
          ness?
175   Ah, change your plans!
       PHILON: I want my glances to
       Dispel the darkness of those deadly dungeons,
       And once I've entered those hollow abysses
       I'll punish those dread demons for their pride.[12]
       Yes, my fair Cloris, I shall shortly join you.
180   Darling, cheer up, you have naught left to fear.
       DORINDE: What passage will you use for your descent?
       PHILON: The earth already gapes beneath my feet.
       I'll clear myself a path in just an instant.
                          Exit.
       DORINDE: My word, he's crazier than I am sane.
185   Meanwhile, let's go see what Cliton will do.
              Exit; enter Cleandre and Amaranthe.[13]
       AMARANTHE: What, you here? Heavens! What will people say?
       You make me tremble, I am terror-stricken.
       What if my father came . . .
       CLEANDRE: Dear Amaranthe,
       No, don't be apprehensive; wait a moment,
190   See what Cliton will do.
       AMARANTHE: How deft he is!
       Good Lord, what cleverness and what finesse!
       CLEANDRE: He wants to play a trick on this Philon:
       He'll be disguised as a poor traveler
       To trap this madman in his mania.
195   But here he comes. Look at his wild expressions.
       Let's move away from here.
              Exeunt Cleandre and Amaranthe; reenter Philon.

PHILON: What, rebels, do
My threats not stun you? You sneer at my misfortunes?
Infernal rebels, are you mocking me?
Yes, I'll destroy you, mighty though you be.
Enter Cliton, disguised as a poor traveler.

200 But isn't that a man I see advancing?
What is it, friend? What do you ask of me?
Have you come to relieve my downcast heart?

CLITON: Sir, do an act of peerless charity
To this poor traveler, back from the next world.

205 PHILON: You come from the next world? Gods, what have I
Heard? Have you seen the beauty I have lost?
Have you seen my Cloris, my fair one, who
Will make my grief eternal by her death?

CLITON: Yes, sir, I've seen her.

PHILON: Alas, what did she tell you?

210 Give me an accurate account at once.
What were her words? Isn't she feeling pain?
My joy is still uncertain on this point.
What terms did she use when she spoke to you?
Was she lodged in a comfortable place?

215 Is she not suffering on that somber shore?
And when she spoke what did she talk about?
What did *you* answer? What was her reply?
Did she declare she'd give her heart to me?

CLITON: If you keep talking, I can't say a thing.

220 PHILON: Yes, speak, my friend, that's what I most desire.
Does she lack anything?

CLITON: She'll starve to death.
They don't give her a single crust of bread.

PHILON: Poor darling! Is it true?

CLITON: Sir, I assure you,
The facts that I relate to you are certain.

225 PHILON: But by what means did *you* return from there?

CLITON: Sir, your Cloris can give you more details.

PHILON: And how could my Cloris tell me of this?
Could I indeed descend to that abyss?

CLITON: Oh, gracious! No, sir, that place is too deep.
230 You'd die of fright before you reached the bottom.
But if you want to rescue your beloved,
I know the means.

PHILON: What welcome news! O God,
What are you telling me? Are you not jesting,
Dear friend? Can we then bring her back from there?

235 CLITON: Sir, it is not by words alone that we
Can rescue her. Do you have ready cash?
This talk surprises you? Know that these demons
Love money just as much as we humans do.

PHILON: I do have money, but is much required?
240 For I wouldn't have enough to satisfy them all.

CLITON: Her ransom will require one hundred gold coins.
But that's for King Pluto; for still more is needed.
Must we not give to Proserpina also?
You never saw such appetite for plunder.

245 PHILON: Alas, for my Cloris what wouldn't I do?
No, no, I will not fail her in her need.

CLITON: Make haste then, sir; you see my time is short.
Release your dear beloved from her torments.

PHILON: Wait, I'll get back to you in just a moment.
                          Exit.

250 CLITON (*alone*): I think the swindle's working splendidly.
I see his love is stronger than his greed,
And yet this love does him a grave disservice.
But he's already coming back.

PHILON (*reentering with a purse*):   Here's money.

CLITON: Ah, sir, you're really diligent.

PHILON: One hundred
255 Louis for Pluto. How much for his wife?

CLITON: You need ten for her. (*aside*) How this delights my soul!

PHILON: One hundred ten then? Here I've got two hundred.
God, how this ransom aggravates me! But
No matter; she is worth more than this sum.

260 That lovely fair will be restored to me.
Then I must take back only ninety coins?

CLITON: Sir, for the pages you'll need six at least.

PHILON: Then I must take back only eighty-four?

CLITON: Sir, and the lackeys? Surely they will beat me.

265 We need twelve at least, for they are numerous,
Or else Cloris would suffer from their malice.
Twelve more for the porters, over fifty strong.

PHILON: A plague on this business! Ah, I'm losing patience!
No matter, though. Cloris will leave that place.

270 I'll give you all the money that you want.

CLITON: Sir, what of Charon, rower of the ferry?
Two louis for him, and much more for the Fates,
For it is they who keep your love imprisoned.[14]

PHILON: Then must my fortune wholly go to Hades?

275 Here, I will give you half a dozen more.
Let's count.

CLITON: And me, sir? Don't I get something for
My trouble?

PHILON: Ah, you go too far!

CLITON: Sir, on
The roads we'll meet some of those wicked spirits
Who'll take our money even if we resist.

280 PHILON: O Cupid, how you test my constancy!
Of my two hundred I am left with six.
It was in vain that I tried to conserve them.
Here, take, I give you both the coins and purse.
I must have recourse now to my cash box.

285 CLITON: Farewell, farewell, sir. In a moment you'll
Once more see Cloris.

PHILON: That's my understanding.
Exit Cliton.

At last, my poor afflicted soul will find
Relief, paid for in cash, in her approach.

Enter Cleandre and Amaranthe.

CLEANDRE: What are you doing here, poor and dejected
290   Lover?

PHILON: I've found the means to be consoled,
Since for a price I'll see my fair again.
No longer will she so resist my suit.
Knowing how greatly she's obliged to me,
She'll be much more receptive to my love.

295 CLEANDRE (*aside*): Ah, Cliton has duped him!

AMARANTHE: Could it be possible?

PHILON: Yes, I'll again behold that heartless fair
Who persevered in persecuting me.
Her eyes on this spot soon will cast their radiance.

CLEANDRE: Who'll bring her to you?

PHILON: Someone from the next world.

300 CLEANDRE (*aside*): My word, his madness never has been
     equalled.

     (*aloud*) And how much did you give for her release?

PHILON: Nearly two hundred louis.

CLEANDRE (*aside*):   Cliton, in truth,
You're much too clever.

AMARANTHE: Sir, your tears will all
Dry up their springs when you behold her charms.

305   But I realize that by our idle talk
We would disturb your sweet contentment here.
Farewell.

Exeunt Cleandre and Amaranthe.

PHILON: I'm grateful to you for this kindness.
It's only Cloris whose presence I love.
Come then to ease my sufferings, fair creature.

310   Come then to make my spring of tears dry up.
Enter Cliton in his normal valet attire.
CLITON: Sir, all good wishes. Have you had tidings
Of fair Cloris? And when will she be back?
PHILON: She'll come soon; I expect her on this spot,
The object of my love.
CLITON: Well, God be praised!
315   You're holding something in your hands, I think;
You're clenching them so hard.
PHILON: See what impatience!
They are gold coins, you inquisitive spirit.
And guess how many? You will get all six.
CLITON: Six in our country come to half a dozen.
320   That's how many you hold.
PHILON: The devil take
The one who told you! He's a fool, an idiot!
CLITON: You've hit upon his name with your first guess.
However, sir, you must not think such things.
Nobody told me.
PHILON: My Cloris advances;
325   I see my darling. Here, Cliton, take these
Louis. You guessed right.
CLITON: Seeing treasures so great,
My eyes are dazzled.
Enter Cloris, Dorinde, and Tyrsis, followed shortly
by Cleandre and Amaranthe.
PHILON: Ah, my dear beloved!
But can I allow another to caress you?
Tyrsis still follows you; you give him your hand!
330 CLORIS: Yes, or else I'd have an unfeeling heart, Philon.
'Tis he who released me from those somber shores
Where I was dying of fear amid sad shadows.
PHILON: He brought you back from that dark shore? And my
Two hundred gold coins did not have that power?

335 CLORIS: What? Your two hundred gold coins? I don't understand.

PHILON: Can I give any clearer explanation?
  I gave for you almost two hundred gold coins
  When you were down below.

CLITON: You stun us all!
  Someone has swindled you.

CLORIS: It's very true.

340 I saw no money.

PHILON: I'm so miserable!

TYRSIS: My word, I pity you to see your mishap:
  You've lost mistress and fortune in a flash.

CLEANDRE (*whispering to Cliton*): Cliton, enough; give him his
  six coins back.

CLITON: Take these, Mister Philon.

PHILON: Thanks, you console me.

345 Farewell, Cloris, farewell, keep your Tyrsis.
  I'll never grieve or worry over this.
  It would cost me too much.

                        Exit.

CLITON: To our ladyloves
  Let's go get married!

DORINDE: God, you're in a hurry!

CLITON: Come on, I'm rich.

CLEANDRE: Let's follow his advice.

350 Such good ideas ought to be acted on.[15]

                    Exeunt.

END.

Marie-Catherine Desjardins

The Favorite Minister

(Le Favori)

The Author

Almost every aspect of the biography of Marie-Catherine Desjardins, better known as Mme de Villedieu, has been the subject of debate. The date and place of her birth, the date of her death, the number of times she was married, even her Christian names have been disputed. Legends, some of them started during her lifetime, portrayed her as a flamboyantly immoral woman whose life was one long list of scandals, who ran away from home to become an actress in Molière's company, whose marriage to Villedieu was bigamous, etc. Some brilliant detective work by three dedicated twentieth-century scholars, Captain Derôme, Bruce Morrissette, and especially Micheline Cuénin, has finally swept away the sensationalist stories. The new and accurate biography that has emerged, solidly based on letters and archival records, reveals a hard-working, sensible, and talented woman who longed for respectability but had the misfortune to fall in love with a man who ruined her reputation and shamefully betrayed her.[16]

Marie-Catherine Desjardins was born in 1640, probably in Paris. Her father, Guillaume, although descended from the lower ranks of the nobility, was virtually penniless, and it was not until he acquired influential protectors through marriage to the lady-in-waiting of a duchess that he finally managed to secure a government position. Around 1650 the family moved to Alençon, Guillaume's native city, apparently due to the chaos during the civil war known as the Fronde. In 1655 the girl's mother obtained a legal and financial separation from her husband and took her two daughters back to Paris. Marie-Catherine was soon introduced to her mother's former employer, and, once her poetic talent was discovered, she was warmly received by many of the leading salons of the day. Her circle of friends and well-wishers would eventually include dozens of cultivated aristocrats and well-known men of letters.

It was one of her noble friends, Mme de Morangis, who propelled the young poetess to fame in 1660 by requesting her to compose a summary of Molière's recent comedy, *Les Précieuses ridicules*, which she had been unable to attend. In a mere twenty-four hours Desjardins produced a witty synopsis, partly in verse and partly in prose. The *Récit* was so admired and so many copies of the manuscript were circulated that several pirate editions soon appeared. Desjardins, having no choice but to issue an authorized edition, chose to work with the eminent publisher Claude Barbin, who would serve as her literary agent and her principal editor for the rest of her life. Besides publishing a collection of her poems in 1662, Barbin encouraged her to write novels, and she would produce some twenty of them, starting in 1661. Many were highly successful. Because Desjardins was trying to support herself through her writing, she paid close attention to shifts in public taste and did not hesitate to experiment with a variety of styles, techniques, and formats.

It is possible that she would never have composed plays had she not been pushed by her literary mentor, Abbé d'Aubignac, author of an influential treatise on dramatic theory. The Abbé probably arranged to have her first tragedy, *Manlius*, performed at the Hôtel de Bourgogne, where it achieved a moderate success in 1662. Unfortunately, the play gained another kind of notoriety when it was cited repeatedly in the course of a long and acrimonious quarrel that pitted the irascible Abbé against France's leading author of tragedies, Pierre Corneille, and the budding journalist, Jean Donneau de Visé. Following the failure of her second tragedy, *Nitétis*, in 1663 and the respectable success of *The Favorite Minister* in 1665, she chose to stop writing for the stage, probably for financial reasons. Even though the plays gained her widespread recognition in literary circles, a dramatist's royalties in those days were far from being enough to live on.

If she needed to earn her living by her pen, it was in large part because of her family's serious financial problems. Her father was an ambitious man whose desire for titles and property far outstripped his income. By 1655, when his wife obtained a legal separation, he seems to have totally squandered her dowry, and her own finances were often precarious, as well. In 1661 Guillaume was briefly imprisoned for debt. Further financial worries would dog the family in the years following. In addition to her steady stream of publications, Marie-Catherine hoped to assure a steady income for herself and her family by petitioning for a royal pension. The influential minister Hugues de Lionne (dedicatee of *The Favorite Minister* and a long-standing supporter) made the necessary arrangements, but the pension was not actually paid until 1676, and then was reduced from 1500 to 600 livres.

As with so many of her fictional characters, Marie-Catherine's greatest sufferings were the result of love. Around 1658 she lost her heart to a dashing young army officer, Antoine de Boësset de Villedieu. It took him a while to respond but he finally did so in circumstances worthy of a novel: returning home from a ball, he found himself locked out of his rooms; he knocked on his friend's door; Marie-Catherine put him up for the night in her room, while she slept in her sister's room; during the night he fell so gravely ill that he could not be moved for six weeks; she nursed him tenderly throughout his convalescence; and he allegedly promised to marry her should he recover. Shortly thereafter they started to live together openly. However, his family, well-to-do and well-connected, opposed his match with a penniless poetess. Moreover, Villedieu was ambitious and in 1663 went heavily into debt in order to purchase a captain's commission. On that occasion, perhaps in hopes of pacifying his relations, he coerced Marie-Catherine into signing a declaration that she was not married to him and never had been.

However, the following year, when she discovered that his regiment had been mobilized and that he had left Paris without even notifying her, she frantically rushed to Provence (with money borrowed from Molière) and managed to find him before he set sail. Villedieu, moved by her entreaties and probably believing that he would be killed in battle, signed an official, notarized statement of intent to be married. Such a contract had binding legal force, but the actual marriage could not be solemnized without consent of the parents, which, as Villedieu clearly understood, would never be obtained. When the captain returned from the wars, he showed no eagerness to honor his promise of marriage, and it may well have been to force his hand that Marie-Catherine began publicly to call herself Madame de Villedieu. Early in 1667, once again desperate for funds at the outset of a new round of fighting, Villedieu resolved to find and marry a wealthy heiress. He thereupon coerced Marie-Catherine to sign a new document desisting from the earlier promise of marriage.

Heartbroken and humiliated, she set off for Holland where her presence was required in a lawsuit involving the family finances, stopping along the way to visit several cities in Belgium. Meanwhile, Villedieu, once again in need of funds, made a whirlwind trip to Paris and committed the vilest indignity of all: profiting from Marie-Catherine's absence, he sold all of her letters to him (mostly passionate love letters) to Barbin, who published them despite the author's refusal to grant permission. Despite her horrified protests from abroad, Barbin refused to withdraw the book from circulation, consenting only to remove her name from an inside page in the second printing. (The title page does not bear an author's name in either printing.) The year 1667 was to provide a staggering series of disasters: the publication of her private correspondence, Villedieu's death in battle, the death of her father, and finally the loss of the lawsuit in Holland.

Even though her marriage to Villedieu never took place, she began as of 1668 to call herself his widow—a title to which his family, with whom she remained on excellent terms throughout her life, never objected. (Nor was there a problem with Villedieu's widow, who had been married to him only a few months; she remarried in 1668.) Around 1672 her bitterness and disillusionment with the world led her to enter a convent at Conflans. However, she was too restless and too addicted to her writing to remain there for long. Finally, her luck changed. In 1677 she married a nobleman of comfortable means, named Claude-Nicolas de Chaste, to whom she bore a son. When her husband died, after only sixteen months of marriage, her kind-hearted father-in-law agreed to take care of her and the child. Soon afterward, for unknown reasons (illness perhaps), she moved to Clinchemore (a family property near Alençon) in order to live with her mother, her brother, and her married sister. She died there in 1683.

The Play

Significance

Marie-Catherine Desjardins was the first woman writer to have her plays professionally staged in the French capital (the premiere of her first play, *Manlius*, in 1662 preceded by one year the Paris staging of Pascal's *The Old Man in Love*), she was the first to be reviewed in a gazette, and *The Favorite Minister* is the first play by a woman to receive a command performance at the French court. The importance of these achievements should not be minimized. Once it was known that the king and court had applauded a work by a female playwright, a barrier had been removed, and dramatic composition was henceforth a legitimate sphere of activity for women. In fact, treatises written about French drama during the latter part of Desjardins' lifetime regularly include her name in lists of recent playwrights. The extent of her success meant that she could not be ignored. Thus, when Abbé de Pure declared, in a passage extolling the glories of the French stage in his generation, that "Messrs. Corneille the Younger, Desmarets, Molière, Quinault, Gilbert, Boyer, Racine and Mlle Desjardins deserve the most justified praise that has ever been given,"[17] he was placing her on an equal footing with the most acclaimed male playwrights of the age.

The fact that *The Favorite Minister* marks a crucial breakthrough for women playwrights does not exhaust its interest for the modern reader. It is also an entertaining and stageworthy play with some irresistible comic scenes. Furthermore, it portrays the transformation of the court under Louis XIV and demonstrates the radical change in values and mentality between the older and younger generations of the French nobility. Written in the same year as the inauguration of Versailles, the tragicomedy admirably captures a notable turning point in French history. Elvira and Clotaire, the self-conscious representatives of the new breed of courtier, quickly transcend the traditional stereotypes of the coquette and the ambitious hypocrite.

Elvira, who endears herself to the reader through her disarming frankness and her light-hearted spirit, unashamedly proclaims a philosophy based on three principles: love of self, love of the court, love of joy. Totally amoral, she rejects all the values of the older generation. Unlike the usual proponents of inconstancy in love, she never appeals to nature as her justification. Instead, she openly recognizes her need for the court as a place to show off her attractions and for men to admire her.

Clotaire, sarcastically described as a court chameleon, is perhaps the most daring figure: a dethroned monarch who revels in his new, subservient role as a courtier. He gladly embraces a life of idleness where the principal occupation is the constant observation of other people. At the same time, he is a shameless opportunist whose ambition, instead of hoping to regain his lost kingdom, is limited to currying favor with his host.

Moncade and Lindamira, representatives of the older, heroic view of the nobility, are presented as restive, anxious to escape the court, uncomfortable with its hypocrisy. But Moncade does not fully realize the debilitating effect the court has upon him: faced with the absolute power of the king and the sycophantic ways of the court, the favorite minister has lost faith in his own abilities and feels that he is nothing more than an insignificant puppet whom the king could discard at any moment. The depression from which he suffers at the start of the play is essentially a lack of self-confidence, despite the fact that his meritorious service to the state and the king's esteem for him ought to make him feel secure.

Even more surprising is the fact that the king also suffers from a lack of self-confidence. He is aware of the discrepancy between his absolute reliance on the hero, whose exploits have maintained him on the throne, and the evolution of the political situation, which has given him expanded authority, while the power of the nobility has waned. He is also caught in an ethical dilemma: how can he reconcile the tyrannical role which the court expects him to play with his personal belief in the older values of justice and magnanimity? Even with absolute power, can he really make a subject happy? The paradoxical solution is that by feigning to exercise arbitrary and unjust authority, he finally succeeds in showing himself to be equitable and in guaranteeing the happiness of others.

Some scholars have suggested that this play could have inspired Molière to compose his own comedy dealing with the transformed role of the French aristocracy, *Le Misanthrope*, first performed in 1666. There might possibly be a grain of truth in this, although according to one contemporary account, Molière had started work on his own comedy by the middle of 1664, roughly the same time he accepted *The Favorite Minister* for performance by his troupe. While there are a number of thematic parallels and even a few textual resemblances, the differences between the two plays outweigh the similarities. Moncade, despite his concern with sincerity and fidelity, shares neither the language nor the personality of the "atrabilious" Alceste. The coquettes, Elvira and Célimène, likewise have nothing in common. Desjardins' play deals with the court more directly, being set in a chateau to which the whole court has been invited, and featuring the king and his most powerful courtiers as the main characters. Although the manners of the court comprise one of the principal themes of *Le Misanthrope*, it is set in a salon, and the characters, apart from the fops Acaste and Clitandre, are excluded from the inner circle at Versailles. By concentrating on complexities of character and ambiguities in human relationships, Molière created a richer and more timeless, but also less political and less harmoniously resolved, comedy.

Source

The principal source for *The Favorite Minister* is *El amor y el Amistad* (*Love and Friendship*) by the Spanish priest and poet, Gabriel Tellez, who wrote under the pen name of Tirso de Molina. It was written in 1621 and first published in 1634. Desjardins could well have obtained a copy, or a plot summary of Tirso's play, from the troupe of Spanish actors who were based in Paris during the 1660s. In any event, she exercised considerable freedom in adapting it, omitting a number of characters and altering two key elements in the plot.

In Tirso's play, Moncada suspects his best friend of being his rival, and it is he, in order to test the loyalty of this friend and of his beloved, who asks the Count of Barcelona to pretend to strip him of his honors and his wealth. In Desjardins' version the trick is the king's idea, and neither the hero nor the audience realizes until the end of the play that the disgrace is not real. In addition to making sweeping changes in characterization and motivation, she introduced political and social commentary that reflected the French, rather than the Spanish, court. The discussions of such moral qualities as constancy, sincerity, loyalty, and gratitude owe little to Tirso, but a great deal to French salon debates and prose writings of Desjardins' generation.[18]

Performance History

According to the seventeenth-century memorialist, Tallemant des Réaux, *The Favorite Minister* had been completed and accepted by Molière's troupe by July of 1664. At that point Villedieu had just been mobilized for the campaign at Gigery, and his fiancée borrowed thirty pistoles from Molière as an advance in order to travel to Avignon to see him prior to his final departure. Why the troupe waited almost a year before presenting the play is uncertain. It is possible that the manuscript given to Molière in 1664 was incomplete; perhaps she asked Molière not to schedule the premiere until her return to Paris. However, after Villedieu's departure with the French fleet, Desjardins spent about half a year in Cavaillon, followed by stops in Lyons and elsewhere, and did not arrive back in the capital until the spring of 1665. Tallemant relates that she quarreled with Molière immediately upon her return, over the fact that he had used her maiden name in the playbills. "Molière gently replied to her that he had announced her play under the name of Mademoiselle Des Jardins; that to announce it under the name of Madame de Villedieu would cause confusion; that he begged her for this once to allow him to call her Madame de Villedieu everywhere, except in the theatre and in his playbills."[19] She agreed, and even when she had the play published the following October, she used her maiden name, both on the title page and in the dedication. (Not until 1668, following the death of her presumed husband, would she start calling herself Madame de Villedieu in her published works.)

Because the records of La Grange (Molière's administrative assistant, who specialized in playing handsome hero roles) have been preserved, we possess detailed information about the performances of *The Favorite Minister*. The premiere took place on April 24, 1665. After seventeen solo performances, it was always paired with a comedy by Molière. It received its final performance on August 17, 1666. In all, Molière's company gave the tragicomedy twenty-six times in Paris and once at court.

Its command performance in the gardens of Versailles on June 13, 1665, was arranged by the Duke de Saint-Aignan, Louis XIV's organizer of royal festivals, to whom Marie-Catherine had been introduced some years earlier by a mutual friend and to whom in 1663 she dedicated her second play, *Nitétis*. It may possibly have been the duke who suggested that Desjardins submit her next play to Molière's company, rather than to the rival troupe at the Hôtel de Bourgogne, who had staged *Manlius* and *Nitétis*. It was certainly his idea to incorporate *The Favorite Minister* into the elaborate festivities of June 13. Scholars disagree as to whether the author was invited, but even if she did not attend it is probable that Saint-Aignan supplied her with a full description of the event and encouraged her to write a poem to commemorate it.

The play was, of course, only one of a number of entertainments offered to the court that evening. Louis also provided a ballet, a concert of vocal music, a ball for the nobles, and a gargantuan supper served on the stage; the court was kept fully occupied until dawn. The play was performed on a "rustic" stage specially built for the occasion, under the supervision of Vigarani, the king's chief theatre architect. If we can take the author's poem literally, the stage, located at the crossing of four paths in the palace gardens, was decorated with one hundred porticos, with a thousand waterfalls forming a dazzling background. Illumination was provided by one hundred crystal torches placed on sculpted myrtle trees, with a hundred more suspended in the air by invisible supports. Surrounding the stage were two rows of cypress trees, sculpted into pyramids and bearing one hundred vases of flowers. Desjardins was probably accurate when she stated that this brilliantly lit and spectacularly landscaped stage awed even the proudest guests. The dramatic effect created by the presence of the court at a play satirizing court manners and by the perfect correspondence between the setting of the performance and the play's decor must have made it unusually effective and realistic.

The signal honor of a command performance at Versailles could hardly pass unnoticed. Besides the author's own rhapsodic description of the festivities in her 195-line poem, "Description of One of the Celebrations Given by the King at Versailles," the *Gazette de France* and that of Robinet duly noted the event. However, since the gazetteers knew that the play was not the principal attraction, they mention it only in passing: the former gives only its title, while Robinet limits himself to this brief comment: "a diverting and beautiful play, by a famous young lady."[20] Desjardins herself decided, whether out of caution or modesty, to refrain from commenting about her own play, noting only that it was "well acted." There have been no known revivals since 1666.

Two curious mysteries remain about the history of this work: its subtitle and the prologue which Molière composed for the court performance. Tallemant refers to it as *The Favorite Minister or the Coquette*. La Grange reverses this order, calling it *The Coquette, or The Favorite Minister* when he records the premiere, and again at the top of the next page in his *Registre*. Elsewhere, he simply calls it *The Favorite Minister*. The subtitle is absent from the entry in the *Gazette de France*, dated June 20, 1665, and from Robinet's account, dated June 21, as well as from the published editions. Whatever the reason may have been, the single title seems to have prevailed soon after the first performance.

The loss of Molière's prologue is most regrettable. La Grange informs us that "M. de Molière made a prologue as a ridiculous marquis who wanted to be on the stage in spite of the guards, and had a laughable conversation with an actress who played the ridiculous marquise, placed in the middle of the audience."[21] Molière was presumably capitalizing on the huge success he had achieved by playing the role of a silly marquis in several of his own comedies. Moreover, by stationing one of his actresses among the spectators, he was accentuating the play's topical aspect as mirror image of the courtly audience. Since the distribution of roles is uncertain, there may be another reason for the decision to write a special prologue for another author's play: Molière, the most brilliant comic actor in his own company, might not have been a member of the cast, but felt obliged to appear at the special court performance. (It is also possible, however, that he took the part of Clotaire.) The exact content of the prologue must remain a matter of speculation.

The Favorite Minister

(Le Favori)

Tragicomedy

Marie-Catherine Desjardins

Actors

THE KING OF BARCELONA.

MONCADE, his favorite minister.

CLOTAIRE, an exiled foreign prince.

LINDAMIRA, beloved of the favorite minister.

DONA ELVIRA, lady of the court.

LEONORA, another lady of the court.

DON ALVAR, friend of the favorite minister.

CARLOS, captain of the guards.

A PAGE.

The scene is on a terrace in the favorite minister's country estate.

. . . .

To My Lord of Lione, Minister and Secretary of State.[22]

My Lord,

It is not in order to have the honor of speaking your praises that I take the liberty to dedicate this play to you, although it is the rule of the majority of authors to proceed in that manner. An epistle seems to me to lack adequate space for a work of that importance, and I am too poor a rhetorician to undertake it. I leave to those who will write the history of the greatest and most just of all kings to give you the place which the glory of his choice made you deserve; and as the character of a panegyric suits neither the playfulness of my poetic skill, nor the weakness of my talent, it is less in order to praise you than to entertain you that my favorite minister and my coquette dare to present themselves before you. If Moncade is happy enough to steal an hour's audience from world affairs, I consider him more honored by that favor than by all those of the king of Barcelona.

> And as for our young coquette,
> If her fondness for flirtation,
> Her affected smiles and glances
> Are lucky enough to please you.

They blame her character in vain;
One can be a coquette for less.

Whatever outcome their rashness may have, I will always have a very
favorable one for myself, if this little offering is received by you as a mark
of the zeal I have pledged to you, and if to the permission to present this
work to you, you add the permission to call myself,

My Lord,
Your most humble and most obedient servant,
Des-Jardins.

. . . . .

ACT I
Enter Moncade and Don Alvar.

MONCADE: At last we're left alone; that tiresome crowd
    Whom my illustrious fortune gathers round me
    Treats me so favorably this morning that
    I can escape a moment, Don Alvar.
5   To the passion that inspires me let's give time
    So sweet. This terrace is where Lindamira
    Resides. Let's try to see her.
ALVAR: You've forgotten
    That it's a bit early for such a visit.[23]
MONCADE: Yes, but I needed to act early to
10   Deceive the overvigilant flatterers,
    And when the favorite, whom they besiege with
    Attentions, has the luck to leave unnoticed,
    When the energetic, punctual busybodies
    Allow him to enjoy some solitude
15   And hide his route from those who'd dog his steps,
    He's either early or blessed by the gods.
ALVAR: What? You still feel this frightful loathing? Still
    Your being in favor overwhelms, torments you?

The luck of seeing yourself so feared, so cherished,
20   So great, can't make you like your rank as favorite?
MONCADE: Although I little value that great title,
     Yet I distinguish honor from disgrace.
     The pleasure of occupying a lofty post,
     Able to serve the state, my friends, my king,
25   And the good luck to receive my master's kindness
     Find my heart properly appreciative.
     But I've little relish in all this good fortune
     When I dare consider what pain follows it.
     If you could learn by some experience how
30   A favorite is viewed by popular opinion
     And what secret snares each man puts in his path,
     My distaste for this rank would not surprise you.
     A man who reaches this exalted station
     Must beware of all, especially himself.
35   For, all too often, lulled by an apparent calm,
     He falls asleep, trusting a wind that wrecks him.
     To enjoy the fruits of perfectly wise statecraft,
     He indulges to the full his sensual taste
     And thinks he's done no outrage to his king
40   When in his home he makes himself king of pleasures.
     Ah, Don Alvar, we must follow other rules!
     There are certain crimes against our sovereigns
     Which, though they're not forbidden by our laws,
     Offend the royal person to the quick.
45   A prince derives absolute power from Heaven;
     The right to command is granted him at birth;
     But that worldly spirit and that tender talent
     Which relate more to urbanity than kingship,
     Since a prince can owe these only to himself,
50   He's more jealous of them than of his power,
     And it's on such points that a prudent favorite
     Above all must avoid being his rival,

That he must watch himself incessantly;
For whatever plans a monarch may suspect,
55   All things for us are equally to be feared,
And his slightest desires are jealous ones.
      ALVAR: In vain you set forth to me this frivolous fear.
You are above such a constraint. Your care
For this state, your high birth, your virtues—all
60   Show you deserve the brilliance of your rank.
Fortune has merely treated you with justice.
Its favors, far from stemming from caprice,
Should have been greater, given your famous deeds.
It's known that you're related to our kings.
65   Ever since the current one rules Barcelona,
Your arm has always been his crown's support.
However excessive you may find his kindness,
Perhaps he owes more to the name you bear.
So take full confidence in your own worth,
70   And don't tire Heaven with your indifference.
Think better of the favors that it grants you,
And don't discourage fate by your contempt.
You show too much, if you must hear the truth.
The perfect friendship that has always linked us
75   Obliges me to speak my mind to you.
Everyone is starting to see with what coldness
You receive shows of affection from the King.
Pleasures, feasts, favors, presents, honors, bounty—
Nothing from him can overcome the deep ennui
80   That constantly is shown in your expression.
Whence comes a sorrow so rude, so unfounded?
You have your king here in your country home;
To dispel your secret sadness he was able
To bring along your ladylove, as well.
85   This prince who likes you, what more can he do
Than to bring the court's elite into your home,

And, in their company, her whom you love?
You're in a palace whose amazing structure
90   Was formed by human skill vying with nature;
And the King, heaping on you so rare a favor,
Made you the greatest gift that monarch ever gave.
This grand variety of hills and plains,
These splendid gardens, marble statues, fountains,
95   These sacred refuges of shade and awe,
This fertile countryside . . .

MONCADE: Alas! Are they
For me, these remote lairs whose charm enchants you,
And all these other goods which in your zeal you praise?
It's true that, judging this place through your eyes,
100 You'd think it the abode of ancient demigods.
Never perhaps with so much art has there
Been pomp and splendor joined to rustic beauty.
Each different spot offers to our desire,
For each hour of the day a special pleasure.
105 But, friend, what use to me is my rich fortune,
If, out of all these beauties, I own none?
Does this fertile country you describe so well
Have any attractions known to me alone?
No cavern is so deep, no lair so dark
110 That I'm not always stifled there by crowds.
Silence is a god I do not know. In vain
Do they laud the attractions of thick woods.
The countless throng of all my courtiers
Deprives me constantly of their cool shade,
115 Of balmy breezes, of the waters' purl,
Of springtime's scents, the singing of the birds.
If Echo, sometimes rising above the din,
Is heard by me, I think it's a miracle.
And with the way fate has treated me till now . . .
120 But here's a new act of cruelty on its part;

All I needed was for Prince Clotaire to come.
Enter Clotaire.
CLOTAIRE: Aha, I've caught you in the act, dear recluse.
The whole court waits inside for you to waken,
And you have got up earlier than the sun.
125   It's to prepare yourself for going hunting.
MONCADE: Sir, I'm not going.
CLOTAIRE: Cruel man! What disgrace,
O gods, you announce to me! O what despair!
What? I'll then spend a whole day without seeing you?
Ah, that can't be!
MONCADE (*aside*):   How very base he is!
130 CLOTAIRE: I'd rather be divided from myself.
I cannot leave you. I'll go tell the King
That if you don't come he can go without me.
MONCADE: Take care you don't, sir . . .
CLOTAIRE: He must give the order,
Even if he's got to come give it in person.
135   I run to implore him.
Exit Clotaire.
MONCADE: Don't trouble yourself,
Sir, for . . . But, O gods, he's far away already.
See in what state he's going to put my mind.
I hoped to devote this whole day to my love;
I've made countless arrangements to get time off,
140   Which he will nullify, feigning to serve me.
Of all my flatterers he's the most unbearable!
ALVAR: It's true he's wrong to find you likable.
His zeal offends you, be it said between us.
What? Can't spend even one day far from you?
145   I must confess, that's genuine misfortune.
MONCADE: All right, then, I agree. Be kind and praise him.
ALVAR: No, since he likes you, he does you too much harm.
MONCADE: He likes me? Gods, that coward is my rival!

Lindamira's eyes have set his heart on fire.
150 But he dares not admit so fair a passion
Because of fears that he'd forfeit my favor
And that perhaps he'd lose me as protector.
So base a terror holds him in its sway
That everywhere he yields her hand to me,
155 Overwhelms me with his indiscreet attentions
And stabs me secretly, the worthless traitor!
ALVAR: A man like him should not inspire much fear.
What could his love and pretense do against you?
A fugitive, conquered, dispossessed, unhappy,
160 Who came to this land to implore asylum,
What hope can he have from a love so vain?
MONCADE: He's a lover and a prince, and she's a woman.
The fair sex, friend, is usually deceitful.
Indeed, if I today must bare my heart,
165 I'm starting to think that Clotaire's love is
A powerful obstacle to my hoped-for marriage.
Lindamira cleverly tries to dissemble,
Seeks other pretexts to postpone the date.
Suspicion born of some mistrust, her year
170 Of mourning, with which she checks my impatience,
Have skillfully defended her thus far.
But there's no hiding things from a lover's gaze.
She waits and waits for our armies to triumph.
The name of queen contains so many charms
175 That if Clotaire's restored to his estates,
She'll shortly lose all memory of my suit.
That's the true cause of her delays.
ALVAR: Do not
Suspect her of so blameworthy a plan.
You ought to know her better, and you wrong her.
180 MONCADE: Alas! Nobody knows what fate may bring.
The law of fickleness is very common,

And Love has its wheel, just like Fortune. But
Lindamira's coming out. Leave us alone.
                    Exit Alvar.
Destroy this day, Love, my suspicions or my life.
                    Enter Lindamira.
185 LINDAMIRA (*reading*): These fields, these woods, this greenery,
        The most ferocious animals,
        The sweetest birds,
        In nature all things love.[24]
    MONCADE (*at a corner of the stage*): She's reading.
    LINDAMIRA: Since love is able to inflame
190   The most unfeeling of its creatures,
        If our hearts are susceptible,
        Alas! Can we hold them to blame?
    MONCADE: That sigh's easy to interpret.
        Ah, happy man who inspires such tender feeling!
195   But she spots me. You, at this hour, in this place,
        Madam? I could scarce believe my eyes. What, is
        There not some mystery in this early rising?
    LINDAMIRA: Indeed, there is, sir. Ordinarily
        I take unequalled pleasure every morning
200   To see the sunrise on this lovely spot.
        The sun, then mixing with dawn, beautifies
        With natural lustre each place that it gilds.
        The sporting zephyrs at such times are seen
        Breathing countless gentle sighs around the flowers,
205   And with their sweet breath scenting all the air,
        They turn the sward green, drying up the dew.
        I give you, sir, an accurate depiction,
        Well knowing that for you such things are new.
        A man who's burdened with the cares of state
210   Rarely enjoys the pleasures of the country.
    MONCADE: It's true that the business to which Heaven binds me
        Is a mighty obstacle to visual pleasure,

But if my sad heart grumbles at that business,
It's not that I long for the goods of nature.
215   To see the sun rise matters little to me.
If I could give more time to love, if thousands
Of urgent signs of my consuming passion
Could prove to you how much Moncade adores you,
If, contrary to what I should wish, favor
220   Left me a few more leisure hours to see you,
In short . . .

LINDAMIRA: Each lover has a different manner.
That of a favorite must be peculiar.
All those superfluous steps, that bustling zeal,
All that affected care from common lovers
225   Are not allowed, sir, to those of your sort.
The useless tribute of their empty passion,
Their tears, their sighs, their great attentiveness
Are fruits, quite simply, of their idleness.

MONCADE: But an idle lover often is more pleasing
230   Than an always busy one, weighed down with care.
For Cupid, patents have less appeal than love-notes.
That god cares nought for ministry affairs.

LINDAMIRA: Have you noticed Cupid treating yours with scorn?

MONCADE: I and my kind don't see what's felt for us;
235   And for a favorite the most pressing worry
Is to have so much attraction on the outside.
His glory often has more friends than he does.
Sometimes he's hated at the same time he's loved.
One can't distinguish, in his good qualities,
240   What's properly his from what is external.
Some people fall in love with what surrounds him,
Who've maybe never thought about his person.

LINDAMIRA: That's being a bit too touchy on this point.
You're simply jealous of your brilliant rank,
245   Without knowing whether it is loved, or you.

If someone mixes them up, do the same.
Provided one is happy, *I* maintain
That one can dispense with asking for the reason.
MONCADE: That precept seems useful and sensible,
250   But in love, madam, it's not admissible.
Love is a goal and object to itself,
Containing and producing both cause and effect.
As soon as its fire sneaks into a soul,
If some other interest mingles with its passion,
255   If one finds charms in the beloved which
Are not the person's, it is not true love.
Then judge whether this point pains me extremely—
Me, whose attractions are all on the outside.
Perhaps my love, my loyalty, my respect
260   Are the least appealing . . .
            Reenter Don Alvar.
ALVAR: Sir, here comes the King.
MONCADE: The King!
ALVAR: Yes.
MONCADE: Heavens!
LINDAMIRA: I'll withdraw. Goodbye.
           Exit Lindamira.
ALVAR: He's downcast and alone.
MONCADE: Run after Lindamira
To learn in what place I can see her later.
           Exit Don Alvar.
How hard to harmonize both love and duty,
265   And how weak is a sensitive heart when one
At the same time serves his master and his mistress.
           Enter King.
KING: Then it's with the sole aim of fueling your sorrow
That you excuse yourself from following me today.
It's to be downcast, moody, melancholic,
270   That you allege to me some public business;

And the joy of being alone means more to you
Than the zealous care of a king who holds you dear.
Such conduct stuns me, and to keep nothing from you,
This gloomy mood is starting to displease me.
275   I'm jealous, seeing that all my favor has
Until now failed to overcome your coldness,
That, though the gods have made us what we are,
Kings can do so little for men's happiness,
Since with all the effort of my sovereign power
280   I cannot make my own handiwork happy.
Make wishes, ask, make trial of my esteem
With anything a subject lawfully
May wish. Hide nothing from me, bare your heart.
Speak, what do you require?

MONCADE: Forgive me, sire,
285   If such a speech leaves me without an answer.
This excessive kindness must confound me so
That I'd believe, great King, I didn't deserve it,
If my mind were left in any liberty.
Yet I must reply; my silence is a crime.
290   I must, magnanimous monarch, on my knees
Swear that my eyes did not reflect my heart,
If they didn't express my happiness enough.
Yes, I attest . . .

KING: Stop, or be more sincere.
These frivolous oaths would make my anger sharper.
295   Speak frankly; also know that all of your
Dissimulation will be of no use.
A hundred sighs let slip, secret complaints
Have been rather good signals of your woes.
I'm not asking for your consent in this.
300   Learn then, to end superfluous talk, that I
Want this result from your obedience,
That my joy and benevolence are at stake,
And that, by persisting in thwarting my wishes,

Today you permanently lose my favor.

305 MONCADE: What a decree, sire!

KING: It's irrevocable.

MONCADE: To what do you reduce me, peerless monarch?
Good heaven, what do you demand of me?
How can I dare make my king my confidant?
O gods, that word clashes with my respect.

310 He can't consent . . .

KING: But I in fact command it.

MONCADE: All right, all right, sire. I must needs obey you.
I shall satisfy you and betray myself.
You order me to.

KING: This delay annoys me.
Speak.

MONCADE: I am jealous of my own good fortune.

315 *I'm* not the one they love; they love your favors,
And, sire, your kindness robs me of all hearts.
To me this would be matter for rejoicing,
If fate left me the heart of my beloved.
I feel how sweet and glorious it is

320 To owe my friends to my king's acts of favor.
In the ardor of the zeal that prompts me, I
Could wish I owed you all the air I breathe,
That I could neither act nor live except by you,
So sweet I find the bonds of my allegiance.

325 But, sire, in love the greatest pleasure is
To owe the loved one's heart to oneself alone,
And it's like a thousand deaths when one's beloved
Can't separate the lover from the favorite.[25]

KING: What? That's the only cause of your affliction?

330 MONCADE: It would be trivial for one not in love,
But love has always had its separate rules.
Vain fancies, nothings, to it mean everything.
And since I here must tell you all my weakness,
If I shared my loved one's heart with my position,

335 Though I had reached the summit of my ambition,
I'd secretly feel sorrow in my soul.
True lovers find offense in everything,
And love's destroyed as soon as it is shared.
KING: What! All my favor, all my tenderness
340 Cannot prevail over so mad a passion!
Then I can't fill this insatiable heart,
And, laden with my gifts, you still are wretched!
When I shower my tenderest kindnesses on you,
Ingrate, aren't all your wishes satisfied?
345 What! I fully give myself to this rash man,
And I mean less to him than a vain fancy,
A haze of love with which he is inflamed!
MONCADE: Ah, sire! Ah, sire! You've never been in love.
KING: No, cruel man, I confess, I loved just you.
350 But since my fondness to your heart means little,
Since, though your king's all, you think you're unhappy,
I abandon you to your unworthy love.
Devote yourself full time to your passion's duties.
Henceforth I plan to choose a person so
355 Appreciative of my favor's effects
That his joy or pain depends on me alone.[26]

Exit King.

MONCADE: Please, sire . . . But gods! After that threat he leaves
Me in disgrace and overcome with worry.
Let's not abandon him and try my best
360 To calm the excess of this boiling rage.

Exit.

ACT II

Enter Elvira and Leonora.

LEONORA: You're mocking me, Elvira, I declare,
To make me leave my chamber at this hour.
Everyone's resting; they will laugh at us.

ELVIRA: Come, Leonora.

LEONORA: But where are you going?

365   Tell me at least, fair early riser, if
It's to arrange a secret love affair
Or to consult the movement of the heavens
That you're leading me at this hour to this spot.
What is it?

ELVIRA: Her worry makes me faint with laughter.

370   It's to accompany me to Lindamira's room.
She must give me a bracelet as reward
If I find her in bed while I hold this bouquet.

LEONORA: On this point, truly, no one equals you.
What good is all this caring for your rival?

375   Her every step you follow eagerly.

ELVIRA: These are love's ruses, which you fail to grasp.

LEONORA: No, I agree. But please tell me of them.
We'll still find Lindamira soon enough;
And then, such worries aren't important. Let's

380   Enjoy the lovely weather for a moment.
To be fully frank, I cannot understand you.
I've sometimes loved, for who can be immune?
You know that in this life we all love in turn,
And even the greatest prude has her hour in love.

385   Love then inflamed me, just like others, and
Like you, I had a rival who was loved.
But either you don't love as others do,
Or my heart is not made as others are.
For as soon as her love was made known to me,

390   I feared the sight of her far more than death.

I shuddered with horror at her very name
And would have eaten her heart, had I been able.
ELVIRA: It's likewise to serve the hatred that inspires me
    That you see me constantly with Lindamira.
395   That way I rob her of the sweet contentment
    Of daring to talk freely with Moncade.
    By the clever pretext of my false affection
    I spoil her pleasures with so much finesse
    That hardly in a whole day, though they don't suspect,
400   Does he find an instant to declare his love.
    Is there a harsher torment for a woman in love?
    I then observe her in her anxiety.
    She becomes annoyed, and almost in a moment
    Her face and eyes alter perceptibly,
405   Her mood turns somber, and her melancholy
    Makes her company boring even for Moncade.
    Thinking she finds him tiresome, he gets jealous,
    And in those moments *I* aim blows at him.
    I try my hardest to be praised by him.
410   My wit is quickened, I get playful, and
    In my fine mood I show off charms that, not
    To flatter myself, Lindamira lacks.
    Is that not clever?
LEONORA: Yes, but also, darling,
    If that's quite clever, it's hardly sincere.
415   And if Moncade should come to notice it,
    Believe me, banish hopes of him forever.
    If love's not founded on a high esteem . . .
ELVIRA: Why, ruses are not criminal in love.
    Those are old errors and superfluous worries.
420   Such high esteem serves only when you cease to please;
    When you've no charms left to appear attractive,
    It's good to try to make oneself estimable;
    For lack of better, you must charm the mind.

But when a young swain surrenders to fair eyes,
425   He limits his love and esteem to what he sees,
And has no thought of getting to the soul.
The secret is to please; we see in fact
That each man always thinks his loved one perfect.
Let's please then in the time of youth and beauty,
430   And not regret to leave esteem for old age.
Let others pride themselves on integrity,
If they desire; *I* want no part of it.
And since I'm destined for it in due time,
I'll wait until my fiftieth year to get it.
435 LEONORA: That's pretty much the doctrine of coquettes.
  ELVIRA: I really don't know whether I'm one or not.
But I adore myself and love to please,
I enjoy attention and I hate concealment,
For others I do less than for myself,
440   And joy in short is my rule and my law.
If that is what is called coquette these days,
It's true, I am one.
  LEONORA: Yes, indeed you are,
And by the laws of pure friendship, I must
For pity's sake give you advice on this.
445   Whether or not it helps you, I can't fail to speak.
Believe me, Elvira, become more sincere.
To do one's duty it's never too early.
Besides, the hope you're forming is quite useless:
Moncade is faithful, Lindamira's lovely.
450   Don't mar the progress of so fair a love.
But here he is.
               Enter Moncade, preoccupied.
  ELVIRA: Observe our conversation.
You'll see if I pretend and if I'm clever.
  MONCADE (*aside*): Avoid seeing me! What boldness or what
    crime

Could bring this great disgrace upon my head?[27]

455   ELVIRA: He doesn't spot me.

MONCADE: What have I done or said?

O gods who see my heart . . .

LEONORA: How upset he seems!

MONCADE: How can you allow my fortune thus to change?

ELVIRA: He sees us, Leonora.

MONCADE (*still aside*):   Unwelcome meeting!

Ah, how I hate that woman!

ELVIRA: So sad and brooding?

460   MONCADE: You see.

ELVIRA: Whence comes that unpleasant humor? At

The pinnacle of greatness which you've reached,

What could give you just reason to complain?

MONCADE: Alas!

ELVIRA: You sigh. Might it indeed be love,

Sir, that would cause your anxieties today?

465   I don't believe it. You, adored by all!

Whoever it is, your passion honors her.

We know too well how much winning your heart

Is worth to repay your love with unjust scorn.

MONCADE (*aside*): The flatterer! (*aloud*) Human misery is so varied

470   That it's not always love that makes us suffer.

A man is often thought supremely happy

Whose heart's dark secret others cannot fathom.

Blind fortune has so little constancy

That none should ever judge by appearances.

475   All earthly things feel its instability.[28]

ELVIRA: Please spare yourself this moral observation.

What good, in the lofty rank where you are seen,

Is imagining a future none can know?

Enjoy the present, which for you is glorious,

480   And leave in the gods' hands what is to come.

MONCADE: He who wants to make full use of his reason

Must think of storms while he is safe in port.
That's where, considering foreseen misfortunes,
The wise man gets prepared, often forearmed.
485 Likewise, the subjects who fill my position
Must constantly imagine their disgrace,
Look on the present as a fleeting moment
Which the next moment is seen to erase.
The amazing downfalls of a thousand favorites
490 Show us to what extent fate makes them frequent;
The image of the past predicts our future.
ELVIRA: Erase this portrait from your memory.
I predict for you, without the aid of magic,
That you'll need never fear anything but
495 Our charms; and, sir, for those with your good looks
It's no great harm to be attacked by us.
If I judge aright the looks from our fair ladies,
They will not cause you any fatal wounds.
MONCADE: I think that on that point my life and death
500 Would both depend rather on fate's caprices;
On its favor or adversity depends
My being happy or miserable in love.
And, to tell all, either I judge amiss,
Or the King's kindness is my main appeal.
505 ELVIRA: What you say, sir, may hold true for some women,
For there are very common souls among us.
When I think of it, for me, I can't deny
I shame to acknowledge my sex on this point.
When I'm called woman, in a certain context,
510 I blush all over, just as with an insult.
MONCADE: Then you'd be constant, and despite misfortune . . .
ELVIRA: You're very anxious, sir, to know that. I've
So few attractions, my zeal and constancy
Have scant importance for you, I think. But
515 Whether they do or not, I invoke the gods—

And if I'm lying, may they strike me dead—
That if fate ceased to treat you justly, no
Advice, torture or fear of execution
Would shake my heart. But why such an admission
520 From Elvira's mouth? To you it matters little.
Charms of more potency would be required . . .

Enter Alvar.

ALVAR: Haven't you learned why they've canceled the hunt,
And what's the sorrow that the King displays?

MONCADE: No, what is wrong?

ALVAR: We all find grounds for fear.
525 He's strolling in this gallery, alone,
So full of his grief and his brooding that
He scarcely sees whatever is before him.

MONCADE: Alone, upset and brooding? Gods, I'm done for!

Enter Clotaire.

CLOTAIRE: What ails the King, dear friend? What grief overwhelms him?

530 MONCADE: I don't know, sir. How miserable I am!

CLOTAIRE: You don't know! That is inconceivable!
If you've no information, then who would have?
You have too great a place within his heart
Not to be informed of all that goes on there.
535 You're being cunning with us. Friend, come, tell us.
Do not mistrust a prince who's yours to command.
If you could know to what extent I love you,
You would regard me as an alter ego.
Would there were need to shed my blood for you!
540 Gods, with what pleasure I would stab myself!

MONCADE: Heaven, can there be such sham?

CLOTAIRE: In place of dying,
Let myriad embraces prove my affection.
But the King will rob me of my only joy;
Carlos comes to seek you.

Enter Carlos.

MONCADE: What's the King doing?

CARLOS: Sir,
545 He's in his room alone and bids me order
You to leave his court and Barcelona by
Tomorrow, and retire to your other home,
Which by his will I give you as a prison.

ELVIRA (*aside*): What, Moncade exiled?

LEONORA (*aside*): Gods!

CLOTAIRE (*aside*): What have I heard?

550 ALVAR: Do you speak truth, Carlos?

CARLOS: This blow's surprising;
Like you I was quite disconcerted by it.
But I've explicit orders.

MONCADE: That suffices.
However rude the blow whose shock I feel,
I obey, Carlos, without complaint or murmur.
555 You can assure the King of this from me.
I did not merit being chosen by him.
He realized fate's error and caprice,
And my disgrace bears witness to his justice.

Exit Carlos.

You, Prince . . .

CLOTAIRE: A quarrel that two of my friends
560 Have both asked me to arbitrate today
Has just this moment flashed into my mind.
I must see to it; my honor is involved;
I must reconcile them. Time presses, farewell.

Exit Clotaire.

ELVIRA: Let's get out of this place fast, Leonora.
565 It's so terribly hot no one can stand it,
And I already feel a horrid headache.
O gods, what heat! Let's hurry off. We're roasting!

Exeunt Elvira and Leonora.

MONCADE: Behold the type of friends produced by favor.
    During the fragile course of a fancied fortune
570   They all bring incense to the public idol.
    One glance, one service, one favor from the King
    Drag all hearts after him with ostentation;
    They run after the crowd, and in great numbers
    Follow the impetuous wind of this good will.
575   This rapid torrent brings both night and day
    All the court's attentions to a favorite's feet;
    And at the first blow that destiny deals him,
    The glitter vanishes, all abandon him.
    As sole advantage of his vast good fortune
580   He's left with naught but a just sorrow. Ah,
    Friend, how I hold that man worthy of envy
    Who places his life's happiness in himself alone,
    Who, shunning the pernicious lure of greatness,
    Knows only his thoughts, his duty and the gods,
585   A man with no friends, living by himself . . .
ALVAR: Stop there! Distinguish me from Elvira and
    Clotaire. I refuse to go by fate, as they do
    And, friend, I'll follow you everywhere, till death.
MONCADE: Follow me? Ah, rather may the cruelest death . . .
590 ALVAR: These marks of my zeal you reject in vain;
    I'll follow you.
MONCADE: What! But the King's disgrace . . .
ALVAR: I see its horror, and see it without fear.
    The King can take only my goods, my life;
    I owe you both and lay them down for you.
595   Resist my help no longer!
MONCADE: But at least . . .
ALVAR: It's done.
MONCADE: Ah friend, most perfect of all friends!
    All right, since it's decreed that fate must crush me
    Both in my false friends and in the true one,

The excess of your affection and their coldness
600   Torture my heart by turns and equally.
I must resign myself to this last torment
And dig a precipice for you myself.
I would have found the cruelest fate too sweet
If I alone had been exposed to its attack.
605   To add the crowning touch to my misery,
All those I cherish must feel its wrath, too.
Since you force from me this harsh consent, find out
If I can see Lindamira for a moment;
I want to bid her farewell. My crime, thank heaven,
610   Should gain for me enhanced esteem from her;
And to inform her, come learn from me whence
Arises this great anger in the King.
                    Exeunt.

ACT III

Enter Lindamira and Alvar.

LINDAMIRA: What you're telling me can hardly be believed.
What! That's the sole crime Moncade's guilty of?
615   The King's great wrath, this exile from the court,
Is based on naught but this effect of love?
ALVAR: No, madam.
LINDAMIRA: To my mind the cause is flimsy,
And monarchs easily are moved to anger.
ALVAR: When kings show kindness they are always touchy.
620   Moncade was not allured enough by favor.
This excess coldness, this indifference
Oft have the look of treasonous contempt.
Princes are jealous of their authority
And want complete control over our fortunes.
625 LINDAMIRA: Till now I did not know that royal power
Had legal right to make a heart its slave.
I knew our duty was to fear and obey,
But as for the liberty to love and hate,
I thought kings left that to individuals,
630   And that love alone should meddle with our passions.
My error vanishes; I start to see
That a king can do whatever he desires.
Yet I don't know if he, without reluctance,
Can ruin a man of such weight and importance.
635   His heart at least should have pleaded for Moncade.
For ten years he has been this state's support.
Twice we have seen unrest in Barcelona,
And he alone shored up the tottering crown.
So many famous deeds speak in his favor,
640   Such great fidelity, respect and fervor!
His wealth, public esteem, position and high birth
Nothing drove his heart to take the slightest license;
He always was obedient to his king's orders

And treated all his wishes as a law.
645 Can this prince have possibly lost all remembrance
Of so many great exploits and glorious deeds?
ALVAR: Whatever a subject does, the King owes him nothing.
We always make him a present of what's his;
And never can one hope, without great rashness,
650 To be rewarded just for doing one's duty.
Let's not complain then. Just see whether you
Can grant Moncade a moment's interview.
LINDAMIRA: Yes, I await him here; you can go bring him.
In my apartment someone might disturb us;
655 We're safer from unwanted persons here.[29]
ALVAR: Don't leave this spot. I hurry to inform him.
Exit Alvar.
LINDAMIRA (*alone*): Cease to trouble me, my too long-heeded pride.[30]
Be silent, you are finally overpowered.
Pride, fear, suspicion, coldness and disguise,
660 Depart forever from my timid heart;
Too long have you all tyrannized my feelings.
Break forth, break forth, my pure and secret passion,
Noble, faithful love that I have fought so long;
Unfortunate slave of an austere virtue, hide
665 Your fires no longer from the man who kindled
Them. Speak, innocent love, 'tis time to appear.
Moncade's unhappy; at this crucial juncture
You'll be less love than magnanimity.
Show yourself in full; the pity that displays you
670 Takes from suspicious eyes . . . Ah, how ill met!
Enter Clotaire.
CLOTAIRE: Madam, having learned that a long banishment
Today was going to rob you of a lover,
I come to remedy this cruel loss
And bring to your feet a tender, faithful heart—

675 A heart, a weak heart pierced through by your blows,
That's never sighed for anyone but you.
LINDAMIRA (*aside*): How cowardly, gods! (*aloud*) The offer is substantial,
And you opportunely seize the favoring moment.
A heart that apes the King's hatred or fury
680 Is an honest present, quite worthy of me.
The man who feels such sympathy for good friends
Persuades his ladylove to yield with ease,
And I must gauge the ardor of your passion
By the way you treat Moncade in his disgrace.
685 CLOTAIRE: Yes, truly, madam, my hatred for Moncade
Reveals my love to you persuasively.
When a heart can hate a rival strongly, it
Must be inflamed with an unequalled love.
The more you know my hatred is extreme,
690 The more you must judge that Clotaire loves you.
LINDAMIRA: Your heart has kept this great passion a secret;
If it's not candid, it's at least discreet.
You're very clever, if you're not sincere,
And feign with skill, if you fail to win hearts.
695 CLOTAIRE: It's true that respect, opposed to my love, has
Long kept my passion bottled up inside.
I hid my sighs, kept back my doleful cries,
But at last my love is stronger than my fear.
I must declare it, 'tis for you I die.
700 At this word arm yourself with all your rigor.
No matter; death brings me less suffering when
Caused by your cruelty than by my long silence.
LINDAMIRA: The King's a great physician for your ailment.
Respect would shortly have snuffed out your life,
705 But the prompt device of sudden fall from favor
Is an effective remedy against silence,
And fortune knows secret miracle-cures

To keep alive lovers who are too discreet.

CLOTAIRE: What! Mocking so sincere a passion to
710 My face! Ah, show me rather all your anger!
In love a show of wrath is less insulting . . .

LINDAMIRA: Ah, you are asking me to be more serious.
Such a request I grant with pleasure and
Agree to show you everything I feel.
715 How dare you bear the title that you bear,
And in my sight exhibit all your cowardice!
You slave of fate, unworthy to be a prince,
After the ignoble conduct you have shown,
How dare you offer me your love and vows?
720 Away, vile courtier, court chameleon,
Forever hide your love and audacity,
And give your presents to some baser soul.
Learn then . . .

CLOTAIRE: That's too much; this excessive fury
Turns to contempt and goes beyond normal rigor.
725 By giving way to this violent outburst,
You authorize my just retaliation.
I know more than one way to take revenge.
I'll say no more and let you think about it.

Exit Clotaire.

LINDAMIRA: From a man of your sort either hate or
friendship . . .
730 Ouch, here's Elvira.

Enter Elvira.

ELVIRA: Why do you seethe with rage?

LINDAMIRA: The pain of finding our century infected
With so much perfidy and cowardice,
To see so few friends in our generation,
And to see self-interest all men's deity.

735 ELVIRA: So that's what pains you. From what I can see,
Love for your neighbor means a lot to you.

What's it to you if social wrongs exist?
Must you answer to the gods for public candor?
LINDAMIRA: No, but if our age had a more noble spirit,
740 My unhappy friends would not be overwhelmed.
Clotaire betrays Moncade in his disgrace,
But would not be so bold, were it a crime.
The label of false friend would horrify him,
Were it abhorred among people of honor.
745 But he readily allows himself this crime
Because it generally passes for wise conduct.
ELVIRA: It's wise indeed, and I for my part hold
That a monarch's anger is a giant burden.
One must avoid it with the utmost care,
750 And the basic love is love for one's own self.
LINDAMIRA: You love yourself a lot?
ELVIRA: Do you do less?
I make my happiness my first concern.
In this life common sense means making oneself happy.
LINDAMIRA: Indeed I thought your soul had more nobility;
755 And knowing how much you valued Moncade,
I thought his fate at least would touch your heart.
ELVIRA: You judge based on yourself, if I think rightly?
LINDAMIRA: Yes, his misfortune touches me; I glory in that.
I deeply pity the state I see him in.
760 ELVIRA: Heaven made your heart more sensitive than mine.
LINDAMIRA: Clotaire reveals a heart so like your own
That I think the gods made them for one another.
I find a wondrous harmony in your humors.
Like him you follow fate's inconstancy;
765 You have like notions of sincerity;
And this perfect couple merits being joined.
ELVIRA: Your spirit is embittered with good reason.
A favorite's suit is stolen from your kind care.
Berate me to assuage so cruel a torment.

770 Come, I'm your friend, and you can speak your piece.
LINDAMIRA: How dare you without blushing . . .
ELVIRA: Gods, what vehemence!
  Just see now what it's like to lose a lover!
  I didn't know this illness was so violent,
  Since I've never experienced it myself.
775 They told me rightly it was very painful.
  But I had a poem for an absent lover.
  Where is it?
LINDAMIRA: Heavens!
ELVIRA: I've got it. (*reads*) "Elegy.
  Ye fates who steal my other half from me . . ."
  Yes, that's the one, for sure. Listen.
LINDAMIRA: O gods!
780 ELVIRA: "You've just decreed that a heart live in two places."
  The style's quite tender.
LINDAMIRA: Fickle, deceitful soul!
ELVIRA: What, that embitters you still more? I don't
  Know any better way to calm your anguish.
  I see I'll have to leave you alone today.
785 LINDAMIRA: Good heavens! Can a woman so well-born
  Have such a heart . . .
ELVIRA: Farewell, unlucky lover.
                          Exit Elvira.
LINDAMIRA (*alone*): If you could judge how shameful it is to
  Throw cowardly insults at unhappy people,
  Whatever torments that my soul must fear,
790 You'd find yourself more pitiable than I.
  But here's Moncade.
                          Enter Moncade.
                          Alas, alas, sir! Then
  It's true that nothing in this life is lasting.
  My eyes inform me then that you're the same man
  That they saw this morning at the height of fortune,

795 And that, when destiny pleases, all this glitter
Fades like a flower in a few hours' time.
By what magic spell can I convince myself
That I see you both unhappy and Moncade?
MONCADE: By a fate whose wrath my heart adores, since I
800 Can flatter myself that I feel it for you.
Yes, madam, heaven seemed to be propitious
Only in offering you this weak sacrifice
From me. This vast greatness, glitter and credit
Made me taste just the shadow of happiness.
805 The only way to make it supreme in this life
Is to give up everything for one's beloved.
At present I taste this perfect happiness
And I feel fully satisfied, as well.
LINDAMIRE: Yes, I approve, sir. Such happiness and glory
810 Will not be lost; they're in my memory.
'Tis there that fortune, hard as it may try,
Can't rob you any more of those rich treasures.
Despite its rage, they constantly will carve
A living image of what I owe to you.
815 My heart, growing enamored of that portrait,
Will make a duty, sir, of loving you.
If you lose this vast power for my sake, you
Lose just an asset subject to fortune's whims;
And to console you for it I here give you
820 A heart that my death only can take back.
MONCADE: Ah, worthy recompense! Ah, peerless glory!
What! When I find myself hated by all,
When the fear of incurring royal wrath is driving
All my friends away, you give yourself to me!
825 Does being unfortunate make me more charming?
Can I believe the evidence of my senses?
LINDAMIRA: Yes, yes, your fall from power attracts my love.
Before today, sir, you were not my own.

Political matters took up all your time;
830   You belonged more to the state than to your mistress.
Your heart, possessed by all these diverse cares,
Confused me often with all other people.
In love such a confusion may be fatal.
I thank you, exile, you remove my rival.
835   Today I triumph; favor is no more.
Moncade can henceforth give me all his heart.
What innocent joys this exile shall prepare us!
Sir, fortune is uneasy and capricious
And jolts the spirit with tumultuous worries
840   That often chase love and its flames away.
On the contrary, disgrace, arousing deep emotions,
Puts us in a tender, languishing condition
Which makes our heart better disposed to love
Than the noise and pomp of courts swarming with people.
845   MONCADE: O gods! What ecstasies of love and pleasure
Inflame my soul with these amorous words!
What, you love me! Alas! What happiness!
But, madam, is this love or generosity?
I tremble, for this great affection has
850   Indeed been hidden from me so artfully,
And you've allowed me for so long to doubt it
That my heart scarcely dares flatter itself.
Some vague suspicion, baneful to my peace,
Tells me that love displays itself in spite of us
855   And that one can't control all one's desires so well
That several signs at least will not escape.
Yet all the effort of a lawful ardor
Let me discover, at the most, esteem.
Two years of attentions have obtained from you
860   Merely the hope of one day being your husband;
Accepting someone's suit without repugnance
Is not always a guarantee of love,

And I have had to doubt until this moment,
Having but that one basis for my hope.

865 LINDAMIRA: Well, doubt no longer, let your fear cease. It
Is true that my excessive scrupulousness
Made me fear that my love would be profaned
By mingling its vows with those of the court.
I feared my soul would be judged so common that
870 I'd be accused of loving you for your fortune.
At last your exile ends this hindrance to my passion.
I love you. It is true, I want you to believe it.

MONCADE: All right then, madam, I shall dare believe it,
This precious love, the source of all my glory!
875 But, gods, unfortunately I believe it
Quite late, since I must leave almost at once.

LINDAMIRA: We'll be far from each other just a few days.
I have, sir, houses very close to yours.
Set your mind at ease; I shall retire there when
880 I'm able to without arousing comment.
Let me arrange concessions to decorum,
And for the rest . . .

MONCADE: Great gods, after this assurance
What's left to ask? Allow me on my knees
To show my joy and love . . .

LINDAMIRA: O sir, arise.
885 If someone sees you, alas, what do you think . . .

MONCADE: Madam, with what rapture you have filled my soul!

LINDAMIRA: I fear we have been seen; let's leave this place.
Depart. Farewell, Moncade.

MONCADE: Madam, farewell.

Exeunt.

ACT IV

Enter Elvira and Leonora.

LEONORA: At the risk of being an irksome friend to you,
890   No, this strange method I can't tolerate.
In one hour's time Moncade's forgotten by you.
That man, so perfect . . .

ELVIRA: He is in disgrace.

LEONORA: For being disgraced, is he no less the same?
What! Your heart feels a passionate affection,
895   And then, with no trouble, you just stop at will.
You change your lovers as one does handkerchiefs.

ELVIRA: And don't you find my method admirable?
My heart loved him as long as he was lovable.
When being in favor made his love worth prizing,
900   When games and laughter followed him everywhere,
I, who love joy and gladness in all things,
Endeavored without ceasing to acquire him;
But in this great reversal, where we find in him
Merely a spirit crushed by grief and sorrow,
905   When he's an object less of pleasure than of tears,
Could I be right in seeing the same charms in him?
Where would my mind and my discernment be?
Come now, give some support to your argument.

LEONORA: You would be showing an intrepid soul,
910   Great constancy . . .

ELVIRA: Oh, let's seek what is solid.
Fie on your constancy! It's out of fashion.
It's just a silly fancy dressed as a virtue.
If our fathers once held to that lunacy,
Our generation's quite cured of that illness.
915   Believe me, Leonora, nowadays at court
They don't give chains to Cupid any more.
Since he's a child, they think him frolicsome.
What was a torment's treated like a game.

LEONORA: It's true, to see you treat his passion thus,
920   One can't deny that it's a game to you.
But on one point I must be satisfied:
Did you not love Moncade before this disgrace?
Was it pretense or not?

ELVIRA: You know me well!
I hate all that is loved, and never love a thing.
925   Whatever might deprive me of the name of fairest
Blindly inspires in me a mortal hatred.
Lindamira seemed more charming than I when
She subjugated the King's chief minister.
As soon as she received this glorious homage,
930   At once she drew upon her all my rage.
But whatever feelings came with this vehement wrath,
I hated her and did not love her lover.
To show you better how I loved Moncade,
I've made a conquest on my stroll just now.
935   For without flattery, or else I'm no judge,
Don Lope has felt the power of my attractions.
By chance I surprised a certain tender glance.

LEONORA: Truly, the more you speak, the less I understand you.
This way of loving and these sudden changes
940   For people of my sort are mystifying.
But I'll concede that point; love has its secrets
That it won't profane with ordinary lovers.
You can change lovers, you can hate him, but
To join Clotaire, Elvira, and betray him,
945   That's the lowest blow a weak, base soul can give.

ELVIRA: Should I not rather share in his disgrace,
And spend the fairest of my days in exile
Through an indiscreet and most unhelpful zeal?
I've taken utmost care to make them believe
950   That I loved Lindamira like myself.
She adores Moncade, and might in her distress

Make some complaint and ruin herself with him.
If her love brings her to such lunacy,
I'll be suspected of complicity,
955 And anyone who slightly envies me
Can bring down all the King's wrath on my head.
I must therefore ward off this calumny
By showing that I am their greatest foe,
And thus adroitly keep myself from danger
960 By my eagerness to do them a bad turn.
For it's a fine recourse for an unhappy lady
To think they'll praise my magnanimity.
What fine ambition! My heart, thanks to heaven,
Wants no part of that title at that price.
965 Let others fathom mysteries so sublime;
I feed not on these idle fantasies.
I know what perfect love and glory are;
But I fear disgrace and greatly like the court.
The most sparkling eyes are dimmed by weeping, and
970 Three days of grieving tarnish many charms.
I like my own a little, and to see them last
I vowed a long time since I'd never weep.
That's how I feel. However I am judged,
I want to have no arguments on this point.
975 If you like grief, let's share between us thus:
You'll weep for me, and *I* shall laugh for you.
Does this course please you?

LEONORA: Perfectly, and you
Oblige me too much. But what does this page want?

Enter Page.

ELVIRA: He's from the new swain. *(to Page)* What do you want?

PAGE: This missive
Will tell you, madam.

980 ELVIRA: It smells like a love-note.
(reads) "Since our moment's conversation

I've noticed, though unthinkingly
A certain impatient sensation
That I cannot identify.
985 I feel emotions brand new to my soul.
My heart has sweet, tumultuous desires.
I don't know what it is, but, madam, I
Think being near you is what the cure requires."[31]
Ah, nothing is more gallant. Friend, I pray,
990 Does this love-letter please your pompousness?
I'm not going out this evening, Page, he'll find
Me. Tell him he can come and he'll oblige me.
                    Exit Page.
All right, Miss Constancy, is love in my style
The most attractive or the most inconvenient?
995 Speak, what's your view?
LEONORA: That hearts so quickly smitten
Grow cold as quickly, and have little value.
ELVIRA: The fine illusion! There now! I'm contented.
Suffice it that he occupies a vacant place.
I leave the rest to fate; some moment will come
1000 That he'd embarrass me, were he more constant.
At least he's sparing me the cruel disgrace
Of being without a lover for one day,
While being young and fair. But here's Clotaire. Well, sir?
                    Enter Clotaire.
CLOTAIRE: Fate seems to try its best on our behalf.
1005 Learn of a project of extreme importance,
Which would have ruined us, were I not prudent.
Defying the King's fury, Lindamira
Joins Moncade in exile and gives him her hand.
ELVIRA: O gods! Who'd have thought it of such a prude?
1010 But how do you know of this unbelievable plan?
CLOTAIRE: From one of her men who likes me dearly, and
Whom I secretly placed with her on purpose.

Now Moncade's exiled to a province where
Lindamira's power almost equals the King's.
1015 That province once belonged to her family,
And maybe this act harbors thoughts of treason.
If that is so, such an adventure, madam,
Will put us in high standing at the court,
The King getting from us this crucial warning.
1020 I pray, consider what rank will await us.
There are no favors that we won't be showered with,
And we can fill the guilty man's position.
ELVIRA: O heaven! Let's haste to give this precious warning.
LEONORA: What, you can go through with this odious crime!
1025 What, this betrayal . . .
ELVIRA: See that heroic lady?
Is it a crime today to practice shrewdness?
Do you know what bad luck and adversity
Attend the name of friend to a rebel subject?
CLOTAIRE: Elvira speaks aright. Yes, it's a maxim
1030 That all his friends will suffer from his crime here.
Believe me, Leonora, it's a tricky point;
We argue too much over a heinous deed.
Let's quickly find the King, but for the rest, madam,
It would be shameful for me to accuse a woman.
1035 It's for you . . .
ELVIRA: Yes, sir, I accept the task.
CLOTAIRE: Let's go. But here the King comes opportunely.
                    Enter King and Carlos.
KING: Just heaven, in this barbarous age must it
Be that a true friend has become so rare?
ELVIRA: Sire, without too much license, might I dare
1040 To bring some tidings to your Majesty?
KING: You may.
ELVIRA: It is quite difficult to believe.
That proud person with a heart so full of glory,

A soul impervious to Cupid's arrows—
In short, Lindamira—is at last in love.
1045   She will accompany Moncade in his journey,
And pity finally masters that great spirit.
It was a heart of steel; love frightened her.
But compassion is all-powerful in great hearts.
KING: Is it possible, O gods? What, that proud beauty,
1050   The height of arrogance?
ELVIRA: Yes, sire, the same.
She'll share her lover's exile.
KING: Who could have
Suspected her of such amazing passion?
ELVIRA: Ah, sire, in every age these model virtues
Are skillful masks to hide suspicious business.
1055   Never put your trust in these hearts made of rock
Which love, it seems, would never dare approach.
One loves no less for knowing how to feign,
And passions held back are more to be feared.
KING: Since you like her greatly, her departure hence . . .
1060   ELVIRA: *I* like her, sire? The gods preserve me from it!
She's going to deserve your just wrath; she
Follows a banished man who has displeased you;
And would my heart dare to consent to like her?
May heaven, I repeat, protect me from it!
1065   I pray, think better of Elvira's feelings.
To justify myself, sire, I dare tell you
That if I judge aright, more than one passion
May play a part in this hasty departure.
I'm not a brilliant mind, but I know women;
1070   I know that spite affects their feelings greatly.
You're wounding her soul in a touchy spot.
I don't grasp principles of state too well,
But in your place I'd fear the worst from her.
See what she's capable of, and give it thought.

1075 CLOTAIRE: If I dare voice my feelings on this point,
That fear is not without foundation, sire.
The high concerns of great kings, such as you,
Rarely descend to the lowly multitude.
Their minds, filled with illustrious concerns,
1080 Think only in passing of their subjects' loves.
But we idle creatures, whose most pressing business
Is usually to study other people,
Notice all things; nothing escapes our sight;
And it's in my capacity as curious idler
1085 That I dare step forward on this point to tell you
That it's good to watch out for Lindamira.
This journey has more than one motive, sire.
Think in what province Moncade has his estate.
KING: You doubtless give me an important warning,
1090 And you will judge that by my gratitude.
This kindness stuns me; I admit between us
I wasn't expecting such great zeal from you,
As you are not my subject.
CLOTAIRE: Sire, your person
Wins more hearts for your rule than does the crown.
1095 One gladly makes fealty to you a duty
When one has the good fortune just to see you.
KING: Prince, you confound me, and my guardian spirit
Shows infinite power on this occasion, for
Your heart should have been won over by Moncade;
1100 He visibly served you with so much ardor.
It was at his sole asking, I recall,
That in the last campaign I aided you,
And later too it was through his great zeal
That you obtained asylum in this land.
1105 A service of such paramount importance,
It seems, ought to have caused you hesitation.
I found you suspect once I dared consider this.

CLOTAIRE: You find me suspect! Me, sire, hesitation!
  If I received good turns from someone else,
1110 The ultimate giver, I well knew, was you.
  By whatever channel they're conveyed to us,
  You are the source; I owe them all to you.
          Enter Lindamira, unnoticed.
KING: Yes, but that friendship that you openly displayed . . .
LINDAMIRA (*aside*): Let's listen.
CLOTAIRE: *I* loved the favor of his master.
1115 He never had a greater charm for me
  Than his good luck as object of royal kindness.
  Indeed, if I today must tell you openly,
  My heart wished you to be less lavish with him.
  Everyone viewed his favored rank with sorrow,
1120 And your best subjects were secretly complaining.
ELVIRA: He's giving you true information, sire.
  Really Moncade's pride was unbearable.
LINDAMIRA (*aside*): The coward!
CLOTAIRE: The whole kingdom was displeased.
LINDAMIRA (*stepping forward*): Yes, sire, it's true; these are impor-
  tant tidings.
1125 CLOTAIRE: O gods! It's Lindamira!
LINDAMIRA: People like these
  Are very needful for all monarchs' welfare.
  Continue, noble counselors, continue;
  Complete the ruin of a friend in distress;
  Set out for us a crime you have imagined—
1130 Just what we'd expect from Clotaire and Elvira.
  Great King, can it be that your Majesty
  Condones such baseness and such cowardice?
  Prince, fount of honor, peerless monarch, can
  You view that hateful couple without horror?
1135 KING: Tone down that vehement anger, tone it down.
  We know the cause of this great indignation.

It's from them I learned of your blissful journey
To which love for Moncade today impels you.
You doubtless heard this, and your anger comes
1140 From seeing an obstacle to such sweet plans.
LINDAMIRA: I knew not the extent of their black perfidy
And have heard nothing of this calumny.
KING: What! Then this journey is mere fabrication?
LINDAMIRA: I don't wish to deny, your Majesty,
1145 That in my taste for calm and solitude
I'd made plans for a voluntary exile,
But in order to relax from court society,
And out of sheer disgust, not out of love.
KING: I ask no further questions on this point.
1150 Enough. One sees few ladies as young as you
Desert the court without regret and sorrow
If love has no part in that secret loathing.
I see all your plots and foresee the results;
And since love rarely has its limits, it
1155 Is good to think at once of countering
Misfortunes that this passion might bring on us.
I'll work on this.
                    Exeunt King and Carlos.
CLOTAIRE: Let's follow the King, madam,
And use his mental state to our advantage.
                Exeunt Clotaire, Elvira, Leonora.
LINDAMIRA: Gods who see in our hearts, inspire the King,
1160 Or make his anger fall only on me.
                          Exit.

ACT V

Enter Lindamira and Alvar.

LINDAMIRA: Moncade under arrest! Ah, cruel disgrace!
Must I believe this woeful news, great gods?

ALVAR: Would to heaven it were easier to doubt it!
But, madam, he was just arrested in my sight.

1165 LINDAMIRA: Ah, there's no remedy for this new ill,
And I feel that my constancy must yield.
This last blow is complete. Alas, he's ruined!
And we're forbidden all hope on this point.
His exile left me room for optimism.

1170 They seemed to keep a measure of decorum,
Sending him to his house with no noise, no scandal.
But if the King treats him as a criminal of state,
Believe me, Don Alvar, his doom is sealed.
Envy and my bad luck have jointly vowed it.

1175 ALVAR: But what will you do next in this deep sorrow?

LINDAMIRA: Oh, in the state I'm in what can I do?

ALVAR: Escape, while it is still allowed to you.

LINDAMIRA: Where can one flee a fury authorized by
A scepter? Where hide from an angry monarch?

1180 No, no, I shall await it all serenely.

ALVAR: But here your ruin becomes inevitable.
Loving a guilty man makes one a criminal.
You must know what claims reasons of state make,
And what power they have on a touchy king.

1185 LINDAMIRA: If of these claims Moncade becomes the victim,
Paying all my blood, I would purchase a crime.
The king, condemning me to follow him
In death, would spare my arm at least one heinous
Deed, and lest the implacable ire of heaven

1190 Deprive me of the good of seeming guilty,
Let's go inform the King of my heart's secret.
I've heeded you too long, dangerous modesty.

Despite your laws I wish, by a frank avowal,
To lose this innocence so opposed to my desires,
1195   And by the happy outcome of a just
Outburst to share my lover's fate forever.
Let's run, let's run to the King; may a vain hope . . .
                    Enter Carlos.
CARLOS: Madam, spare yourself this trouble, if you please.
Await him in your room; he's on his way there
1200   And has just ordered me to keep you there.
LINDAMIRA: This violence is given a fair pretext.
CARLOS: I carry out such an order with regret,
But the King's commands . . .
LINDAMIRA: They seem on this occasion
To be in league with my passion. The King
1205   Obliges me more than he realizes
By treating me as equal to Moncade.
This honor was not due me, but to earn it
I'll try my best to imitate him well.
I know this hero never was guilty but
1210   In having loved too much her he judged lovely.
I'll follow this example; till my death
I hope to share his crime and destiny.
Assure the King of this. *(to Alvar)* You, whose noble heart,
I dare believe, is envious of my glory,
1215   Receive, to drive away these jealous feelings,
The advice that I received from you just now.
Illustrious friend, flee from this land. I see
That heaven is declaring war on it.
Its denizens, no doubt, have angered the gods;
1220   They cannot suffer virtue in this place;
And since virtuous souls must tremble here,
'Those who resemble you are in great peril.
ALVAR: Ah, madam, hide this seething indignation.
Tone down the excess of this vehemence.

1225 LINDAMIRA: No, no, dear Don Alvar, the time to feign is past.
  When hope is gone, there's nothing left to fear.
  CARLOS: But, madam, the King will be there before us.
  If you please, we must . . .
  LINDAMIRA: Yes, Carlos, that's enough.
  Let's go.
                    Enter King.
  CARLOS: Forgive me. Gods! The king advances.
1230 We must have made him lose all patience with us.
  LINDAMIRA: You see, sire, I am going to withdraw,
  And Carlos is my witness that I don't complain.
  KING: Stop, stop, you're necessary to me. You
  Have too much of a share in all this business
1235 To be deprived of the joy of witnessing it.
  You, Carlos, listen.
  CARLOS: I'll take care of it.
                    Exit Carlos; enter Clotaire.
  CLOTAIRE: Despite all your contempt, I swear to you
  That, madam, I fully share your anxieties.
  LINDAMIRA: Your heart could be dispensed from such a trouble.
1240 My cares are not as great as you dare think.
  KING: Now gently! We have learned from your own mouth
  How excessively you love that guilty man.
  You vainly try to hide from us the passion . . .
  LINDAMIRA: No, no, sire, if you wish, I shall confess it.
1245 Is it a crime to love a great-souled hero
  Who has won esteem from all the universe?
  CLOTAIRE: Sire, after such a speech, what are you waiting for?
  KING: You give these titles to the object of my wrath.
  The amazing power of a foolhardy passion
1250 Dares go to such lengths to defy my anger!
  LINDAMIRA: Why, sire, you are the one who caused that passion
  That rages in my heart in spite of me.
  It's by placing Moncade on glory's summit,

By making him gain numerous victories,
1255 By giving honor to his glorious exploits
That you made him so charming in my eyes.
Had not you showered him with your favor, his
Great gentleness, loyalty, lack of presumption,
His zeal and his respect for your Majesty
1260 Would have shone less to my discerning eyes.
The highest virtue sinks beneath royal favor:
It's a slippery slope where the firmest fall;
Yet I have seen him bear your many favors
Without seeing his heart waver for one moment.
1265 I've seen him as a conqueror without rashness,
A favorite without pride, a courtier yet sincere.
You've known him to be so, yet you're surprised
That after that Moncade has charmed my mind.
CLOTAIRE: But, madam, he conserves from all that glory
1270 No more than the sad memory today.
No more is he the object of a great king's kindness,
Lifted almost to equal status by his love;
He's the doomed target of an august wrath,
Which through submission we must all deem just.
1275 Knowing this glorious prince, you must belie
For him whatever your heart and eyes tell you.
Yes, you must judge that a fair-minded monarch
Treats no subject as guilty without cause.
Knowing the King, when I see this disgrace,
1280 I hold Moncade tainted by a hundred crimes;
I deem him rash, ambitious, treasonous;
I think the virtue that he showed to us
Is a deceptive mask, used to hide from all . . .
ALVAR: Ah, sir, can such words come from you? What have
1285 I heard, great gods? What, such a slander comes
From Prince Clotaire? Ah, blackest perfidy!
KING: What vehemence, Don Alvar . . .

ALVAR: Forgive me, sire,
 If it escapes my heart despite my respect.
 When I see Moncade accused here by a prince
1290 Whose life and whose country he has conserved,
 And for whom so many times with so much kindness
 He urged your Majesty to do him service,
 I can't deny it; not even your august
 Presence can force me to keep silent now.
1295 I know Moncade well; it is I, sire, I
 Who can best answer for his loyalty.
 I alone have seen his plans, have read his thoughts.
 Men hide their faults from the objects of their love.
 One might presume, adoring Lindamira,
1300 That he feigned virtues to win her esteem.
 But I, who would observe him with great care,
 And whom he always loved equal to himself,
 I am the one, great King, who, seeing him accused
 In my sight, must repel this insulting blow.
1305 CLOTAIRE: This anger and this vehemence reveal
 Their factions, sire, their criminal collusion.
 I told you so; he has been buying hearts,
 Winning your subjects, paying them with your favors.
 Judge by this single case what he can do
1310 And what avail your rank as monarch is.
 LINDAMIRA: Yes, traitor, the favors he had from the King,
 Making his merit and his loyalty shine,
 Indeed produced the ardor that inspires us.
 CLOTAIRE: Great gods, what more can she say after that!
1315 LINDAMIRA: But if he had absolute power on our hearts,
 It was because he fully did his duty.
 ALVAR: Yes, sire, he did; I know his innocence,
 And if I dare defend him in your sight,
 I give myself up to your Majesty, great Prince,
1320 As guarantor of his fidelity.

Yes, if he is convicted of the slightest
Thought that could truly harm your authority,
I yield myself, sire, to the cruelest death . . .
LINDAMIRA: That honor's due to me; don't take it from me.
1325 Yes, Don Alvar, it's for me, whom he loves,
To answer for him like an alter ego.
All-just, all-good King, suffer me on my knees . . .
KING: We'll settle your fate. Here he is. Stand up.
Enter Moncade and Carlos.
Come, wretched man, come see by a hundred patent proofs,
1330 What your secret intrigues are arousing here.
Come see those of my court whom I most cherish
Competing to be sacrificed for you.
Look at Don Alvar; approach, consider her
For whom I am less king than father,
1335 And whom I've taken care of since her birth,
Who makes my rights yield to those of her love:
Lindamira, object of all my esteem,
Wants to share your crime and follow you in exile.
She loves him who offends me; she admits it
1340 And for this guilty love betrays my plans.
Would anyone have thought that such a passion . . .
MONCADE: Ah, sire, judge better of her soul's desires
And don't condemn with such severity
A weak gesture of magnanimity.
1345 It's that alone, sire, that makes Lindamira act;
Love has no part in the zeal inspiring her;
Whatever outburst she may make today,
It's pity, it's kindness, but it isn't love.
Enter Elvira and Leonora, at a distance.
ELVIRA: You see, Leonora; let that suffice for you.
1350 Joy always, everywhere, in all things: that's
My motto. But here's not the place to preach it.
Let us withdraw.

KING: Come forth, you may approach.
Your presence will be necessary here;
I need witnesses for what I want to do.

1355   LINDAMIRA: Yes, to make my glory shine in sight of all,
Approach, Elvira, you are needed here.
Knowing your ability to keep a secret,
We make you witness of my love today.
I thank you, sire, for this obliging service,

1360   And I would like the universe as witness.

MONCADE (*aside*): O gods, she'll ruin herself!

LINDAMIRA: I'll fearlessly admit . . .

MONCADE: Ah, don't believe her, sire, this is pretense.
Knowing what power she has over your heart,
She feigns this obliging ardor out of kindness,

1365   Presuming that perhaps a king who loves her
Will grant my pardon for her great love's sake.

LINDAMIRA: There now, I've said too much; you try in vain.
Thanks to my confession, we will have one fate.

KING (*to Moncade*): How did you manage to seduce such a person?

1370   Was it in hopes that you'd usurp my crown?
For this great heart indeed has never loved.

LINDAMIRA: He did his duty and has served you well.
It's thus that one seduces truly noble hearts,
And not by hopes that they'll commit some crimes.

1375   Know me well, sire; what can inflame me is
His lofty virtue; that's what makes me love him.
That's the glorious, sole cause of a love so pure.

ELVIRA: What a silly thing this perfect love is!
Long live convenient love and good, calm friendship!

1380   MONCADE: In the gods' name, madam, show less pity; you
Make my woes sharper as your zeal increases.
Be less magnanimous and be more prudent!
Alas, before this sad day who could have told me

That her too great love would be my main misfortune?
1385 LINDAMIRA: I know that excess will make me a criminal,
But my greatest desire is to appear one.
Sire, if today I've made one person guilty,
I intend in turn to be guilty for him.
His love displeased you; mine does likewise. If
1390 He said so, I own it; we love one another.
Order the same penalty; let equal passions . . .
KING: Well! After that, is our Moncade content?
Will he still feel that his joy is imperfect,
And can't his king give him just what he wishes?
1395 MONCADE: What, sire! This anger was just pretense . . .
KING: How,
Moncade, could you have judged it otherwise?
You're innocent; I treat you as if guilty.
Yet you, who know I'm a fair-minded monarch,
You see me as unjust and dare to think so.
1400 Ah, that suspicion's what I should resent,
And if Moncade didn't have the knack to please me
In all things, that's what should arouse my anger.
LEONORA: What a reverse!
ELVIRA: What have I done?
CLOTAIRE: Vain pretension!
KING: Now learn the secret of my intention. Since
1405 For ten years you've made known to me that never
Has subject loved his master more than you,
No subject likewise has been cherished by
A king more fervently than you by me.
I saw you afflicted by a melancholy
1410 That was the sole hindrance to my peace of mind.
I learned its cause and I now make it cease.
No doubts have any further right to harm you.
I swore by the rights of the holy diadem
To show whether what's loved is my favor or you.

1415 I keep my word and on this glorious day
All—friend, beloved, king—will make you happy.
LINDAMIRA: O King, the most incomparable of kings,
May this great day make you remembered always.
MONCADE: May I deserve this excess of your kindness
1420 By shedding all my blood for your Majesty.
(*to Alvar*) And you, illustrious friend, whose most uncommon
Soul seems impervious to fortune's arrows,
Let's henceforth share the favor of my king.
ALVAR: I've satisfied my heart, served just myself.
1425 KING: Let's complete our work by ordering your wedding.
CLOTAIRE: What's this? What have I done? O rage, despair!
Exit Clotaire.
MONCADE: Prince . . .
KING: No, leave him to this just hysteria.
He has well deserved such stinging self-reproach,
And his example must serve as a sign to all
1430 That no one clearly views a monarch's heart,
And that to get out of so great a danger,
There's nothing like nobility of soul.
But let's go finish this.
Exeunt all but Elvira and Leonora.
LEONORA: Well, crafty one,
Will you take a great share in the public feasting?
1435 ELVIRA: All this is not worth any conversation.
Don Lope's waiting; he's my consolation.
Exeunt.

END.

Anne de La Roche-Guilhen

All-Wondrous

(Rare-en-tout)

The Author

Anne de La Roche-Guilhen was born in Rouen and was baptized on July 24, 1644.[32] On both sides of her family she was descended from the lower ranks of the Huguenot nobility. She was the great-niece of the poet Saint-Amant and was distantly related to the memorialist Tallemant des Réaux. Nothing is known of her early life, but she probably received a solid education. She undoubtedly could read Spanish, for her earliest literary work was a translation of Perez de Hita's history of the Spanish civil wars. This work was probably completed by 1666 (the date when the dedicatee, the Spanish ambassador to France, left his position), although it was not published until 1683. In 1674 she published her first novel, *Almanzaïde*, the first of some twenty volumes of fiction which she was to produce. Judging from the number of reeditions, translations (mainly into English), pirate editions, and false attributions, her books must have sold well. Indeed, she openly admitted in the preface to one of her last novels that she wrote primarily in order to make money.

Several major gaps remain in our knowledge of Anne's whereabouts. The family was still residing in Rouen in 1664 when her mother died; she was in London in 1677 for the premiere of her only play; she was present when her father died in Paris in 1682; from 1687 until her death she was based permanently in London. Also, whereas she had her earlier works published in Paris, during the last twenty years of her life she sent all her books to publishers in Holland. She probably first came to London in December of 1675, in the entourage of the Duchess de Mazarin. In 1675 Anne had dedicated her second novel, *Arioviste*, to this lady's sister, the Duchess de Bouillon, and later the same year she dedicated her next novel, *Astérie*, to the Duchess' cousin, the Countess de Quintin (who, like the novelist, was a Protestant). Moreover, Lady Sussex, sister-in-law of the

Duchess of Grafton (the dedicatee of *All-Wondrous*), was a close friend of the Duchess de Mazarin. According to a note in Desmaizeaux's 1705 edition of Saint-Evremond's correspondence, Anne was in the service of the Duchess of Grafton, presumably either as a companion or as a French tutor, at the time King Charles II commissioned her to write a musical play for his birthday celebration. It is conceivable that Saint-Evremond knew the novelist and could have suggested her name.

It is likely that La Roche-Guilhen remained in London thereafter, with only occasional trips to France for family reasons, but that it was not until the revocation of the Edict of Nantes that her younger sisters, Marie and Madeleine, both invalids, came to join her. Beginning in 1686, the three sisters received a pension from the Royal Bounty, a government fund set up to aid Huguenot refugees who had fled to England. Even though, as members of the nobility, they received the second highest category of allowance (the highest going to clergymen), the sum was barely enough for them to live on and Anne continued her prolific literary activity. She outlived Marie, who died in 1700, and Madeleine, who died in 1705, and was buried on February 26, 1707.

It is difficult to form an idea of her personality. Based on her prefaces and occasional editorial comments in her novels, we know that she was an intelligent and conscientious writer and that she was deeply committed to her Protestant faith. Beyond that, there is only conjecture.

The Play

Significance

Only a dozen years after the performance of *The Favorite Minister* at Versailles, *All-Wondrous* was performed in London for the English court. The honor was even more exceptional, because King Charles II actually commissioned the play and because the author was a foreigner. The royal recognition occurred, just as in France, only a few years after the initial acceptance by English professional acting companies of works by women playwrights.

All-Wondrous, besides playing a minor but intriguing role in the history of opera in England (see next section), helped set some trends in French comedy. It is one of the first plays to comment on the sudden and intense popularity of opera, beginning immediately with the appearance of Jean-Baptiste Lully's first *tragédie-lyrique* in 1673 and continuing unabated throughout that composer's career. Authors and performers of spoken plays, alarmed by the competition from the new music-dramas, soon realized that they offered an unlimited field for parody. While few went as far as Saint-Evremond, whose comedy *Les Opéra* (published 1705 but written decades earlier) showed young people going mad from love of opera to the point of wanting to sing all the time in real life, La Roche-Guilhen does present a temperamental young singer who disdains to speak when she is not singing and will not tolerate the company of any person who is not musical.

In addition, this play is apparently the first French comedy to give a starring role to the *petit-maître*, or fop, a character type who would enjoy a long vogue with Parisian audiences. The new popularity of seducers, rakes, and fops in literature undeniably corresponded to changes in seventeenth-century society. The rise of the salons and the increasingly dominant role played at court by women made it ever more important for men to possess the requisite social graces and to devote considerable effort to pleasing the ladies.

The *petit-maître* is a male flirt whose pursuit of ladies is motivated solely by a narcissistic desire for admiration. Able to act convincingly the role of the passionate lover, he seems to lack sexual desire altogether and shows no interest in entering bedrooms. Whether he "romances" one woman at a time, or several, depends on how effective he considers such a strategy to be in gaining for him the universal recognition that he craves. In the interests of poetic justice, playwrights always make sure that the fop is unmasked and abandoned by the ladies, and that he will be barred from marriage (the normal resolution of comedies) unless he repents and changes his ways.

La Roche-Guilhen was able to anticipate the popularity of this character type, even if her play failed to influence the emerging dramatic tradition. Her fop, totally self-assured and aware of his true motives, can make fun of his valet's more genuine and down-to-earth passion and remains unruffled at the end of the play. Inheriting the love of hyperbolic expression from the braggart soldier tradition, All-Wondrous frequently boasts of his prowess in love, war, and music. Yet his claims for himself are not shown to be completely fraudulent. He does indeed have a good voice, has received musical training, and knows how to charm the ladies. If there is no confirmation that he is brave and has fought in battle, nothing is said to disprove those assertions, either.

All-Wondrous is also noteworthy as one of the last specimens of a hybrid genre, the comedy-ballet. This form consists of a spoken play with some singing allowed within an act, punctuated by interludes of chorus and ballet bearing at least a tenuous connection to the main plot. Generally, characters who spoke could not sing, and vice versa. Since these works were almost invariably royal commissions, they featured a prologue and epilogue containing fulsome praise of king and court. It was Molière who created the hybrid in 1661 with *Les Fâcheux*, and the form achieved phenomenal success from the start because of Molière's comic genius, Lully's gifts for music and choreography, and Louis' love for magnificent display. However, the comedy-ballet was destined to flourish for less than two decades. During the 1670s Lully turned his attention to the composition of tragic operas;

Molière died suddenly; and the king, delighted with the new works that were sung throughout, stopped commissioning works in the hybrid form. Lully accelerated its decline by persuading Louis to protect the monopoly of his newly-created opera company by banning other theatres from using more than a handful of professional singers and instrumentalists. This restriction, combined with the general public's wildly enthusiastic response to Lully's operas, made it increasingly unprofitable for acting companies to perform comedy-ballets. A handful of writers, led by Thomas Corneille and Donneau de Visé, persevered and continued to write hybrid plays, while some of Molière's comedy-ballets were revived either with new music or with no music, but by the early 1680s the form was largely abandoned.

The play is topical in yet another way: it sheds light on Franco-English relations in the 1670s. The prologue, which depicts Charles II as the champion of peace (as opposed to the prologues of French operas and comedy-ballets, which constantly hail Louis XIV's military successes), indicates the degree to which many Europeans, including large numbers of Frenchmen, were weary of war. La Roche-Guilhen also suggests that a fair number of Frenchmen were, like herself, moving to London. No reason is given in the play for the sudden departure of Climene and her father, although religious and financial causes may be the most probable explanation. Certainly, we are not to suppose that the father has crossed the Channel merely to escape from his daughter's suitor. On the other hand, La Treille claims that it was not uncommon for French girls who had lost their honor to move to England in hopes of finding a husband or a protector (vv. 595–600). In addition, London was a center of musical activity, with concerts often held in private homes or on the Thames, and, given the number of French musicians resident there, French musical style must have exerted some influence. Concerts play a major role in La Roche-Guilhen's comedy: It is during a concert at the home of another French émigré that the hero first meets Isabelle, and both of the interludes are concerts organized in honor of the heroine, the first presumably by Tirsis, the second by All-Wondrous. Even the names of the singers may suggest a kind of friendly contest between musical styles: Isabella happens to be the first name of the play's dedicatee, the Duchess of Grafton, in whose entourage the author had been for some time. Climene was the stage name for one of the most famous French sopranos of the day, Mlle Brigogne. The juxtaposition of English and French airs during the meeting of All-Wondrous and Isabelle in Act II, implying respect for both styles, forms the center of the play.

All-Wondrous *and the Early History of Opera*

If the birth of opera took place during the 1590s in Italy, the idea of a totally sung drama failed to catch on in France or in England for almost a century thereafter.[33] The composer Robert Cambert and the poet Pierre Perrin were the pioneers in France: following the success of their short, experimental *Pastorale d'Issy* (1659), they renewed their collaboration to produce the first full-length French opera, *Pomone*, in 1671. Perrin also secured a royal patent to found an official French academy of music. However, Cambert's arch-rival, Jean-Baptiste Lully, having grasped the new genre's potential, bought the patent from Perrin (who had quickly found himself imprisoned for debt) and, for all intents and purposes, expelled Cambert from the country. The hapless composer moved to London, where his former pupil, Louis Grabu, had been employed at court since 1665.

Charles II, who had been favorably impressed with the performances of Italian opera and of French machine plays which he had seen during his years in Paris, showed great eagerness to enlist the services of foreign musicians at his court and to reproduce some of the musical forms, including opera, which he had come to enjoy. At various times during his reign he attempted to launch Italian and French opera companies in London, most of which never got off the ground. The project which came closest to fruition was the "royal Academy of Musick," under the direction of Cambert and Grabu. In 1674 Grabu wrote a new opera entitled *Ariane* (reusing a Perrin libretto which had earlier been set by Cambert) and had it performed at court on March 30 in honor of the Duke of York's marriage. Grabu also received permission to borrow from the theatre at Whitehall whatever scenery he needed to stage a group of French operas; however, he was required to return it in fourteen days. The Royal Academy was thus able to give public performances of *Ariane* and several works by Cambert (*Pomone* and a new "divertissement" dedicated to King Charles). The French operas appear to have been badly received, and Cambert's company was allowed to dissolve. Even worse, Grabu lost his appointment at court in September of 1674, and there is no record that Cambert ever received any employment at court. The latter died (penniless, it is said) early in 1677. Grabu did not get another chance until 1685, when he composed the music for Dryden's unsuccessful opera, *Albion and Albanius.*

It has been suggested that English musical taste was undergoing a shift at about this time, with French music losing ground to Italian. However, it should be stated that Italian opera had no more success in London than the French, despite the enthusiastic welcome accorded to visiting Italian singers. The English spectators of the Restoration, although willing to accept increasingly large doses of music and dance into spoken plays, continued to balk at the notion of a work featuring continuous singing. Even though the period produced the first real operas in English, especially Purcell's masterpiece, *Dido and Aeneas* (1689/90), these works received only a few private performances and failed to inaugurate a new national tradition. Curiously, spectacular plays with extensive music, which in France would have been called comedy-ballets, were referred to by the English as operas.

Unable or unwilling to resurrect the Royal Academy, yet nostalgic for French opera, Charles commissioned a comedy-ballet, *All-Wondrous,* for his birthday in 1677. It is hard to tell whether this was simply a case of indulging his personal taste, or whether Charles hoped to rekindle interest in French music. If the latter is correct, the king's hopes were cruelly dashed by the audience's hostility to the new work. The composer, Jacques Paisible (or Peasible, as he styled himself in England), retained his position at court, but would never again receive a large-scale dramatic commission. With the possible exception of what seems to have been the visit of a French troupe in 1685–86, French opera disappeared from the London stage with the failure of *All-Wondrous*, clearing the way for the eventual triumph of Italian opera there in Handel's day.

Performance History

The only known performance is that at Whitehall before the court of Charles II on his birthday, May 29, 1677. Paisible conducted the orchestra, drawn from the ranks of court musicians. The singers and actors were imported from France; it is tempting to speculate that Mlle Brigogne played the role of Climene. Unfortunately, the audience failed to appreciate the new work, either because the performance was disappointing, or because they disapproved of French music and/or the use of the French language. The one surviving account of that performance is in a letter written by one John Verney to a relative on May 31:

> On Wednesday his Majesty's birth night, was some gallantry at Whitehall, where was acted a French opera, but most pitifully done, so ill that the king was aweary on't, and some say it was not well contrived to entertain the English gentry, who came that night in honour to their King, with a lamentable ill-acted French play, when our English actors so much surpass; however the dances and voices were pretty well performed.[34]

Unfortunately, Paisible never published the score for this work, and it has not survived.

All-Wondrous

(Rare-en-tout)
Comedy
Mixed with Music and Ballet

Performed Before His Majesty
on the Royal Theatre of Whitehall

Anne de La Roche-Guilhen

Actors

(in the play proper)

ALL-WONDROUS, Gascon.
LA TREILLE, All-Wondrous' valet
ISABELLE, English singer.
CLIMENE, French singer.
FINETTE, Isabelle's servant.
TIRSIS, French singer.

Actors

(in Prologue, Epilogue, and Interludes)

EUROPE.

THE THAMES.

CUPID.

NATIONS, TRITONS AND NEREIDS, YOUNG LOVERS,
SHEPHERDS, SHEPHERDESSES, SATYRS.

The scene is in London, on the bank of the Thames and by Isabelle's house.

· · · · ·

To My Lady, the Duchess of Grafton.[35]

Madam,

The respectful devotion I have for your Grace inspired my plan to put your name at the head of this work, as it is destined to divert his Majesty and all his Illustrious Court, and since you make yourself distinguished in a manner surprising for an age when one is ordinarily unknown to the world. I do not doubt that it will be favorably received if you honor it with your protection. It is so rare, Madam, to find all the fine qualities that you possess in such a small number of years that one must have a well-established reputation for sincerity in order to persuade of these truths those persons who have not had the advantage of approaching you. My own sincerity must not be suspect, since it is neither feelings of self-interest nor a tendency to flattery that makes me speak.

> I know the lustre of your youthful beauty
> Only from a rather great distance;
> But your eyes have a power that can
> From near and far surprise and capture hearts.

But, madam, although I have seen your lovely person only in a crowd that did not allow me to show myself as an individual, you did not make any the less impression on my heart. There are a thousand reasons that make you estimable: the worthy choice that one of the Greatest Kings of Europe made in your favor for a Prince who has the honor to be of his blood, the dignities that the merit of My Lord your Father exercises so advantageously, the admirable education that you are receiving in your family, and an infinity of others. But you have something that touches more perceptibly and that comes from you alone.

> Yes, one finds in you everything that charms:
> Gentleness, beauty, wit and learning;
> And you have nothing of a child
> But that innocent look so apt to cause
> Love. Cupid is depicted at your age;
> He touches people's hearts like you;
> But on beholding your face, he
> Would be jealous, if he did not adore it.

I do not want, if possible, to fall into the fault that makes the majority of dedications unpleasant. I fear your Grace is already tired by the

length of this one, and the misfortune of being boring is almost inseparable from these sorts of things. But, Madam, this is the weak spot of tender
hearts: when they like a subject, they have difficulty in finishing; and if I
heeded my heart, I would importune you further. Do me the favor of
being persuaded that if feelings took the place of something, those which
you have inspired would repair all the faults of the present which I take
the liberty of offering you, since I am with all the respect and passion possible,

Madam, of your Grace,
The most humble and most obedient servant,
La Roche-Guilhen.

PROLOGUE[36]

The stage represents a countryside in which Whitehall Palace
is discovered. The Nymph of the Thames, supported by her urn, is
approached by Europe, who comes to entreat her to persuade
the King to be the arbiter of peace between all her princes.

EUROPE: It is upon your tranquil shore
    That against Bellona in her fury[37]
    I come to your Hero to seek refuge and
    For my vast empire to implore his favor.
5   Of all the kings whose birth I've seen
    He only reigns today over happy subjects.
    The whole world knows he is magnanimous,
    And Glory took great care to spread his fame.
    While your sisters find their billows agitated
10   And the frightened Rhine hides underneath his waves,
    You see your waters flow in perfect peace,
    And with prosperity your banks are filled.
    In this happy state, bear to your glorious King
    The tears of Europe in distress.
15   Describe to him, Nymph, the woes that overwhelm me
    And make his noble heart concerned about me.
THAMES: I've seen him sigh at the piteous tale
    Of your misfortunes, whose report has reached him.
    His noble soul pities the wretched state
20   To which the storm of Mars reduces you today.
    If his sagacity equals his courage,
    Queen, do you feel some terror still?
    He'll banish horror from your ravaged fields,
    And with his favoring care drive off the storm.
25   Through his wise counsels we will see an end
    To this long, bloody warfare. We'll
    See you again, peaceful and flourishing,
    Put on a crown made from our myrtles.

But it is just by reputation
30   That you know the Hero whose laws I adore;
And when you see him, you will be so charmed
That you'll prefer him to your other kings.
When he can relieve a wretched person's woes
He tastes true happiness,
35   And there is no way to exhaust
The boundless fountain of his goodness.
No one comes here, distraught over refusals,
To swell my waters with his tears.
We live without alarm under the sway
40   Of him whose virtues we devote ourselves to praising.
Of these precious advantages
What other nymph or stream would dare to boast?
The Ocean scorns the homage of their waves[38]
Ever since so much blood has polluted it.
45   I'm not afflicted by Ocean's disdain;
I alone convey my waters to his palace.
The powerful Thetis showers wealth upon me,[39]
While she feels indignation toward my sisters.
Make no mistake; if I have so much sweetness,
50   If on my banks I see in a rich mixture
The treasures of the Indus and the Ganges,
I owe all this good luck to my King's labor.
EUROPE: You banish my anxieties
Through such a charming conversation.
55   In your lovely secluded haunts
I plan henceforth to lead a tranquil life.
But if I devote myself to this dear island,
Where, Nymph, I see so many attractions
Already, I still have a mother's feelings
60   Which I do not renounce.
Your Monarch must, as arbiter of our princes,
At last restore calm to our troubled peoples.

No longer captives in their sad lands, may
They triumph over the fate that keeps them crushed.
65   Peace is required for my repose,
And if I obtain it now from this great King,
Placing all my glory in reliance on him,
There's nothing that I would not do for his.
THAMES: I see him making his way here;[40]
70   Good fortune favors you.
Already you're surprised by his appearance;
When you see him better, how will you react?
Since destiny sends him to us,
Let's profit from this precious time,
75   And to provide him pleasing entertainment
Let's make our joy burst forth.
EUROPE: You nations who obey my laws, appear!
Come demonstrate your skill
And mingle with your gestures
80   Shouts and choruses of gladness.
Let the sound of his name fill the universe!
Join forces on land and on sea;
Sing in a thousand different places
That his virtue for all must charming be.
A crowd of Nations comes out from both sides of the stage and they
conclude the prologue with songs and dances.
85   CHORUS: Let the sound of his name fill the universe!
Let's join forces on land and sea;
Let's sing in a thousand different places
That his virtue for all must charming be.
SOLO VOICE (*to the Thames*): If Europe on your banks appears
today,
90   If we accompany her eagerly,
Nymph, be not astonished.
Your illustrious Hero well deserves this homage.
ANOTHER SOLO VOICE: I've left behind the shores of Spain

To follow Europe to this spot.
95   You know what favors she hopes to obtain;
Great King, accede to her desires.
THREE SOLOISTS: He alone can give us satisfaction.
Ye peoples, let us seek to please him.
Let the sound of his name fill the universe!
100   Let's join forces on land and sea;
Let's sing in a thousand different places
That his virtue for all must charming be.
CHORUS: Let the sound of his name fill the universe!
Let's join forces on land and sea;
105   Let's sing in a thousand different places
That his virtue for all must charming be.

                                Exeunt.

ACT I

LA TREILLE (*alone*): Though just a simple servant, Madam
    Thames,
    Allow my soul to moralize on your banks.[41]
    I come not, downcast and weary from sighing,
110   To teach your lovers how to show despair;
    More reasonable matters fill my thoughts.
    However, Cupid's wound is in my breast,
    And as so many lovers, heaving sighs,
    Have oft informed you of their amorous secrets,
115   I feel the same desire urge me this moment.
    You see a person filled with tenderness.
    O listen to my tale and remember it![42]
    I'll speak in proper order, hiding nothing.
    I make no claims for an illustrious birth.
120   My father, porter in an important household,
    Made me possessor of a lackey's patent,
    And I fulfilled my charge quite honorably.
    But in eight years my master, as sole wages,
    Gave me the stewardship of some old clothes.
125   I was already brave, and, leaving him,
    I joined the service I am in today.
    It was last winter, late December, when
    Mister All-Wondrous made me his manservant.
    All-Wondrous—aren't you surprised by that great name?
130   You'll see him soon; he's following my steps.
    We are to meet upon your lovely shore.
    He's Gascon, handsome, skillful, full of courage,
    Noble, but so susceptible to charms
    That a mere song can force him into love.
135   Of this I'll give you quite a fine example.
    One night, as we passed by the Marais du Temple,[43]
    A voice till daybreak captured his attention,
    And he formed a passion for an unknown woman.

I was heartily enraged: I'm a bit timid,
140   The cold was stinging, and the night quite damp.
I won't lie to you; I was terrified,
For naturally I'm afraid of darkness.
In vain to drag him off I badmouthed music.
I wasted all my rhetoric for hours.
145   At last we left behind that wretched place,
But never was swain of fiction more in love.
I had to use my ingenuity
To find the building where the singer dwelt.
My zeal succeeded; God knows what fine language
150   Signaled at once his budding passion. He
Didn't waste his words; the lady was responsive;
Encouragement took care to ease his pain.
Perhaps a more real favor was involved.
But Mister Destiny did not stop there,
155   And on these lovers' passion declared war.
Climene, one fine morn, left for English soil;
She had to give in to a father's wishes;
Though moved to tears, though sighing, 'twas in vain.
Departure was so prompt that the lady's message
160   To my master brought the news too late. I thought
He would go hang himself or else take poison,
And never did a lover show less reason;
We had to pack our travel bags at once;
He'd surely die unless he made the journey.
165   It was quite smooth, but on arrival here,
His sorrow increased, far from being relieved.
We could not find out what fortunate house
Possessed our fair soprano in its bosom.
I searched both night and day, but having learned
170   That a Frenchman oft had concerts in his home,
I cleverly slipped in and found Climene.
The concerts were held once a week. What joy

My master had, how many hugs expressed
To me the ardor of his eagerness!
175 What raptures, pleasures when I informed him of
The place where shortly I would introduce him.
To get him in I'd made all the arrangements;
A valet I'd made drunk aided my plans.
To Climene's lodgings we were given entry,
180 And Lord All-Wondrous safely came inside.
But his eyes, dazzled by a newfound lustre,
Joined battle with his heart's fidelity.
The father of Climene had struck a friendship
With an old Englishman of quite good birth
185 Who had an only daughter, loved her dearly—
Young, beautiful, and singing like an angel.
My master, with her at the concert, could
Just barely cast a glance on poor Climene.
He left with a crowd in order to avoid
190 A visit or a private conversation.
I'd read all his inconstancy in his eyes.
I thought my duty was to reprimand him,
But he implored me for the rest of the day
Not to oppose myself to this new love
195 And to agree again to use my skill
To gain an interview with his young mistress.
I sought out her maid and was so charmed by her
That my master never fell in love more quickly.
My heart, which isn't made of bronze or rock,
200 Sighed for her beauty at the first approach.
I felt a passion stealing all inside me
Which soon will overcome my energy.
I found her of an easy-going nature
And rather well versed in the ways of love.
205 It's to converse with her that I've come here.
But I see my master; he looks serious.

Enter All-Wondrous.

ALL-WONDROUS: Well, haven't you seen the lovely Isabelle?
How I love her, La Treille, how fair she is!

LA TREILLE: That's well and good, sir, but Climene has lost
210   Then all the power she had over your heart.

ALL-WONDROUS: Yes, for the English beauty I leave her today.

LA TREILLE: Well done on your part.

ALL-WONDROUS: I am filled with merit
That makes me triumph over the greatest charms.
My very name, my valor . . .

LA TREILLE: I don't doubt it.
215   But let's be logical. What's your intention?
Do you think your business is advancing well?
Climene's the type of girl who'll take offense,
And I foresee problems that we must avoid.
Beware her anger.

ALL-WONDROUS: I, fear! You insult me.
220   I intend to vaunt my fickleness to her face.

LA TREILLE: And you think you'll immortalize yourself this way?

ALL-WONDROUS: Has she commanded you to tyrannize me?
I kiss her hands; the past belonged to her,
But the future will be lovely Isabelle's.

225   LA TREILLE: And at some concert Isabelle in turn
May well lose out in just such a reversal.
Behold, young beauties, what fate threatens you:
Just when you think you reign, you're in disgrace.
Love promises all things, reneges on all;
230   With him the present's worth more than the future.

ALL-WONDROUS: All your remonstrances don't serve my purpose.
I like Isabelle and plan to make her like
Me. Let Climene shed tears and moan and groan;
Time can give remedy to her suffering.
235   We're just two steps away from Isabelle's house.
When she comes out, I want to approach her. How

Do you find my air? It's rather vanquishing,
And well I know how hearts are captured. You
Don't answer me?

LA TREILLE: No.

ALL-WONDROUS: Why?

LA TREILLE: What's there to say,
240 Since you enthrall every fair maid alive?
Profit from a talent that you must hold dear.
Isabelle appears, so hurry to approach her.
With your fine air you shall be all the rage.
Occasion smiles on you, she is alone; now courage!
245 Finette, though, follows her; how sly her eye is!
Enter Isabelle and Finette.

ALL-WONDROUS: Madam, you see a Gascon of renown,
Wounded a thousand times and so covered with glory
That his acts will one day honor history;
But all of this will be less sweet to him
250 Than the happy privilege of loving you.
Refuse him not the consent he asks of you;
I know indeed the favor will be great.
Isabelle looks at All-Wondrous contemptuously and walks away
from him without speaking, followed by Finette.

LA TREILLE: You're speechless, sir, at this reception. Have
You fully understood what she has told you?
255 Are you not charmed by such eloquence? That's
Paying your inconstancy in gallant style.

ALL-WONDROUS: You judge too quickly. Would you want her to
Agree at once to everything I ask?
I was expecting no other response.
260 A girl at her age has great modesty;
Also, my martial air inspires respect.

LA TREILLE: Where love's concerned I find such acts suspicious.
Her eyes are scornful; I think she disdains you.

ALL-WONDROUS: To clear this up, consult her waiting-maid.

265　　Try to discover where her coldness comes from;
　　　Whether it's hate, contempt, naïveté, modesty.
　　　In short, assist my love and praise my merit.
　　LA TREILLE: *You* speak, she's coming back. No, she avoids you.
　　Isabelle returns with a man who gives her his hand. She sings.
　　ISABELLE: Cease, languishing hearts, from aiming to please me.
270　　I like happy liberty,
　　　And if love is a necessary evil,
　　　I don't submit to its necessity.
　　TIRSIS (*sings*): In vain, to appear unfeeling,
　　　You wish to resist love's sway.
275　　But, believe me, only he's invincible,
　　　And you may love one day.
　　　　　After singing, Isabelle and Tirsis reenter her house.
　　LA TREILLE: This singer surely threatens your love. It's
　　　Some happy rival, he has a courtier's air.
　　ALL-WONDROUS: And mine is warlike. Zounds, I jeer at him!
280　　LA TREILLE (*between his teeth*): To tell the truth, his presence is
　　　　offensive.
　　ALL-WONDROUS: I leave you; spare no pains on my behalf.
　　LA TREILLE: Go then, my zeal does not want witnesses.
　　　(*alone*) I scarcely trouble myself for his new love,
　　　But mine indeed wants to be satisfied.
285　　Good, here's Finette. Damn, how lovely she is!
　　　　　Reenter Finette.
　　　My dear, a word or two.
　　FINETTE:　　　　　　　　Don't stop me. I
　　　Must take care of certain things without delay.
　　　A party thrown for Madam by the Thames
　　　Will feature instrumentalists and fine voices.
290　　We next will see, accompanied by six oboes,
　　　A dance of fishermen to a pleasing tune.
　　　Doesn't that sound like an admirable party?
　　　So let me go and don't become a nuisance.

We have to tidy up and curl our hair.

295 LA TREILLE: Even if I run the risk of angering you,
You shall not pass.

FINETTE: All right, what do you want?

LA TREILLE: To tell my reasons, speak to you of my passion,
Tell you all the hurt your lovely eyes have done me.

FINETTE: You talk just like a book; your speech enchants me.

300 LA TREILLE: Not to be vain, my love's quite eloquent,
But expressing oneself well is not enough.

FINETTE: And what then is required?

LA TREILLE: To make you love me.

FINETTE: My heart's too favorable to you already.

LA TREILLE: You do me too much honor. Devil take me,

305 If people died of joy, I'd be already dead!
(aside) I must make an effort in the Gascon's favor.
(aloud) Tell me, for what reason did stern Isabelle
Seem so rebellious to my master's speech?
He loves her to the point of fury. If

310 Your lady shuns him, I fear for her honor.
These devilish Gascons have a raging spirit;
He's one of the greatest rogues that roams the world.
But tell me, should he act the role of Tarquin,[44]
Is she the type to kill herself for honor?

315 Would she at once follow Lucretia's footsteps?

FINETTE: I don't believe her virtue is so tigerish.
Our century has seen few of those rare outbursts.
In extremities the soul would justify the body;
Intention takes the place of good excuse.

320 You're not criminal unless you consent to crime.

LA TREILLE: Wow, what reasoning! How did you learn so much?

FINETTE: I've always frequented the finest wits.
I used to serve, in Paris, a young countess[45]
Who knew all things and read incessantly.

325 All of the learned men were her admirers.

Around her you would see a troop of authors
Who oft came to consult her on their works,
And I didn't waste such great advantages.
But to return to your dashing Gascon, he
330 Approaches Madam in a silly way.
Were he, in short, the tenderest of lovers,
Were he more valiant than great Alexander,
Had he more graces and more charms than Cupid,
If he can't sing, his efforts will be wasted.
335 Without music no one enters our good graces,
And my harpsichord alone procures my place there.
As for your Tarquinizer . . .

LA TREILLE: If he need but sing,
My master certainly . . .

FINETTE: May God preserve us!
If he sings like he speaks, he will work wonders.
340 My poor La Treille, we must have the sublime.
His very accent is disheartening.

LA TREILLE: Today
Our opera stars are all from Gascony like him.[46]

FINETTE: Too bad.

LA TREILLE: Why too bad? You are acting scornful.

FINETTE: You're very wrong, but I'm a connoisseur,
345 And my refinement often brings misfortune.

LA TREILLE: My master's singing will be to his credit.

FINETTE: All right, we'll hear him; if he's any good,
Music can put his suit in proper order.
But you, the worthy servant of such a master,
350 Regale us with some little ballet air.
You sing apparently, and when my keyboard
Has joined with your voice . . .

LA TREILLE: Ah, my dear Finette,
If one day I could concertize with you,
What sweetness for me, and what charming pleasures!

355   FINETTE: La Treille has good taste.

     LA TREILLE: You're adorable.

     FINETTE: Can one praise people with an air more pleasing?

     LA TREILLE: You merit better, and you must admit

       That those who know you can't praise you too highly.

     FINETTE: You'll turn my head; I'll think myself too lovely.

360   LA TREILLE: Ah, think it without fear.

     FINETTE: My mistress calls me.

       I must leave you. Farewell, I'll see you soon.

     LA TREILLE: If you permit it, I'll come back tonight.

       Mention my master and defend his love.

     FINETTE: I'll do it without fail.

     LA TREILLE: Farewell, my dearest.

                      Exit Finette.

365   (*alone*) My word, my heart is throbbing. Ah, cruel Love,

       Allow me to breathe gently for a moment.

       I used to fault my master for being amorous,

       And I couldn't prevent myself from doing the same.

       Unlucky voyage! O contagious country!

370   But by despairing I'm no better off.

       Come on, La Treille, summon up your constancy.

       Finette is surely flattering your hopes.

       What could alarm you? Were there a hundred rivals,

       The rogue has eyes and sees what you are worth.

375   Let's run to seek my master and let him know

       The path he must take to gain happiness.

                      Exit.

INTERLUDE I

The Interlude of the first act is an amorous dispute of
Tritons and Nereids on the banks of the Thames.
Some fishermen who are spreading their nets on the shore,
delighted to see the divinities, express their joy
in a pleasing dance.

A TRITON (*sings*): Young and beautiful naiads,
    From our watery strands
    Banish cruel resistance;
380   Follow Love's commands.
    Its games all give enjoyment,
    Pleasures follow in its wake,
    And you are far too lovely
    Their acquaintance not to make.
385 A NEREID: Thetis disapproves of sighing
    And bans that tiresome practice in the sea.
    A TRITON: She wouldn't dream of telling you
    She made a mortal happy formerly.
    ANOTHER TRITON: Ladies would like to seem demure
390   When Love, an enemy to age,
    Shuns fair ones as their years advance.
    But the name of prudes may often
    Allow some small returns
    To former habits.
395 A NEREID: What, even at the gods you shoot
    The barbs of your satire?
    A TRITON: Does being part of the heavenly realm
    Mean they don't have a heart and eyes?
    THREE TRITONS: When pleasurable youth
400   Lends you some of its charms,
    Profit from fleeting time;
    Once lost, that asset never comes again.
    As soon as old age is seen

Chasing away your youthful lures,
405 Love in disgust abandons you
And carries his darts' power somewhere else.
A NEREID: Lovers who seek to please,
Do you know what is needed
To touch young maiden's hearts?
410 What we want is constancy,
And quite often we reward
Those who show perseverance.
A TRITON: You do us wrong,
Lovely Nereid;
415 The love that guides us
Binds our fate to your alluring charms.
A NEREID: You swear to be faithful,
And at that very moment
To some fairer naiads
420 You sometimes go to make the selfsame vows.[47]
THREE TRITONS: Make love, follow our lessons;
To Thetis' laws take care not to surrender.
In Ocean's realm, Nymphs, Tritons, all
Pride themselves on being tender.
425 A TRITON: Will you always be coy
While we are languishing?
TWO NEREIDS: Cupid wants to be deferred to;
In vain would we resist him.
CHORUS: Let a victory so fair
430 Increase his fame today.
                          Exeunt.

ACT II

Enter All-Wondrous and La Treille.

ALL-WONDROUS: You say I must know how to sing to please her.
    Thank heaven, I have the power to satisfy her,
    La Treille, and if her eyes don't favor me,
    Her ears perhaps will do me less injustice.

435   LA TREILLE: I think like you, but it's not in the bag.

ALL-WONDROUS: My voice for certain guarantees success,
    And Lambert found me singing like the angels.[48]

LA TREILLE: You know still better how to sing your praises.

ALL-WONDROUS: Perhaps you think I speak from vanity,

440   But I'm fair-minded and I know my worth.

LA TREILLE: Phoebus be praised, Phoebus and the nine Muses,
    Folks who're no blockheads, as you know, and whom
    It's good to invoke in matters musical,
    For they might take offense on points of honor.

445   If they wished to bestow some of their gifts on me,
    Finette's love would increase a thousand times.
    She knows her music and would like a lover
    To at least play preludes on an instrument.

ALL-WONDROUS: This rogue moves me to laughter with his pas-
    sion.

450   LA TREILLE: Ow!

ALL-WONDROUS: Are you feeling ill?

LA TREILLE: No, I'm just sighing.

ALL-WONDROUS: You're sighing? Zounds! You can't be serious.
    Are sighs created for the likes of you?

LA TREILLE: And why not, if you please? Have I not breath,
    A heart and feelings to express my pain?

455   These Sirs of the nobility seem to think
    Poor servants aren't part of the human race;
    They only have the right to try their luck
    And we've no heritage from Madam Nature.
    But they're mistaken, and we are, like them,

460   Quite apt at cultivating love affairs,
    And very often chosen by good Fortune
    For favors great!
    ALL-WONDROUS: Shut up, you bother me.
    Isabelle is taking long; I'm dying to see her.
    Night's falling meanwhile.
    LA TREILLE: I am in despair;
465   You'll stay alone, I do not like night's shadow,
    And I fear some painful mishap for my back.
    ALL-WONDROUS: Fear by my side, you coward! Don't you know
      me?
    Each blow my hand gives leads to certain death.
    Remain here, scoundrel, with full confidence.
470   LA TREILLE: Get beaten senseless, but far from my presence!
    I agree wholeheartedly; you are a warrior.
    For my part, I like wine better than laurels.
    Gather some in this place and request the Thames
    To favor you with her thickest branches. If
475   You pay with just a hundred cudgelings,
    My word, that's not expensive.
    ALL-WONDROUS: Ah, Sir Knave,
    My patience you have finally exhausted,
    And I shall thrash you soundly right away.
    LA TREILLE: Don't trouble to; someone's coming. Calm yourself,
480   And change your fury for a gentler air.
    It's your beloved, Isabelle the divine.
    ALL-WONDROUS: The Queen of Love was never so fair as she.
    Since it's by singing that I must approach her,
    Let's start with a persuasive aria.
             Enter Isabelle and Finette.
485   (*sings*) Young wondrous maid,
    To a sighing hero's lyre
    Deign to lend an ear,
    Look favorably on my desire.

Ye gods, what glory
490   To have triumphed my heart o'er!
Never was victory
More worthy of the conqueror.
LA TREILLE: Finette, what say you? Can he sing?
FINETTE: Brilliantly.
I see no further obstacle to his passion.
495   LA TREILLE: Then we can see each other.
FINETTE: Yes, of course.
LA TREILLE: Up close.
A concert at our house is being arranged;
My master plans to invite Isabelle to it,
And you as well.
FINETTE: I've news for you.
LA TREILLE: About
Whom then?
FINETTE: Climene. She's just left our house, and
500   My mistress was the target of her anger.
She says your master is a perjured traitor,
Who shamefully insults the oaths he swore,
And Isabelle, if she allows his suit,
Should fear fickle treatment from that faithless heart.
505   LA TREILLE: Let her keep on denouncing perfidy;
It makes a pretty subject for a play.[49]
But the Gascon's coming forward, shunned no longer.
FINETTE: Music, La Treille, has mighty powers.
LA TREILLE: Even
In Hades people pride themselves on singing,
510   And Cerberus the dog barks musically.[50]
FINETTE: He must have studied to amuse King Pluto.
LA TREILLE: In Lully's opera he assisted Charon.
His role was lovely, though the slanderers
Spoke ill of it.
FINETTE: How critical the French are!

515   But Isabelle sings; let's quietly approach.

ISABELLE (*sings*): When handsome Tirsis I behold,
    My eyes grow dim, I blush;
    When he is absent, I'm all sighs.
    I think about him night and day;
520   I fear all things that I desire.
    These agitations from my love arise.

ALL-WONDROUS: What charming accents! O thrice happy night,
    Continue favoring my plans, I pray.
    My word, you're wonderful in every way,
525   And my ardent love can't pardon me for not
    Having at least a hundred hearts to give you.
    Since you like my voice, I place it at your service.
    With mastery of the art I do performing.
    I know some brand new, gallant English airs;
530   I'll sing for you some of the finest ones.

Sings an English air.

ISABELLE (*answers him with another song*).[51]

FINETTE (*to La Treille*): How do you like that?

LA TREILLE: I don't know the language.

FINETTE: Be still, your master picks up his oration.

ALL-WONDROUS (*while Isabelle is singing*):[52]
    What charms! what pride! what bearing! what a voice!
    What pleasure and felicity I feel!
535   My soul goes into ecstasy and rapture.
    I'm dying, Madam; stop, I beg of you.
    With two more notes you'll cause me to expire.
    Allow my love some time to breathe. I am
    Charmed, conquered, rendered tender, faithful by
540   The eyes, the voice, the wit of Isabelle.
    My noble birth, my wealth, credit and valor,
    My worth, my arm, my passion and my greatness,
    I dedicate to her, and for her glory
    I want to engrave our names in Memory's Temple.

545 Don't you know where that is, La Treille?

LA TREILLE (*laughing*): Why, no, sir.
Who would have taught me?

ALL-WONDROUS: You are making fun.
I owe you punishment; I'll pay my debt.

FINETTE: Must you get angry in your present state?
Madam is peaceable, loves gentleness,

550 And violent outbursts fail to touch her heart.

ALL-WONDROUS: Then I forgive him; let him thank you for it.
Night's sudden fall makes me leave here. Tonight
A lovely concert is performed in my house.
Your mistress will attend?

FINETTE: Assuredly.

ALL-WONDROUS: And you?

555 FINETTE: I never leave her side.

ALL-WONDROUS: I must invite her.
(*to Isabelle*) My love prepares you gallant entertainment.
It's to your taste, consists of charming airs
Sung and accompanied by instruments.
My house is just a short distance from yours;

560 May we expect the honor of your presence?

FINETTE: Fearful of promises, Madam says nothing.
But I give my word.

ALL-WONDROUS: You make me furious.
Let her decide the matter that I ask.

FINETTE: I speak at her command; she bids me to.

565 ALL-WONDROUS: Ah, that suffices, I drop my resistance.
Her silence always means she's not refusing.
La Treille, stay here to escort the ladies.
Do me a favor: speak of my passion, too.

LA TREILLE: You've won her heart.

ALL-WONDROUS: Farewell for just a moment.

570 I go to excite my singers to be brilliant.

Exit All-Wondrous; Isabelle goes into her house.

FINETTE: Speak of the Gascon; didn't he make you laugh?

LA TREILLE: I don't have time to; I must sigh for you.

FINETTE: Your love, if sad, will put me out of humor.
I thrive on merriment; that's all I like.

575   La Treille, sprinkle some water on your embers.

LA TREILLE: Your heart speaks calmly since it is indifferent.
But since to please you I must be amusing,
Let's speak of Lord All-Wondrous.

FINETTE: Truth to tell,
He's an eccentric; there is no one like him.

580   My mistress, though, is starting to relent.
Through music he will gain esteem with us.

LA TREILLE: Where the devil did she pick up what she told us?
Not speak to people, what a silly mania!
For me that would cause endless pain and trouble.

585 FINETTE: I'm used to it now and am no longer bothered.

LA TREILLE: Is she a deity rich in doubloons?
Is she generous and does her hand upon
Her servant liberally drop heaps of them?

FINETTE: Mind your own business. It's not selfish gain

590   That keeps me in her service.

LA TREILLE: Then what does,
I ask? You'd be the first and only French girl
To serve an Englishwoman for her beauty.
Don't pride yourself so on unselfishness.
More than other ills, it's poverty I fear.

595   But might you not be one of those painted beauties
Who, having lost those flowers they failed to guard,
Move to England, arm themselves with modesty
And take the first match that might do them honor?
So many of them have left France and come here

600   Whose sole real motives are of such importance.

FINETTE: You reason rightly, and I find you kind.
You greatly honor me with such suspicions.

Insult a very virtuous girl like that!

LA TREILLE: Excuse my frankness.

FINETTE: It's too late.

LA TREILLE: I'm furious.

605   My dearest, by the love which you've inspired,

Don't push a desperate heart beyond all limits.

Your coldness is a dreadful torture for me.

You know there are fires, swords and cliffs around,

And if I were to slay myself for you,

610   Would you see your charms augmented by my death?

FINETTE: You play the madman, when you've insulted me.

LA TREILLE: I'll swallow poison.

FINETTE: I want my revenge.

LA TREILLE: You've got enough already, tigress, and your pride

Has no humaneness for your faithful lover.

615   O hear my sighs, see my tears flow! With them

I want to wash away the insult to your charms.

I'm feeling faint.

FINETTE: Alas, I think you're dying!

LA TREILLE: Yes, to death's palace I go to lament

My woes.

FINETTE: My soul relents; you may take heart,

620   And for another time postpone your voyage.

LA TREILLE: Finette, then you forgive me?

FINETTE: Certainly.

LA TREILLE: My word, I was about to make my will.

I'd leave my wealth to you upon life's end.

FINETTE: Go, keep it for yourself, I don't desire it.

625   In brief, if you want to expunge your crime,

Never say anything that might offend me.

LA TREILLE: No, I intend to speak of my love only.

FINETTE: I have to go attend to Madam's coifs.

We'll be back soon; your master waits for us.

630   Don't you want something more?

LA TREILLE: No, I'm more than content.
                    Exit Finette.
        Such animals lose their temper very quickly;
        But I too was at fault: to doubt her virtue
        Meant putting her to shame; that was quite brutal,
        And to tell her to her face, more beastly still.
635   To speak that way I must have lost my mind,
        And I deserved a stronger punishment.
        Let's drop the subject; she's forgiven me,
        And here she is again.
                    Reenter Isabelle and Finette.
FINETTE: Have you soliloquized?
        Let's go, walk before us to your master's house.
640   Madam does not want to be recognized.
LA TREILLE: Don't be uneasy, I'll be most discreet,
        And I'll impose the secret on my master.
                    Exeunt.

INTERLUDE II

*The scene changes here and shows the house of All-Wondrous,
who gives his mistress the entertainment of a very
pleasing concert, with a ballet of matachins.*[53]

A LOVER (*sings*): Too fortunate night, charming shadows,
    Come to protect my love; give me
645   For pity's sake those pleasures that the day
    Refuses to my loving passion.
    It's said you look with favor on
    All tender secrets that lovers confide to you.
    Alas, if you deny me this,
650   Take what remains of my life, too.
ANOTHER LOVER : If your beloved
    Does not do what you want,
    Mine is a raging tigress
    Who greets my suit with scorn.
655   I've sighed for quite some time
    But her rigor is no less,
    And Cupid's empire has not yet
    Favored my heart with its gentleness.
A WOMAN : Thus it is that through the world
660   In song our cruelty you proclaim.
    Hardly have you declared your flame
    When you want us to respond in kind;
    And if you gain an audience
    With hearts that lack experience,
665   You pay them with indifference,
    Once they no longer can resist.
TWO WOMEN : When constancy
    Succeeds to hope,
    One is happy under Cupid's direction.
670   All things please and charm;
    Never does an alarm

Warn of a sad change of affection.

THREE MEN : When hope succeeds
 To constancy,
675 Fickle desires are never found.
 Love's chain is worn without vexation.
 Love causes no sufferings
 Where pleasures also don't abound.

SOLO MAN : Cease, O cease to be so cruel
680 When for your sake we breathe our sighs.

A WOMAN : Lovers, start being faithful;
 A sweeter lot will be your prize.

CHORUS: Let's fall in love; Cupid invites us to.
 Without him life is naught but languishing.

Exeunt.

ACT III

The scene changes back to the set of the Prologue and Act I.

685   CLIMENE (*alone*): Black furies, fatal jealousy,
     On the ingrate who insulted me just now
     I must avenge myself; O teach me how
     By teaching me that he's betrayed me.
     If yielding to his charms was sweet,
690   Will his punishment bring less contentment?
     No, no, then, just resentment,
     Come spur me on to seek my vengeance.
     You spread your poison, barbarous love,
     Into the souls of innocents;
695   I lived in peace till by your treacherous flame
     My reason was defeated.
     Quite far from thinking to complain,
     I would take pleasure in my illness.
     I thought I had no cause for fear,
700   But I must blush; by you my heart was cheated.
     Cowardly lovers, faithless sex,
     You deserve the cruelest torments
     Known within the realm of love.
     To punish such a criminal heart
705   Requires the direst agony;
     Death is far from cruel enough.
             Enter All-Wondrous.

ALL-WONDROUS: Do you feel ill, or is it some unease
     That makes you, madam, thus seek solitude,
     Or do you come to this remote location
710   To hide from mortal eyes your many talents?
     I willingly agree to be displayed;
     If I've great worth, I show it joyfully.
     It's gaining fame here, and I think at court
     Its impact on the ladies may be lasting.
       Climene, furious at such a speech, walks away from
     All-Wondrous without speaking. He continues as follows:[54]

715   What frenzy leads this damsel to avoid me?
          What was her plan and what did she intend?
          Had she hoped that a cowardly repentance
          Would once again enchain me to her love;
          That, quick to ask forgiveness, bathed in tears, I
720   Could sacrifice love of Isabelle to her charms?
          That's not my manner; I act differently.
          I wished to flaunt my change of heart before her,
          And with good reasons prove to her that my soul
          Can, when it likes, dispose of my loving heart;
725   That such a man as I, free in his actions,
          Must follow passions only for his pleasure;
          That if my heart prompts me, I can be fickle.
          Should All-Wondrous be seen reduced to bondage?
          Should his great name be subject to that insult?
730   No, I must save my brow from such disgrace.
          At present I'm in love with Isabelle,
          But I might change for someone fairer still,
          And depending on how Cupid guides my view,
          My victims may be running certain risks.

          While All-Wondrous is speaking, Isabelle is listening to him
               and shows her contempt for him by her gestures.
               Then she goes back into the house and he continues.

735   Whene'er I cast my eyes on my whole person,
          I must not lie, its merit startles me.
          The ladies are quite right to favor me,
          And their pliancy is not to be despised.
          My servant comes here staggering. La Treille,
740   I think you've been consulting with the bottle.

                    Enter La Treille.

LA TREILLE: Me, sir? Not at all.

ALL-WONDROUS: No matter, change the subject.
          To make us take to drink love has strong reasons.
          I haven't yet seen Isabelle appear.
          Besides, I've an appointment with a Countess.

745   Finette might come out; do not leave this place.
I'll leave you here alone.

LA TREILLE: So much the better.
You'd cut a very sorry figure here.
Being kept waiting so long is not auspicious;
Such conduct brings disgrace to your high rank,

750   And at all times one must keep one's dignity.

ALL-WONDROUS: Farewell then.

Exit All-Wondrous.

LA TREILLE (*alone*):   Heaven favor you. As for me,
I dedicate myself to the Thames' bank.
The choice is wise, I'm not so very wrong.
Luck follows me, Finette already comes.

755   Am I not mistaken? I see in her face
The infallible portent of some displeasure.

Enter Finette.

Sweet object of desire, your eyes are languishing.
Is that not an effect of the pains I feel?
What can upset you? Has your whimsical singer

760   Not given you an annoying talking to?
Speak openly if you wish to oblige me.
Tell me of sorrows I want to relieve.
For a lover who's beloved there are no secrets.
Think of my passion.

FINETTE: You, think to shut up.

765 LA TREILLE: O dear, what looks, what words, what a tone, what
      pride!

FINETTE: No longer will you impose on my good faith.
He who deceives me once gets no second chance.

LA TREILLE: Finette, is this a jest?

FINETTE: It is no jest.

LA TREILLE: Explain more clearly, or I shall be frantic.

770 FINETTE: You still pretend to be the man of honor.
I must admit, your impudence is brazen.

Your master has not told you his perfidy!
That lover should be hanged and drowned!

LA TREILLE: Ah, gently,
Finette! What has he done?

FINETTE: His guile is splendid:
775   To swear he loves and is consumed by passion,
Perhaps to place himself in Madam's heart,
And afterward declare that he'll desert her
As soon as his inconstancy finds a new love.

LA TREILLE: Finette, I give my word; this is just slander.

780   FINETTE: Madam was listening; he spoke in her presence.

LA TREILLE: That testimony's strong; I can't reply.

FINETTE: You should at least have come to give me warning;
But to let us both be duped, have you no shame?
What love! what a lover!

LA TREILLE: But, Finette, for your part
785   I'm criminal for having failed to speak.
I would have needed to have all revealed to me,
Since I was in the dark.

FINETTE: Pure nonsense!

LA TREILLE: What,
You, cruel one, wish to espouse your lady's quarrel?
Is it my fault if my master deceives her?

790   FINETTE: Yes, she accepts the hand of a worthier lover;
Their wedding is tonight. Tomorrow I
Contract a pleasing marriage with another.[55]
Your sighs and your vows, you can take them elsewhere.
Complain, get angry, choke yourself, if you like;
795   I won't make inquiries of your future actions.
Since your fine master has botched his business, yours
Shall have the same fate, if you please. My wedding
Will be fashionable. I invite you to
The feast; my pity grants you that one favor.
800   Farewell, console yourself.

Exit Finette.

LA TREILLE (*alone*):   O hateful Discord,[56]
Killer of sweetness, enemy of reason!
Thus in all hearts you spread your horrid poison.
To charm your snakes we must be found displeasing.
Through your vile offices I'm quite at ease!

805   And you, cruel Love, whom my innocent heart
May well call author of the ills it suffers,
If ever I catch your quiver and your arrows,
My vengeance will wreak furious havoc on them.
Finette abandons me and you allow it!

810   Ah, how I'd like to beat you black and blue!
If I grab you one day on land or sea,
I shall make mincemeat of your long blond hair,
You little knavish dog, you foe to peace!
But see, the faithless man comes opportunely.

Enter All-Wondrous.

815   ALL-WONDROUS: Behold, I'm back. What did you see? Can I
Not learn from you some news of Isabelle?
Did you find Finette? Did you learn anything?
But your sole answer is to look surprised.
Whence come these sighs? Why are you sad?

LA TREILLE: Can one

820   Be otherwise on losing one's beloved?

ALL-WONDROUS: What's this you tell me? Have I heard correctly?

LA TREILLE: I'm in despair, I'm in a faint! Ah, give
Me back my heart!

ALL-WONDROUS: What do you mean?

LA TREILLE: I've lost my heart; that ought to be enough.

825   ALL-WONDROUS: I fail to understand you; speak more clearly.

LA TREILLE: You snatched it from me by your senseless outburst.
But your star's governed by the same ascendant:
Finette shuns me, while you lose Isabelle.
Behold the unbearable fruit of your errors,

830   And the cruel effect of the bad luck that dogs me.

To loudly boast of being a fickle traitor,
To turn it to account before one's mistress,
To own one's perfidy and glory in it!
Indeed, the lovers' guild should punish you
835   For infidelity and heinous acts.
You thought to show your talents to advantage,
But people heard you, and Climene today
Has found support against your inconstancy.
Don't hope for pardon; Isabelle's so furious
840   That, to be revenged on you, this very night
A more discreet lover will wed her, and
Finette, damn it, will be married tomorrow.
You've got yourself to blame; indeed, your boasting
Ought to have earned you fifty bastinadoes.
845   ALL-WONDROUS: Did you say "bastinadoes?" For such talk,
My arm might turn my fury into action.
Do you think I care whether or not I'm jilted?
If I fall in love, it's in the proper way.
Be smart, and learn from me. You must agree
850   That a grieving lover's worthy of his fate.
Since love brings so much trouble, I renounce it;
I much prefer to reap the plains of Mars.
For me, there's less fatigue in twenty battles
Than in one day's service to the law of love.
855   Once I decide to please, I find it easy:
People run after me in town and country;
I'm always hard pressed by a mob of hearts,
And my slightest glances are assured to conquer.
LA TREILLE: What splendid reasoning! In the state I'm in
860   Such wild delusions do not serve my purpose.
Alas, my poor heart, I no longer find you!
Finette detains you. Why . . .
ALL-WONDROUS: This is excessive.
To cure yourself, use my philosophy.
Believe me.

LA TREILLE: If my wisdom trusts it henceforth,
865   May I be thrashed! It has cost me too dear.
      Death . . .
ALL-WONDROUS: From his sorrow I must rescue him.
      La Treille, you must leave behind those baneful thoughts.
      Make a small effort; time will do the rest.
      And to console you, here's my solemn promise
870   Never to scold you when you make me angry;
      And also tomorrow you'll get twenty ducats.
LA TREILLE: With you words are more numerous than deeds.
      Gold has great power. Maybe that precious metal
      May ease my rigorous torment.
ALL-WONDROUS: Come, I promise
875   Them to you, hero's word of honor.
LA TREILLE: Courage!
      Already you see hope relieving me.
ALL-WONDROUS: I'm overjoyed. Let's think only of leaving.
      For the rest of the day let's entertain ourselves.
      That's how a noble heart behaves in love.
880   A common lover deserves humiliation.
      To moan and sigh, what a tiresome practice! As
      For me, I cannot tyrannize my passion.
      It's true that, everywhere I distribute it,
      The offering, once received, gets instant payment.
885   The gods befriend me; I'm their darling boy.
      Mars some years back made me his favorite.
      When Cupid wants to charm, he picks my face.
      I speak the Muses' language gallantly.
      I often dabble in Apollo's games,
890   And to his violin I join my voice.
      Since Isabelle leaves me, to her detriment,
      Let's go to other lands to spread my talents.

EPILOGUE

*The scene changes at the end of the last act and represents
a small wood. Cupid makes a speech to the ladies which serves
as an epilogue, and afterward he calls forth shepherds
and satyrs to come conclude the entertainment with a
pastoral festival.*

CUPID (*to the ladies*): Charmed by the sight of so many beauties,
    I renounce my mother's tutelage
895   And leave the isle of Cythera
    To taste in this land other kinds of bliss.[57]
    In the sweet rapture that inspires me,
    To prove that a choice so fair has
    But one legitimate excuse,
900   I have with pleasure just torn off my blindfold.
    How your charms have enlarged my realm!
    How many faithful subjects you have given me!
    To you I owe my power, enchanting fairs,
    Worthy to have Cupid himself sigh for you.
905   Therefore, I promise that the tenderest hearts
    Shall gladly come to offer you their homage,
    And that the greatest of my delights
    Will be your least advantages.
    Do not intend to arm yourselves
910   With a fierce austerity.
    Virtuous souls have no qualms about loving,
    And when it pleases me, I touch them.
    There's nothing criminal in the commerce of
    Hearts, when the practice is sincere,
915   And those who bind themselves to me by solemn oath
    Engage in just an innocent rite.
    Then do not blush for following my laws,
    You youthful beauties, faithful lovers.
    The gods themselves submit to them,

920 And nothing makes monarchs exempt.
Shepherds, come, let nothing stop you.
Leave for a moment caring for your flocks.
Devise new forms of pleasure and
Here celebrate my festival.
925 You, satyrs, come forth from these woods.
Leave behind your gloomy haunts
And come to blend your voices with
The sweet sound of musettes.

Shepherds, shepherdesses, and satyrs appear from the two sides
of the stage and finish the comedy with songs and dances.[58]

TWO SHEPHERDS: Let's hasten to where Cupid calls us;
930 Let's follow what he gently will ordain.
Come, shepherds, with new festival
The greatest of all kings let's entertain.
CHORUS: Come, shepherds, with new festival
The greatest of all kings let's entertain.
935 A SHEPHERD: Come, lovely shepherdesses,
To blend your tender songs with our gay dances.
A SHEPHERDESS: If our innocent concerts
Steal a few moments from him,
Glory, let your envy cease.
940 You sovereign of his desires,
Allow a bit of time for pleasures
And the rest of his life enjoy in peace.
A SHEPHERD: How charming Cupid is!
How sweet to follow him!
945 A heart that's all unfeeling
Does not deserve to live.
Let's join our tender sighs
To the sound of our musettes
And give voice to our desires
950 Through dainty songs of love.
A SATYR: Why should one follow Love?

We only like to laugh.
In his rigorous realm
There's suffering night and day.
955 It's Bacchus whom I wish to serve;
He only suits a satyr's needs.
A SHEPHERDESS: The pleasures of the god of lovers
Are not made for wild, brutish souls.
He lets the mouths of the profane
960 Despise the sweetest of his moments.
But if you can slander,
His arrows can punish,
And sometimes we see a satyr
Sighing and moaning for his favors.
965 SATYR: How haughty a coquette is!
If she's at all attractive,
She gives way to despair
When males do not surrender.
A SHEPHERD: Take your unfeeling heart off to the wilds!
970 You enemy of love, seek out your fellows.
We, charmed by his adorable
Laws, cherish all, even his rigor.
ANOTHER SHEPHERD: It's so sweet to please,
It's so pleasant to love!
975 Young hearts, yield to passion's flames.
Cupid loves those who revere him.
SATYR: Ah, how alluring are the charms of Bacchus!
It's so pleasant to drink!
Happy is he who can follow his path.
980 My glory comes entirely from his service.
A SHEPHERD: Love's pleasures cause a thousand sweet sensations.
SATYR: And wine brings pleasing madness with its vapors.
SHEPHERD AND SATYR: Let's love/drink.
985 Let's go through life that way;
Without envy or sorrow

Let's follow Cupid's/Bacchus' teachings.

A SHEPHERD: While our tender age
    Lets us fall in love,
    Let's yield to the charms
990   Of so sweet a custom.
    Let's not wait until old age
    Brings its coldness to our veins.
    To passion let's give all our care;
    Thus fate for the greatest hearts ordains.

995 ANOTHER SHEPHERD: Great Cupid's empire let's obey;
    Come and give honor at his altars.
    To it must everyone, gods and mortals,
    Prince, shepherd, satyr, faun give way.

CHORUS: Great Cupid's empire let's obey;
1000   Come and give honor at his altars.
    To it must everyone, gods and mortals,
    Prince, shepherd, satyr, faun give way.
                Exeunt.

             END.

Catherine Bernard

Laodamia, Queen Of Epirus,
(Laodamie reine d'Epire)

The Author

Catherine Bernard was born in 1662 in Rouen, the daughter of a prosperous Huguenot merchant.[59] Some of her biographers state that she was the niece of Corneille, but no proof of this relationship has yet been uncovered, and, assuming that the claim is true, it is puzzling to find no mention of it during her lifetime. She moved to Paris at an unknown date and was quickly received into elegant society, where she gained the friendship and protection of Mme de Maintenon (who later married King Louis XIV) and Mme de Pontchartrain (wife of the influential minister, later Chancellor of France). In 1685, shortly before the revocation of the Edict of Nantes, she made a well-publicized conversion to Catholicism. However, if her abjuration endeared her to her protectors at court, it angered her family. The will of her maternal aunt warned that Catherine Bernard would forfeit her share of the inheritance if she persevered in her new faith, and the rest of her family may have cut her off, as well.

In the course of the next dozen years Bernard produced four novels, three of which were very successful, two tragedies, which were both staged at the Comédie-Française, and a considerable quantity of occasional verse. The honors she garnered for her work were most impressive: she won the poetry prize at the "Floral Games" of Toulouse several times; she won the poetry prize of the French Academy on three occasions (in 1691, 1693, and 1697); and she was elected to membership in the Accademia dei Ricovrati in Padua, which had opened its doors to women some decades earlier.

Despite her celebrity, Bernard found her earnings insufficient to live on. A modest royal pension, which was not always paid, did not prevent her from sinking into poverty. Eventually, her friend Mme de Pontchartrain rescued her with a very substantial pension, but the devout benefactress imposed strict conditions: Bernard was obliged to renounce writing for the stage and to burn much of her early verse. She wrote virtually nothing for the rest of her life, and her death in 1712 passed largely unnoticed.

The attacks against her literary reputation began in 1730. The *Mercure galant*, in criticizing Voltaire's new tragedy, *Brutus*, compared it unfavorably with Bernard's play on the same subject. From then on, Voltaire, together with Abbé Trublet, never missed an opportunity to cast aspersion on the dead poetess. They claimed that Fontenelle had helped her with all her compositions and that he had written all or most of *Brutus* himself.[60] Following Fontenelle's death in 1757, editors of his collected works included Bernard's tragedy under his name. Later enemies hinted that *Brutus* was really the work of Marie-Anne Barbier (this attribution even found its way into the catalogue of the Bibliothèque nationale). The absurdity of this accusation is glaringly apparent because Barbier herself directly refuted it back in 1702 (see the preface to *Arria and Paetus*, later in this volume). The charge that Fontenelle collaborated in the writing of *Brutus* may, however, contain a grain of truth. That illustrious academician, even if he was not her cousin, was probably a good friend (although Bernard's biographers, who all refer to this friendship, never provide evidence for it). Given the remarkable improvement in style between *Laodamia* and *Brutus*, plays which were only about two years apart, it would not be surprising if she turned to a more experienced poet for advice. Nevertheless, the testimony of Barbier, who was writing while Bernard was still alive, must stand against the word of hostile critics writing long after her death: Catherine Bernard was indeed responsible for the works published under her name. She signed the dedication of *Brutus*, and, in fact, the reviewer of the *Mercure galant* gushed, after seeing the play's premiere, "Ladies today are capable of everything."[61]

Absolutely nothing is known about Bernard's love life, if indeed she had one. But in her depiction of that passion, she was an austere moralist and a sensitive observer. In the preface to her first novel, *Eléonor d'Yvrée*, she announces that she will not permit happy endings in her fiction, in order to warn her readers against the dangers, suffering, and disorders caused by love; even if a love is pure and reasonable, it must be punished. Much of the melancholy and sadness of her prose writings carries over into *Laodamia*. In *Brutus*, where the tone of Cornelian heroism predominates, the condemnation of love is still more severe. Although she can make no claim to poetic genius or profound originality, Bernard was certainly a sincere and serious-minded artist.

The Play

Significance

Laodamia deserves a place of honor in the annals of French women dramatists: it is the first full-length play by a woman to be staged at the premiere theatre of Paris, the Comédie-Française. (That company, founded in 1680 as the result of a merger of the existing rival troupes, would hold a virtual monopoly on serious dramas in the capital for over a century.) I have chosen it over Catherine Bernard's second tragedy, *Brutus*, despite the fact that the latter was even more popular and is stylistically superior, because *Laodamia* is more innovative and more overtly feminist.

Although *Laodamia* conforms perfectly to the structural and stylistic conventions of French classical tragedy, it contains several notable departures in the area of characterization. First of all, Bernard depicts a woman as virtuous, conscientious, and able to keep her passions under control, without embracing the austere and self-assertive stoicism of Corneille's Roman heroines. The title character is a hard-working and well-intentioned ruler, but not an ambitious queen or a brilliant politician; she is brave, but not a warrior, and must rely on male generals; she can make hard decisions, but she agonizes at great length over them. In short, she is an admirable but not extraordinary figure, who demonstrates what a normal woman is capable of achieving in an essentially unheroic and male-dominated world. Her sister Nereis is also a figure of great dignity who likewise finds the courage to sacrifice her personal happiness for the sake of the public good.

Gelon is a more conventional figure, one of a long line of polite, chivalric, and self-effacing heroes in French tragedy of the later seventeenth century. Nevertheless, Catherine Bernard manipulated the convention in order to raise questions about the type of heroism he represents and to set off the moral superiority of the ladies. He feels not the slightest allegiance to family or state, is devoid of political ambition, and seeks only personal glory through his exploits and the love of his lady. Gelon moves in a world of civil war, conspiracy, and murder, filled with unscrupulous opportunists coveting power, yet he remains aloof from it all, uninterested in anything save his personal drama. We tend to wonder, as he ascends the throne of Epirus at the end of the tragedy, what kind of ruler he will make. Moreover, compared to the ladies, he is too ready to become alarmed and to weep at the slightest provocation. He is not ashamed to call his behavior "weakness" (v. 169) and to wallow in it.

The other noteworthy innovation in *Laodamia* is the exceptionally close bond between the two sisters, whose affection does not waver even when they discover that they are in love with the same man. Although several other tragedies of the 1670s and 1680s had shown two sisters as rivals in love, the earlier plays show one sister eventually betraying the other, albeit reluctantly, and they concentrate on the ladies' love, rather than on their sisterly tenderness. In Bernard's play, both sisters refer constantly to their close relationship and would rather sacrifice their own happiness than hurt the other. Rejecting the misogynist view of women as incapable of friendship due to the allegedly greater hold that the passions have upon them, Catherine Bernard made her heroines splendid examples of friendship under pressure, and in the process contributed to a revaluation of woman's nature.

Historical Background

The plot of *Laodamia* is almost entirely fictional, loosely based on a passage from a little-known Roman historian named Justin. In Book 28 of his *Abridgment of the Histories of Trogus Pompeius* he relates how Olympias, daughter of Pyrrhus, king of Epirus, became regent after the death of her husband, Alexander (who was also her brother). Alarmed by the attempts of the Aetolians to wrest from her the tributary province of Acarnania, she appealed for help to Demetrius, king of Macedonia. To secure the alliance, she gave this king her daughter, Phithia, in marriage. However, the first wife of Demetrius, whom he divorced, was so angered by the popularity of the new wife that she departed to the court of her brother Antiochus, king of Syria, and provoked him to make war against her husband. Meanwhile, the Acarnanians, anxious to rid themselves of the Aetolian invaders, and distrusting the Epirots, appealed to Rome. The Senate thereupon sent ambassadors to the Aetolians, ordering them to withdraw their garrisons from Acarnania. However, the Aetolians, aware that Rome was still shaken by Carthaginian invasions and by the recent burning of their city, proudly defied the ambassadors and proceeded to ravage the whole province of Acarnania. Unable to rely on Demetrius, whose army was busy elsewhere, Olympias sent her last surviving son, Ptolomy, to head an expedition against the Aetolians.

But Ptolomy fell ill and died on the way, and his army turned back. Olympias died of grief shortly after. Such is the chaotic state of affairs at the point when the play begins.

Unfortunately, Justin's account of Laodamia is so brief and so unclear that it could hardly provide adequate guidance even for the most scrupulous of playwrights:

> There remained of the blood royal no more but only a young maid called Nereis and her sister Laodamia. Nereis was married unto Gelo son of the king of Sicily. And Laodamia flying for her safeguard to the altar of Diana, was there by the concourse of the people slain. The which offense the gods immortal revenged and punished with continual slaughters of that nation, and well near with the utter destruction of all the whole realm. For first and foremost being punished with dearth and hunger, and being [shaken] with civil discord, last of all they were in manner quite consumed by the wars of foreign nations, and Milo who killed Laodamia falling out of his wits, so mangled his body sometime with iron, sometime with stones, and in fine so rent and tore his own bowels with his teeth, that within 12 days he died most miserably.[62]

It is not clear whether Laodamia was in fact the older of the remaining sisters, or whether she was crowned queen, following the deaths of her mother and brothers. Nor is it specified whether the marriage of Nereis to Gelo was arranged before or after the death of Olympias, or why the Sicilians failed to come to the aid of the Epirots. We are not told who Milo was, or why he assassinated Laodamia.[63]

As for the historical Gelo, we learn from Pausanias (*Description of Greece* VI.12) and Polybius (*Histories* VII.8) that he was the eldest son of Hiero, king of Syracuse. Hiero came to power in 275 B.C. and reigned for fifty-four years, during which

time he kept his land at peace. He made an alliance with
Pyrrhus of Epirus, sealing it with the marriage of his son Gelo to
Pyrrhus' daughter, Nereis. Gelo, an obedient son whom his
father made co-ruler, died in 216/15 B.C., shortly before Hiero
and aged more than fifty.

It should be remembered that Catherine Bernard did not
have access to the tools of nineteenth- and twentieth-century
classical scholarship, nor would she have necessarily used them,
even if she had. She may well have chosen the episode from
Justin precisely because of its vagueness and because the characters were virtually unknown, thus allowing herself the opportunity to invent a plot of her own choosing.

Performance History

The premiere took place at the Comédie-Française on February
11, 1689, making it the first full-length play by a woman author
to be staged by that company. It was performed a total of twen-
ty-three times that year, which made it a respectable success by
the standards of the day. Beginning on March 2, an afterpiece
was given with the tragedy, despite the author's wish that the
troupe postpone doing so as long as possible. *Laodamia* stayed
in the repertory for two more years, receiving two more performances in 1690 and one more in 1691. (*Brutus* would be even
more successful, with a total of forty-three performances by
1699.) The Marquis d'Argenson, one of the play's rare champions in the eighteenth century, attempted to convince the
Comédie-Française to revive it, but in vain.[64] There have been
no known revivals since.

The date of 1689 for the first performance, derived from the
Mercure galant and the brothers Parfaict, and confirmed by
Joannidès and by Bernard's biographer, Eugène Asse, has occa-
sionally been disputed. Eugène Cassin, writing in 1845, placed
the premiere on February 11, 1688 (perhaps a printing error).
The *Nouvelle Biographie universelle*, in a volume published in

1853, calls the play *Léodamie* and places the first performance in 1690. René Godenne, who also spells the title *Léodamie*, claims that the premiere took place on February 16, 1685. Since none of these scholars has brought to light new evidence to support their alternative datings, there is no reason to challenge the traditional date of 1689.

Laodamia, Queen of Epirus

(Laodamie reine d'Epire)
Tragedy

Catherine Bernard

Actors[65]

LAODAMIA, Queen of Epirus.
NEREIS, her sister.
GELON, Prince of Sicily.
SOSTRATE, Prince of Epirus.
PHOENIX, minister of state.
MILO, confidant to Sostrate.
ARGIRA, confidante to the Queen.
PHAEDRA, confidante to the Princess.

The scene is in Buthrotum, capital of Epirus, in the royal palace.

. . . . .

ACT I

Enter Queen, Princess, Argira.

QUEEN: Go, Sister, leave me to my sadness, go.
  Vain are your friendly efforts to allay it.
  For your consideration I am grateful,
  But tears and evil fortune are my lot.

5 PRINCESS: Madam, you see your armies are triumphant.
  Can victory then hold no charms for you?
  Cannot this last success, just now achieved,
  Cheer up your thoughts, if only for a moment?
  These hymns of joy, resounding through Epirus
10 This day, condemn your soul's distress and anguish.[66]
  Whose wishes are fulfilled more than your own?

QUEEN: 'Tis true, but fate, by its sad kindnesses,
  Hastens the hour that dooms the rest of my life,
  When I must be enslaved under a harsh decree.
15 Attale, returning as a haughty victor,
  Will press a marriage that my heart opposes.
  Yet I consent to it: my crown demands
  Protection and support from a strong husband.
  The fierce Aetolians, bent on my destruction,
20 Have long maintained a state of war against us.
  We must oppose them with an equal force.
  My father ordered me, alas! to wed Attale,
  Prince of Paeonia, ally of the Romans,
  Who, he believed, would keep me on my throne.
25 By not obeying, I bring on myself
  New enemies who pose a threat to Epirus.
  I sacrifice myself. How could my heart not feel
  Its woes, joined to the welfare of my state?

PRINCESS: If the order of our father, the late king,
30 If harsh constraints due to reasons of state
  Do not permit you any other husband,
  Madam, this duty will become more pleasant.

Now that the prince returns covered with glory
From his great victory over the Aetolians,
Deign to consider that such deeds of arms
Might have deserved the honor of your choice.
QUEEN: Well, if he has achieved such great renown,
I'll see him, prouder and no more lovable,
Ask for my hand with greater arrogance,
With no better success in touching my heart.
This ferocity which dominates his manner,
His restless nature, quick to take offense,
Make my unfortunate heart rebel against him,
Though Heaven has sentenced me to be his bride.
Have you not seen what evil humor rules him?
The Prince of Sicily, whom I intend for you,
Already feared and famed for myriad exploits,
Was helping us too much toward victory.
Attale, who found such high renown offensive,
No more could bear to see this rival in the army,
And to rob him of victories assured,
He sent him back to us on specious pretexts.
Unworthy motive! What extreme injustice!
What torment my marriage to that man will be!
PRINCESS: Madam, I empathize with all your suffering.
I pity your misfortunes.
QUEEN: You don't know them.
Your heart till now has only had experience
Of a mutual love, happy since its beginning,
Which, never thwarted, cannot to your wishes
But offer dreams of a future happier still.
Filled and possessed by such enchanting bliss,
How could you even conceive of my misfortunes?
PRINCESS: One of the strongest ties binding me to you
Is that serene, sweet happiness you speak of.
I owe to you, I constantly remember,

The Prince of Sicily and his tenderness.
Gelon, a warrior with no ladylove,
Became my suitor by your happy choice.
Your orders made him offer me his heart.
70 Soon after genuine love completed your work
And reinforced the sweet bonds started by you.
But no less is my heart beholden to you,
Madam, and my affection for you strengthens,
The more this love spreads charms upon my life.
75 QUEEN: Enjoy, my sister, these innocent charms,
And may you never feel distress like mine.
Such sad discussion must be torture for you.
Leave me alone to give way to my sorrow;
This melancholy's too unsuitable
80 To the charming sweetness that makes your lot happy.
Go, free yourself . . .
PRINCESS: Madam, have I offended?
QUEEN: No, sister, your affection I am sure of,
But despite myself I feel my sorrows growing.
In my present state I must have solitude.
                    Exit Princess.
85 ARGIRA: What, madam, does the presence of a sister
So tenderly beloved now upset you?
QUEEN: Alas, shall I confess? But what can I hide,
When I see the climax of my woes approaching?
Learn, then, to what ills I shall be a prey.
90 You know my great affection for Nereis,
But soon, O gods! Gelon shall wed this sister,
And Gelon is secretly lord of my heart.
My father Alexander's final treaty
Mandates my loveless marriage to Attale.
95 I must fulfill his absolute decree;
A thousand reasons of state further require it.
My crown is shaky, and my people are rebellious,

Already worn out by a cruel war.
Should I bring still more enemies upon them,
Rebellious subjects will think all's permitted.
The interest of the throne, to which I'm chained,
Makes this cruel marriage a necessity.
But my heart rebels and fights incessantly
Against a father's will, reasons of state.
Alas, how happy we would be, Argira,
If always dangerous passions were required
To wait at least, before they first arise,
Until an eager lover showed his ardor!
But oft a spark that dominates our heart
Precedes the signs that *should* kindle our love,
Fuels itself and will commit us further
Than the tenderest treatment that we might receive.
Such is my involuntary love for Gelon.
No sign of hope ever graced this secret torment.
Meanwhile I saw that he loved no one else;
He might yet turn his preference toward me.
My heart, in spite of me, with eagerness
Seized on a hope so false, so unsubstantial,
And, dazzled by the charm of a vain error,
Erected a strong barrier to my duty.
To rid me of the error that my weakness cherished,
I arranged a match for Gelon and the princess.
How much it cost me! How my aching heart
Was torn apart by an internal struggle!
How hard I tried! I thought, harsh on myself,
That love is cured as soon as it turns hopeless.
My trying to make him fall in love succeeded
Too well. My rival's are the profits! Alas!
This love I fostered has grown to such excess!
It took no more to rob me of all hope.
O ineffective aid for my weak reason!

I thought their love would cure me of my own,
And find myself obsessed with jealous sorrow.
What a remedy for love! That jealousy . . .

135 ARGIRA: Perhaps it will at last effect a cure
When Gelon's love has roused your indignation.
But, madam, it is he that now approaches.

Enter Gelon.

GELON: You know what love sprang up upon your orders,
Madam, and that fair flame, authorized by you,

140 May find excuse for too much eagerness.
My suit to the Princess does not displease you.
Must the wedding be postponed, though nothing hinders?
And must my happiness . . .

QUEEN: It is not in doubt,
Prince; Attale is coming back and I owe him

145 My hand. I plan that here on the same day
A double wedding will shine with more splendor.
And for the little time you must delay,
Your love must surely not complain too much.

GELON: Madam, I beg you let me then reveal

150 A secret cause for my desire for haste.
If we must wait for Prince Attale's return,
I fear to find that he'll oppose my love.
He is to sit on the throne where Heaven placed you.
To judge by the feelings he has shown too well,

155 I've no illusions he'll show me his tenderest
Affection, as he sees himself near to the throne.
Should he intend to stop the match I wish for,
How many devious means he might employ!
How many secret schemes he might devise!

160 O heaven! if my happiness were thwarted,
How I'd regret the unforgivable mistake
Of failing to use this propitious moment.

QUEEN: Prince, you expect that when Attale returns,

I'll cease to occupy my wonted rank
165 And be deprived of influence and power?
GELON: Madam, allow a lover's unease of mind.
He worries easily; the more we value
A good, the more it seems about to escape us.
I beg you sympathize, approve my weakness.
170 I always think Attale threatens my love.
But even had I no cause to fear his coming,
Is two or three days sooner naught for love?
If only you knew well its sovereign power,
If only you felt the charms I can't resist!
175 But at least a love that owes so much to you
Has some right to expect . . .
QUEEN: Well, be content.
The wedding your heart desires, Prince—for tomorrow.
GELON: What words of thanks could ever be sufficient!
QUEEN: There is no need; go to my sister, Prince,
180 And share with her the sweetness of your future.
                    Exit Gelon.
Ah, let him wed her, let a speedy marriage
Forever quench my hapless flame, Argira.
Let him wed her. Why did I wish to delay
The scheme I had so carefully prepared,
185 The only way to crush a love too fatal?
ARGIRA: Yes, thus you'll put out love's remaining fires,
Madam. Too long now have you struggled for you
Not to make virtue triumph in the end.
QUEEN: Triumph it will. I was too deeply wounded
190 When he revealed to me his raving passion:
A silly haste, an ill-founded suspicion.
I leave him to the love that obsesses him.
The ingrate did not know that his impatience
Seemed to my heart a mortal injury.
195 He made not the slightest effort to discern

The secret feelings underlying my words.

ARGIRA: What, would you want that? Don't you always hide
From him and the princess your too loving heart?

QUEEN: True. Neither my eyes nor my mouth have ever
200 Betrayed signs of my involuntary love.
I bear the harshest, self-imposed constraints,
But still I'd like the man who loves me not
To penetrate my feigning, guess my secret,
And, pitying me deep down, perhaps respect me.
205 But the error of such hope would be extreme:
He's too preoccupied to guess my love.
With firmer heart, if possible, let's submit
To the joyless marriage that's prepared for us,
And not expect to find appreciation
210 For heroic efforts in surmounting passion.
Heaven! I still shudder at my coming fate.
Attale is coming; each instant he draws nearer.
But what does Sostrate want? Is this a time to vex
Me with a useless love that makes him odious?

Enter Sostrate and Milo.

215 SOSTRATE: Sad tidings have just been delivered here,
Madam. Attale is dead.

QUEEN: He's dead! O gods!
And what foundation is there for this news?

SOSTRATE: One of his men, arriving from the army.
Attale, in haste to see you and to bring you
220 His laurels, rode ahead of his warriors.
But near Paeonia a cruel band
Attacked the prince with criminal intent.
Attale succumbed, madam, to all their blows.
Heaven, by allowing it, shows its displeasure.
225 Today the whole state will share in your grief.

QUEEN: Attale has perished and his death is certain!
How sudden a change for me and for the state!

Let's seek more confirmation of this news.
> *Exeunt Queen and Argira.*

SOSTRATE: It's done, dear Milo, I applaud myself.
230   I managed this plot with so much artifice
That henceforth I am clear of all suspicion.
The path to power opens for me at last.
The objects of the passion that consumes me—
The throne I claim, the Queen whom I adore—
235   Attale, too fortunate, would have robbed me of,
Had I not dared to act for my own good!
Free from suspicion I'll enjoy a crime
Which love and glory justify too well.
Let's profit from it, dear Milo, and make haste.
240 MILO: Sir, have no doubt, the crown belongs to you.
The nearness of your kinship to the Queen
Assures to your desires the sovereign sway.
SOSTRATE: The Queen has always treated me with coldness,
Although her ardor for Attale was weak.
245 MILO: How could she view your love more favorably?
Attale for her was a mandatory choice.
Your suit, too full of danger, she avoided;
Her heart, enslaved, dared not make its own choice.
SOSTRATE: I must inform you of my secret fear:
250   Another love in her heart might harm my chances.
MILO: Another love! The very sharpest eyes
In this court, sir, have never seen that love.
SOSTRATE: My eyes are sharper than any in this court.
Love and ambition lend me their keen insight.
255   Not that I'm certain of what I perceive;
I don't so much know, Milo, as believe it.
I sense it, and a secret loathing ever
Shows to my heart the man the Queen prefers.
In short, it seems to me that she loves Gelon.
260 MILO: What foolish fancy causes you alarm?

Gelon offers sole devotion to the princess.
The Queen permits it; such clear evidence . . .
SOSTRATE: The Queen was duty-bound not to oppose it
So long as Attale, alive, was her betrothed.
265   Under a long and harsh restraint she kept
Within her soul a passion unrevealed.
Is it not possible, Milo, that this death,
Of which I learn today with so much rapture,
May have for her a charm still more pronounced?
270   Did she so much as shed one tear? Or breathe
One sigh? Perhaps at this moment her eyes
Saw on the throne a place for her beloved.
Ah, should she delude herself with such a hope,
Should another love deprive me of the ingrate,
275   My arm will be fatal to both of them.
I have not worked so hard to serve a rival.
Yes, rather sacrificed to my just wrath,
They'll see what it means to make a heart despair.
Naught will I spare: I have courage and friends,
280   A long-established plan to reign, a just
Claim to Epirus; and if I can't be master,
At least I'll keep another from the throne.
MILO: Fear nothing, sir, rely upon your rights.
Is this prince, like you, descended from our kings?
285   While his older brother reigns in Sicily,
He, banished from his land, a stranger lacking
Aid and support, finds refuge in Epirus.
SOSTRATE: I know my rank and ancestry count for me.
The throne with justice can't be taken from me.
290   But I fear the daring and intrigue of Phoenix.
He hates me, and fearing to become my subject,
He might to Gelon's project lend support.
Being thoroughly devoted to this rival,
For his own interest he will have to serve him.

295 Under his reign he'd see his own power grow.
Let us forestall his plans, having foreseen them.
This insolent minister, whom the Queen esteems,
Is going to serve her love and brave my hatred.
Dear Milo, let us act with tireless zeal.
300 The throne and Queen have for us too much appeal.

Exeunt.

ACT II

Enter Princess and Phaedra.

PRINCESS: Attale's demise is only too assured.
    The Queen is rescued from an odious marriage.
    Gelon tomorrow joins his fate with mine.
    My happiness is perfect; naught is lacking.
305   My sister's anguish was an obstacle,
    But Heaven performs a miracle to save her.
    Although Attale's death ought to inspire pity,
    It yields in my heart to sisterly affection.
    How the Queen has suffered! How much she has wept!
310   Her tears disturbed the sweetest charms of my love.
    I've wished a hundred times within my heart
    To suffer her woes and let her have my joy.
    Do you conceive the horror of a hated spouse?
    Perhaps—worst pain of all—she loved another.
315   She objected to this loathsome match too strongly:
    One does not hate so much unless one loves.
PHAEDRA: Whom could she love? Sostrate, who worships her,
    Shows us each day the anguish that devours him.
    A lover who's belov'd, is he unhappy?
320   No, when he's forced to keep his love a secret,
    His complaints at least are of another sort.
PRINCESS: The honor of the crown has strange constraints.
    The Queen might have concealed her heart's fond secret
    Under the cruel facade of a proud rigor.
325   Sometimes one makes the man one loves unhappy,
    The better to dissemble one's own suffering.
    But Cineas, Iphis, who court her favors,[67]
    Still seem to us captivated by her charms.
    They make this all too clear by their behavior.
330   And though their rank gives them little claim to her,
    Their virtues and great love might touch her heart.
    Perhaps this very day we'll know this secret.

The Queen, at liberty to break the silence,
Owes it to my affection to confide.
335   Can she hide from me . . . But see, she approaches.

Enter Queen.

When all your kingdom has its eyes on you,
While, curious, it seeks to learn whether
Your sadness stems from politics or love,
Will you permit your sister here, madam,
340   To probe your feelings deep within your heart?
You did not love Attale, and his death saves you
From a duty which your love found cruel to follow.
You sometimes would admit as much to me.

QUEEN: The grief that always follows on a death,
345   The sudden change occasioned by Attale's,
His loss which may be fatal to my land,
All keep my heart from feeling at liberty.
This heart is less enslaved, but no less troubled.

PRINCESS: But you at least are freed now from the fear
350   Of suffering the pain of a forced marriage.
Now that Attale is dead your heart's your own;
And should it feel the tender passion, it
Must yield at last to its ruling emotion.
Who'd stop you? You're free and a queen. Perhaps
355   All your desires are bound up with ambition.
But if you aren't in love, you lack a joy.

QUEEN: Would that I were indifferent, sister, truly!
Would that the throne were impervious to love,
Because so rarely can one be happy there.

360   PRINCESS: No duty blocks your wishes anymore.
How sweet to think that you have a beloved!
I love; permit me, madam, to declare it:
This conformity of passion and of feeling
Creates a bond between all those in love.
365   Love! Cupid owes you all of his delights

As a reward for all the tears you've shed.
O crown today your charming conqueror!
What joy to give a scepter with one's heart!
QUEEN: 'Tis not yet time for you to think me happy.
370 My ostensible felicity's deceptive.
My fame and love can scarce be reconciled.
PRINCESS: Your fame? How can you be convinced of that?
QUEEN: Fear for my fame leads to this inner struggle.
In my rank can I follow my emotions?
375 PRINCESS: Sostrate, I see, has failed to win your heart.
Perhaps a luckier man managed to charm you,
And nobler virtues, though in lesser rank,
Legitimize your feeling for this suitor.
Yet, madam, you repel your heart's desire.
380 You fear his rank might cancel out his virtues;
But why torture your heart with a vain scruple?
Are you queen merely to tyrannize yourself?
When crowned, the man you love will be respected.
Since he won your heart, he has well earned the throne.
385 QUEEN: I've said too much, my heart could not keep silent.
But you'll not learn what man has won my heart.
My sister, let us drop this dangerous subject.
In my condition flatter not my wishes.
But I see Sostrate. I must avoid his presence.
Exit Queen; enter Sostrate.
390 SOSTRATE: I see that she leaves you, madam, to flee me.
When one's unhappy, how one is unwelcome!
But don't you fear something?
PRINCESS: What fate awaits us?
SOSTRATE: I give you an unpleasant, but vital warning,
Madam; this is no time to keep things from you.
395 The Queen has long inspired my amorous feelings.
Though my despair has possibly revealed this,
My jealousy was still unknown to you.

I must let you know what poison makes me die.
Perhaps your lot will be as sad as mine.
400   Madam, Prince Attale is dead; we need a king.
PRINCESS: Sir, I can't understand what you've been saying.
SOSTRATE: The Queen, obeying Alexander's order,
        Agreed to wed a man she did not love.
        His death cannot have caused her any sorrow.
405   Thus, when I broke the news to her, at first
        She seemed to listen with little emotion.
        But since then, sad, uneasy and confused,
        Her mind keeps forming and rejecting plans.
        She has the right to give the crown as she
410   Sees fit, but her liberty seems to amaze her.
        Her heart finds some embarrassment in using
        It.
PRINCESS: Well then, sir?
SOSTRATE: Can one fail to suspect it,
        If Gelon were the man she loves in secret?
PRINCESS: That she loves Gelon! Ah, that cannot be.
415   From her I received him; she gave him to me.
        Our love was born by her express command.
SOSTRATE: 'Tis no less certain, madam, that she loves him,
        And you in vain seek to delude yourself.
PRINCESS: Who told you of this?
SOSTRATE: Trust my jealous fury.
420   A lover spurned knows all of his misfortunes.
        A thousand times I've caught the loving lady
        Attentive to the charms of her subduer.
        Despite her caution I saw her eyes avow,
        Her mouth applaud, her heart sigh for this love.
425   PRINCESS: Then how, sir, does it happen that this passion
        Which you discovered was never seen by me?
SOSTRATE: You were belov'd, and your lover and you
        Were always fully absorbed in your sweet bliss,

Quite unaware of other people's passions;
430   Your mutual love hid from you all the rest.
Content with his heart, you'd not think to seek
Whether someone in secret wished to steal him from you.
One must have jealous eyes to spot a rival.
I, whom a fatal passion has enlightened,
435   I who pursue a heart and cannot win it,
I've sought the cause and managed to discover it.
PRINCESS: You must admit your proof is rather doubtful.
SOSTRATE: Ah, you rely too much on deceptive friendship.
Your interests, madam, are the same as mine here.
440   Secure a captive who may break his chains.
The crown has charms to make a man unfaithful;
The Queen will offer it, forestall her plan.
I'll do my utmost to defend your love,
But you in turn, madam, must take some action.

Exit Sostrate.

445   PRINCESS: What shall I think? I saw the Queen's agitation.
I did not tremble, being too prepossessed.
Alas! He is loved, Phaedra; all signs confirm it.
The secret she hides and her nonplussed look,
Sostrate's ill fortune and his jealous rage,
450   Gelon's good looks, is anything more needed?
Go, run, tell him to come, inform him of my grief.

Exit Phaedra.

(*alone*) Heaven, have you destined me for such great woes?
My sister, whom I love so, does she betray me?
Does she burn with passion for the man I love?
455   Yet, have I ample grounds to fear this danger?
If the Queen loved him, why order our betrothal?
This reasoning, which I've always accepted,
Why does it fail to satisfy my heart?
Fear and suspicions I knew not before
460   Have come to overwhelm my tranquil heart.

What bursts of cruel emotions grip my soul!
Is it you, baleful Jealousy, I feel?
Will you spread all your fury on our thoughts?
Will you uproot affection from our hearts?
465 But why give in to my distress? Let's not
Accuse the Queen on a jealous man's advice.
Too soon I've heeded odious suspicions.
Let's wait at least for further evidence.

Reenter Phaedra.

PHAEDRA: I couldn't see Gelon; he was with the Queen.
470 Your wedding is postponed, and for that reason
The Queen, alone in her study, summoned him.
PRINCESS: He's with my sister! The marriage is delayed!
No word of this to me! Ah, sure misfortune!
Now all is lost, I feel the unlucky omen.
I see, Phaedra, that our wedding, just postponed,
475 Alas, in a few days will be forbidden.
PHAEDRA: The Queen is noble and she loves you, madam.
And when she sees the anguish in your soul,
Even if she's in love, honor and pity
480 Will still force her to follow sisterly affection.
If Gelon's faithful, what can she devise?
She'll have respect for a love so tender. You
May hope soon to enjoy full ease of mind.
Constancy always is the virtue of a hero.
485 PRINCESS: Ah, Phaedra, heroes only heed their glory,
And love for them is but one type of victory.
Perhaps he'll sacrifice me with no anguish,
Alas, and I for him would have sacrificed all.
Then he'll be offered the throne and all its charms,
490 While I can only give my love and tears.
What disparity! And why, O unjust Heaven,
Since I love a hero, can't I make him king?
PHAEDRA: But . . .

PRINCESS: Do not contradict my mortal grief.
Could I imagine he'd be faithful to me?
495   If he were constant, he'd incur ill fortune.
The Queen would avenge the spurning of her love—
A woman in love, insulted, on the throne.
These are all the disasters I must fear,
Dear Phaedra, and you see the least one is
500   Not to be his, although I find him faithful.
I can remain no longer without seeing him;
At least let's hear him and learn his position.
Let's go. We must determine our deadly woes.
Let's learn for which misfortunes we must weep.
Enter Phoenix.
505   Stop, Phoenix, stop. What reason brings you here?
You who have always known the Queen's designs,
Why has the date of my wedding been postponed?
PHOENIX: The sad death of Attale, which grieves this court,
Is sufficient cause, madam, for this delay.
510   That's one reason that I was coming to tell you.
There is another which I dare not mention,
But, madam, after all, why hide it from you?
PRINCESS: Speak out, my soul is steeled for all misfortunes.
PHOENIX: The people give their voice this day to Gelon.[68]
515   Perhaps this signifies events to come.
'Tis thus that Heaven pronounces its decrees.
PRINCESS: Is it not rather secret conspirators
Who have produced this tactless show of support?
For one may doubt, however great his merit,
520   That such zeal would break forth without a leader.
PHOENIX: My heart, you know, has never used disguise,
Yet I'll admit I did not intervene
In the people's warm show of support for Gelon.
The fruits of his valor everywhere resound.
525   I saw in every heart my enthusiasm,

But I made it speak and did so without crime.
If his virtues need any more assistance
To advance the course of his great destiny,
I'll bring to it the zeal which naturally
530   A hero so worthy of the throne inspires.
Do likewise, madam, help to make him king.
But it is not for me to dare to teach you.
Yourself . . .

PRINCESS: Did he dictate this message to you?
Gods! Gelon wants to reign, I understand this speech
535   Too well.

PHOENIX: He loves greatness, although a lover,
And the state's welfare must balance his desires.
Great masses are inviting him to reign.
See the sudden effects his merit causes,
Madam, and what I further foresee today,
540   And judge yourself if he can fail to be king.

PRINCESS: O Heaven!

Exeunt Princess and Phaedra.

PHOENIX (*alone*):   Your firmness, Phoenix, is required.
'Tis your hate today that you must satisfy.
Sostrate wishes to reign; you must prevent it.
If your plot fails, he'll have the power to punish
545   You. I will serve the Queen! When I named Gelon,
Her great delight showed me that she loves him.
I enable her to dare follow her heart,
Despite her consideration for her sister.
Let's act at once; a moment's sometimes useful.
550   Let's crown the Prince of Sicily today.
He'll owe the throne to me, I'll be his stay.
For him I'll do my all and expect all from him.

Exit.

ACT III

Enter Queen and Argira.

QUEEN: I am at liberty to bare my soul to you;
 All things conspire to advance my love, Argira.
555 I find thousands of voices in his favor;
 They indicate the man my heart should love.
 But though my subjects strive for my happiness,
 They can't give me the heart that I desire.
 Just now I saw Gelon, whom I had summoned,
560 But never could I speak to him, Argira.
 The sudden news that his wedding was postponed
 Produced a deathly sorrow in his face.
 He still knew not that people want him as king.
 I wished to tell him and failed despite myself;
565 I feared, too timid, in breaking this news
 To show the interest love gives me in him.
ARGIRA: Speak, madam, for a throne has charms too sweet,
 And soon you will see Gelon at your feet.
 Would he give up all for a frivolous love?
570 One sacrifices love, never the throne.
 'Tis better to be king than a perfect lover.
QUEEN: What? He'd pretend to love me just to reign?
 Ah, if his passion for me's not sincere,
 I shall be able to detect such falseness.
575 No, if the throne is his only desire,
 Let him expect never to gain his wish.
 What am I saying? Am I grown so fastidious?
 This heart, which feels all of love's weaknesses,
 Could it reject the homage of this suitor
580 Because a crown contributes to his passion?
 And would I not account myself too happy
 To bear the sham appearance of his love?
 I fear, at whatever price the ingrate loved me,
 My heart would be enraptured by his attention.

585 ARGIRA: Could he resist such great love, madam?
QUEEN: Alas,
     Why did I not at least let his heart act freely?
     If I myself had not formed his betrothal,
     Perhaps he would have loved me, or loved no one.
     Perhaps he loved the princess to obey me.
590 Let him restore this heart I ruled too well.
     But do I really wish to steal him from my sister?
     A sister who bases all her happiness on me?
     Could I be so cruel to take away her lover?
     I know what he inspires; she'd die from this.
595 She loves me, and my heart, sighing in secret,
     Saw many times the extent of her affection.
     A thousand times my sorrows touched her deeply.
     As a reward I shall betray her love.
     Alas! in vain I blame my treachery.
600 I've tasted the dangerous poison of hope.
     When I see the way become clear for my love,
     I feel that all my self-reproach is useless,
     That I will stifle honor and pity's cry,
     That love outweighs affection in my heart.
605 But no, Argira, let's offer resistance,
     Restore my reason by removing hope.
ARGIRA: Don't you owe something to yourself, to the state?
     You'd be committing a crime against it, madam,
     If, able to give it as master a great hero,
610 The only one that can be recognized here,
     You placed the sceptre in less worthy hands
     By your too great adherence to vain scruples.
     Reason and justice, madam, favor you.
     The Princess for the state must sacrifice;
615 Let her today make test of her moral strength.
     You have suffered and struggled even more.
QUEEN: I tremble, Gelon comes. What do I resolve?

Enter Gelon.

GELON: Madam, the reports that here are circulated
   Might have made me look suspect to you, but
620   I come to swear to you that my deep respect
   And my inviolate, pure loyalty to you
   Detest and disavow such insolence.
QUEEN: Prince, you've no need to justify yourself.
   When one can place one's trust in virtue alone,
625   One scorns to get involved in base intrigues
   And leaves such acts to less heroic souls.
   Even the people's show of feeling is pardoned;
   For anyone but you, I'd have condemned it.
GELON: How must I express my thanks for your great goodness?
630   Would all my life-blood could settle the debt!
   I have not shed enough of it for you.
QUEEN: We know how much, Prince, you have done for us.
   You see too that the Epirots have shown
   That for your valor they want you as master.
635 GELON: Still other warriors, madam, have earned their choice.
   Sostrate above all has a legitimate claim.
   The supreme advantage of being from your race
   Ought to confer on him the whole state's vote.
QUEEN: They do not name him.
GELON: Is it for the people
640   To name the man, madam, whom you must love?
QUEEN: When one's objective is the empire's welfare
   One must often ratify the people's choice.
   The people are enlightened by their true interests:
   One must be a hero to be worshipped by them.
645   Their choice by their advantage is determined,
   And when honor holds sway in a Queen's heart,
   That heart which does not follow blind emotions
   May base its feelings on so sure a choice.
GELON: Ah, madam, what a choice when the mob decides!

650 The people, often guided by mere caprice,
　　May foolishly love one of meager worth.
　　QUEEN: Agreed. Perhaps they act that way today.
　　　　I've not yet seen a great and noble soul
　　　　Reject vigorously a proffered crown.
655 　What man who could command prefers to live a subject?
　　GELON: Honor, for which a noble heart ever strives,
　　　　Is not inseparable from the joy of ruling.
　　　　It may be detached without incurring scorn.
　　　　'Tis sometimes glorious . . .
　　QUEEN: 　　　　　　　　　　I see your disdain.
660 　You think the sovereign power is beneath you,
　　　　But when you scorn the offer of a crown,
　　　　The scorn may fall on her who makes the offer.
　　GELON: Of this crime, madam, no one can accuse me.
　　　　Your lofty virtues never could allow it.
665 　I might have engaged in the opposite crime,
　　　　But you yourself prevented me from doing so:
　　　　You placed my heart into a powerful chain,
　　　　You made me love your relative, your sister.
　　　　And I indeed needed against your charms
670 　The counterweight of charms equally strong.
　　　　Witness to your virtues, every day I might
　　　　Be led from admiration into love.
　　QUEEN: It is not love we wish to make you feel,
　　　　Gelon, you need not thus defend yourself.
675 　I'm queen, and wish today to make a king,
　　　　But my sole guide will be reasons of state.
　　　　Since your love binds you to another fate,
　　　　Enough, I've nothing more to say to you.
　　　　　　　　　　　　Exit Gelon.
　　　　I'm so ashamed! Where shall I hide, Argira?
680 　How I will punish him for winning my heart
　　　　And having by my fault perceived my weakness?

What words I've spoken! Heaven, with what skill
The ingrate made me repeat them countless times!
Alas! was he seeking to remove all doubts?
685   No, his sole aim was to defend himself
And made me speak to keep from understanding
Me. With what artifice, what vain evasion
He cast aside a meaning I kept urging!
Ah, I feel love is giving way to spite!
690   ARGIRA: Madam, if he returns and asks for mercy . . .
QUEEN: Argira, he would come in vain, I hate him.
But alas! I know too well he'll never come.
At least let's give a master to our state,
Who'll make him recognize by countless troubles
695   The nature of the pride of sovereign power,
Which now he treats with such disdain. Do they
Think he alone is worthy of the crown?
The kingdom would have fallen very low . . .

Enter Sostrate.

SOSTRATE: Stop fleeing from a prince who must follow you.
700   Madam, you know how great a love I've hidden.
'Tis the hardest task a lover can perform.
I did it, though, with no hope of pleasing you,
And when lucky Attale was to wed you, I
Pined away without showing it was for you.
705   In short, if sometimes you through my disguising
Have seen my woes without hearing my complaints,
Allow me to address you with respect now.
Attale is dead, madam, and I burn with love.
QUEEN: Yes, Prince, I've managed to observe your conduct,
710   And of your feelings I am well informed.
SOSTRATE: How happy I would be if you could see my heart,
My sincerity, the ardor of my love.
Others in you may only love your crown;
Beware of all those who surround you. I

715 Though, I loved you without scheming or hope,
When another was about to marry you,
When love could give me no reward but tears.
You see what power your charms had over me.
QUEEN: Now I am free and wish to make a king
720 Who's worthy of the throne and of me also.
SOSTRATE: If love's excess deserves any reward,
And if one can count on its perseverance,
Should not a heart, never wounded except
By you, dare think that it is worthy of you?
725 QUEEN: I esteem your love and shall give you your due.
SOSTRATE: Might I hope that one day, smiling on this love . . .
QUEEN: You may believe you have perhaps no rival
To whom your love will not prove fatal, Prince.
SOSTRATE: Madam, what ecstasy . . .
QUEEN: This must suffice you,
730 Prince. Go.

Exit Sostrate.

Argira, alas, what have I told him?
ARGIRA: You see my astonishment; until this day . . .
QUEEN: See how a wretched love sweeps me along.
Ah, all I hoped for was a speedy vengeance.
I wished to humble an insulting ingrate.
735 At that fatal moment was I thinking of
Sostrate? Did I want to crown that odious suitor?
I find him even more hateful, Argira,
Since he stumbled on a favorable moment,
Since he made me succumb to my blind anger.
740 My hatred shall at last all fall on him.
What! I'd wed him to ruin the man I love?
If possible, let's not take vengeance on ourselves.
But why take vengeance? Have I reason to?
What crime must I avenge? What is my plan?
745 Gelon loves my sister, he's a faithful suitor.

Indeed he scorns the crown for her sake. He
Won't reign if it means breaking his word. How I
Would love him to commit that crime for me!
                    Enter Phoenix.
PHOENIX: Forgive me, madam, if my impatient haste
750   Disturbs the august privacy of your secrets,
But Heaven today showers its blows upon us.
Paeonia still ready to attack us,
Calling Attale's sudden death assassination,
Shows eagerness unequaled to avenge it.
755   A champion, proclaiming war in this land,
Is calling men and gods to witness for
This crime committed near Paeonia.
They want Epirus this day to be punished.
Their allies, most of all the Romans, surely
760   Will want to aid their unjust enterprise.
The people are frightened; in this circumstance
It would be dangerous to rouse their protests,
And for a thousand reasons you must give them
A king whose fame is apt to win them over.
765   Gelon so glorious, so great, so awesome,
Will make himself belov'd of your warlike peoples,
And striking terror in your enemies' hearts,
He'll make your subjects conquerors and well-ordered.
But pardon, madam, if the zeal that moves me
770   Makes me dare . . .
QUEEN: Your zeal merits commendation.
The obstacles are great, your reasons, solid.
Leave me to ponder all these diverse thoughts.
                    Exit Phoenix.
Let's go, I see my sister. To abide
Her sight, my soul is wracked with too much emotion.
                    Enter Princess.
775   PRINCESS: What, the Queen avoids me! Everyone, alas!

Abandons me. Stop, madam, do not flee me.
O listen to a wretched sister's sighs.
She comes to lament to you the torment that
Overwhelms her. Look upon my woes with pity.
780   I fear already I've lost your affection,
And yet I come to ask that you restore it.
I come to show the anguish that devours me.
Although you are the cause of my mortal grief,
I am so used to opening my heart to you
785   That it wants to share with you its secret pain.
I lament even to you the hurt you do me.
They say (and this report fills my heart with fear),
They say that Gelon is to rule this land,
That I will be condemned to eternal weeping,
790   And that you, madam, have decreed this fate.
QUEEN: Who is already giving you such a fright?
PRINCESS: Love, a tender heart that feels all its misfortunes,
Sostrate, who feeds my sorrows by his fears.
We have the same woes, make the same complaints.
795   But you now, madam, by your embarrassed air,
Are you not showing more than what he told me?
Perhaps I speak to you imprudently,
But I've full confidence in your affection.
Guile is ill-suited to prove my loyalty.
800   'Tis my sincerity must speak for me.
QUEEN: These feelings, sister, tend to disconcert me.
'Tis only by my tears that I can answer.
Do not pry too much into my deadly secret.
PRINCESS: Ah, with regret my timid heart discovers,
805   That it is true; I doubt no longer, madam.
Your heart no longer heeds sisterly feeling;
Another passion destroys it today,
And my steadfast love, whose firm support you are,
For you will henceforth be a source of anger.

810   My grief by its excess might well displease you.
        These tears which I won't manage to hide from
        Your sight, may well embitter, rather than touch you.
        Alas! what feelings will each of us have?
        You mar my happiness; I must fear yours.
815   QUEEN: I hope for none, my sister, dry your tears.
        PRINCESS: You love, you reign; I foresee my misfortunes.
        Deliver me, I pray, from this great anguish.
        Say whether you love him and he loves you.
        You see your sister falling at your feet.
820   QUEEN: What are you doing? Alas, Princess, arise.
        I am perfidious, unjust, ungrateful.
        Call me all these names, if their horror pleases
        You. Yes, I love your suitor; I deserve them.
        But this love still has made me venture nothing.
825   Gelon inspired in me the deadliest passion
        Perhaps that ever burned within a soul.
        Despite this love you were scheduled to wed him,
        But fate seems to arrange things otherwise.
        Attale is dead; the people have made known
830   The need they feel to have him as their master.
        And I, to oppose our mighty enemies,
        Must have a king whose valor fortune favors.
        More for these reasons than from personal esteem
        I wanted to secure him; that's my whole crime.
835   But I must admit, nothing can shake his faith;
        For you he scorns the glory of being king.
        Yet you're alarmed about his loyalty.
        Be reassured, Sister, you are too belov'd.
        PRINCESS: Such an excess of love makes me enchanted.
840   I was not sure that he could love so well.
        But you love him, alas! What avails his passion?
        You, madam, are the mistress of my fate.
        QUEEN: I've said already it is not my love

Which, Sister, will decide our fates today.
845 The state is threatened; the Paeonians
Already have allied with the fierce Aetolians
Against us. Rome too will take part in this war.
Shall I not have concern for my frightened people?
They want as king a prince who loves you. Speak,
850 What can I do in this extreme distress?
Perhaps I would have spared you suffering
By disavowing what I feel for him.
I, loving you, could not resolve to keep
Silent, and you wanted me to be sincere.
855 Enough, I'll leave you.
PRINCESS: Ah, Heaven, if your harshness
Dooms me to suffer, may you choose my misfortune.
                    Exeunt.

ACT IV

Enter Princess.

PRINCESS: Unhappy Princess, are you well resolved?
  Will you bear the sight of your lover in tears?
  Have you correctly gauged your force, your reason?
860 Do you not fear that your heart will betray you?
  Will you be cruel, inhuman, if need be,
  To cause the most faithful lover to despair?
  I have both his love and my own to surmount.
  What anguish! Ah, I feel my heart revolt!
865 Honor, reason, virtue, come to my defense.
  I implore against myself all your assistance.
  Restore a sad calm to my worried mind.
  Come break a knot which you yourselves have joined.

Enter Phaedra.

PHAEDRA: You see me, madam, trembling and uneasy.
870 In my zeal I panic at the fate awaiting
  You. All the people clamor to have as king
  The glorious hero who stays true to you.
  His passion for you angers and embitters
  Them. Everywhere I see sinister omens.
875 I tremble, I shudder.

PRINCESS: Phaedra, be at ease.

PHAEDRA: Would you be any calmer than I, madam?
  Who could give you such assurance? All will be
  Ruined for you.

PRINCESS: Don't believe appearances.
  You'll see everything calmed in a moment, Phaedra.

880 PHAEDRA: Who then could bring about so great a change?
  I beg you, madam, deign to tell me. What!
  This happy marriage which your heart desires . . .

PRINCESS: It's cancelled, Phaedra, but all will be calmed.

PHAEDRA: Ah heaven! How your words start to alarm me!
885 Sadness is painted in your somber looks;

It brings into my heart fear and distress.
Save me, madam, from this cruel anxiety.
PRINCESS: Only too soon will you learn everything.

Enter Gelon.

GELON: What! Will I always see you bathed in tears?
890   My love and loyalty have no charms for you?
Can they not calm your anguish for a moment?
What, my Princess, your weeping starts again?
PRINCESS: 'Tis only by my tears and my great sorrow
That I can demonstrate now that I love you.
895   I'd like to bestow on you, sir, with my troth,
Those honors which today you refuse for me,
Certain that with my hand they'd touch your soul.
GELON: Ah, madam, as naught I count all those honors.
The gift of your hand, your love alone delight me.
900 PRINCESS: Alas! my hand, Prince, never will be yours.
GELON: What say you, madam? Heaven! I'm thunderstruck!
Explain yourself, I beg.
PRINCESS: Prince, we must be resolved.
For the last time I speak to you in this place.
Receive a lover's cry: Farewell forever.
905 GELON: What sudden horror grips my very soul!
Farewell forever! You snatch away my life.
Where am I? Have I rightly understood?
Just Heaven! Do I deserve farewell forever?
PRINCESS: I must, it is required. The Queen's my rival;
910   You are called to the throne. My fatal passion
Would block the wish expressed by all our subjects,
Might rob you of the fruit of your great battles,
Would give the lie to Heaven which declares for you.
Ah, what more could a barbarous hatred do?
915   No, no, appreciate the love felt for you:
You'd be my husband if I loved you less.
GELON: Then your love is concerned thus with my fortune?

Have, madam, a more ordinary heart.
Love has small share in these lofty sentiments.
920 Cease having this insulting care for me.
Show me those outbursts and those jealous tears,
Those sorrows which just now I found so charming.
You did not oppose to me the throne and greatness,
To which with so much coldness you consign me.
925 You were afraid to see me wed another;
You wanted to unite my fate with yours.
That is true love, and I was charmed by it.
PRINCESS: My heart has never loved you so much, Prince.
I now, sir, have a love that's genuine.
930 My passion until now was hardly rational.
I feared to be betrayed; my fatal error
Put all my effort into guarding my conquest.
Alas! jealousy is quite unscrupulous.
In loving you, I was unjust, ungrateful.
935 You seemed perfidious to my jealous mind.
Doubting your loyalty, I wished to be yours.
My nervous love would take the crown from you;
This love, now reassured, gives it back to you.
Alas! forgive me for my selfish wishes,
940 This anxiety, this eager care to harm you,
These sorrows, these suspicions, even this pleasure
That your refusal of absolute power
Gave me.
GELON: No, my Princess, let's not quench our passion.
Restore your love to me; that's all I want.
945 PRINCESS: Since I'm belov'd and have acknowledged it,
'Tis time I thought of how I might deserve it.
For me you are renouncing the sweetest honors,
But I do even more by renouncing you.
Rule; you owe an example to other kings.
950 Think how the universe has its eyes on you.

One day you'll blush . . .

GELON: Your virtues, basic fairness,
  Your troth, all bind me to fidelity.
  If one must wear a crown to love you, I
  Expect my sword can conquer one for you.

955   But 'tis not in the land your sister rules
  That glory awaits me.

PRINCESS: Sir, can I be yours?
  Shall I see the populace enraged against me,
  Reproaching me for my sad country's woes?
  The victories, the goods they'd lose through me,

960   And what they'd suffer under another's yoke?
  Source of so much misfortune, with such omens,
  How could our marriage find the gods propitious?

GELON: And shall *I* have naught to reproach you for?
  My woes alone, you ingrate, cannot touch you.

965   Why, what care I for peace or war, for the fate
  Of a disobedient people, of the world?
  I wanted only you. Your heart belonged to me.
  Where shall you then bring this heart and your troth?

PRINCESS: 'Tis at the altars where Diana's worshipped

970   That I intend to spend the rest of my life.
  You will forget my too fatal, too sweet name,
  And if, despite my care, I still think of you,
  If my tranquillity cannot be perfect,
  At least by my retreat your ease is certain.

975   GELON: Gods, your retreat! I'll manage to prevent it.
  There's nothing that can hide you from my sight.
  I'll go to every place on earth, have no
  Doubt, to disturb your heart's profoundest peace.
  I'm justified by your oaths which I want to

980   Uphold. Heaven itself cannot restrain me.
  Legitimate despair makes violence permitted.
  And if you scorn my love and constancy,

Cruel woman, you will see your raging lover
Destroy all, be avenged and die before you.

985 PRINCESS: I feel my woes too deeply in your sight, Prince.
The more I delay, the more my strength abates.
Farewell, enjoy in peace your destined future.
May you be happy, since it costs me dear!

GELON: I see it is no longer time for threats;
990 It is for me to ask for mercy, madam.
What, despite my tears, my sighing, my despair,
Can you resolve never to see me more?

PRINCESS: Ah, Prince! Hide your sighs and your tears from me.
When you attack me with such weapons, you
995 Reduce me to despair; my deadly plan
Becomes more difficult and no less certain.
I'll die from it, but time must bring you comfort.

GELON: Can you thus leave?

PRINCESS: I must sacrifice myself.
Will you have no thought for the state, for our gods?
1000 Consent, if possible . . .

GELON: I'd see you leave!
At least defer a plan so deadly! In
This pressing woe, 'tis the only hope that's left me.
Reflect, madam, you drive me to despair.
My death is certain once you have departed.

1005 PRINCESS: What say you? Heaven! What is my destiny?
All right, I grant you this one day. Perhaps
My reasons will be more appreciated.
But finally you make me doubt my strength.
Just now I had resolved to leave you; I
1010 Delude myself no longer. Your grief kills me.
But gods! What has my heart allowed itself?
I grant you one day, since I've promised it.
But when it is expired, however great
My anguish, I'll show strength equal to my weakness.

1015 Do not be weaker; suffer me to be wretched.
I leave; Sostrate is coming.

Exit Princess; enter Sostrate.

SOSTRATE: Sir, you triumph.
May I have the advantage of speaking here
With you? When, sir, will I have to do you homage?
Will you deign soon to accept my respects?

1020 GELON: Your homage, sir, would be too suspect for me.
I'll not put myself in a position to claim it.

SOSTRATE: You must deny it till you fully succeed.
One endangers one's plans by making them too public.

GELON: If I had such plans, without flattering myself,

1025 I think, sir, I could thwart your aspirations.

SOSTRATE: Who knows it not? You've power to destroy me.
How can you be resisted when my only title
Is to be the last descendant of our kings?
I admit this title's weak compared to yours.

1030 GELON: You ought to reign, but others are being named.
Epirus of your rights judges amiss.
You're descended from their kings; I am a stranger.
However, in this circumstance you see
That its vote in fact is not assured for you.

1035 SOSTRATE: Its favor is for you; reason, for me.
But it's for the Queen alone to choose a king,
It seems to me you value her vote little.
You place your glory in pleasing just the people.
Yet your ambitious plans would be endangered,

1040 Sir, if the Queen put value on her kin.

GELON: Ah, sir, on this point I've nothing to say.
I leave to you the throne your heart aspires to.
But once again, if I wanted to reign,
You could not easily resist me. Yet

1045 My love forever separates me from it.
I have no wish to rule, and I declare it.

What I do perhaps is of sufficient weight
To be worth adding to your other titles.
Exit.

SOSTRATE: This haughty speech . . .
Enter Milo.

MILO: The Queen's about to come.
1050 She wants to speak to you, sir.

SOSTRATE: He reveals
By his proud look that he's sure of her heart.
Insolence always means that one is happy.
The Queen, however, gave me to hope that I
Would be preferred above all of my rivals.
1055 Again let's learn what I've managed to gain.
Let's speak, let's urge. We must lose all, or reign.

MILO: Yes, make your doubtful hopes settled today.
The people are assembled in the nearby square.
Their love for Gelon has made some discontented.
1060 Follow your project, sir, there still is time.
You see your friends ready to venture all.
Their number's greater than had been expected.
They'll all assemble at the slightest signal.
Find out what the Queen has resolved for you.

1065 SOSTRATE: Their aid will be good if everything fails us,
But I yield to the hope the Queen gives me.
No doubt she hesitates in spite of love.
She dares not come before this court showing no
Regard for her kin or loyalty to the Princess.
1070 She's queen and must subdue or hide her weakness.
Let her tremble, if she must heed her desires.
I won't permit a rival to be happy.
My jealous heart ponders a dreadful vengeance.
Of what is a spurned love not capable?
Exit Milo; enter Queen.

1075 You see that the people trespass on your rights

And are ready, madam, to dictate your choice.
Make haste to stop the progress of this boldness.
Name, show a master to this rabble, madam,
And the disobedient, fearing with good reason,
1080   At once will recognize their queen and king.
QUEEN: It is not arrogance, but prudence, Prince,
    That can stop a proud people's insolence.
SOSTRATE: It would be dangerous to be mistaken here.
    The storm is still weak; it can be dispelled.
1085   But if, by a weak and soft-willed patience, you
    Allow its violence to reach its height,
    Your power, madam, once it has been weakened,
    Will never be reestablished as before.
    Create a king whose very name inspires
1090   Legitimate respect in too proud subjects,
    Who is descended from a race that's used
    To seeing itself equally feared and loved in
    This land. I'll dare here to recall your promise.
    Everything speaks for me: my respect and fondness,
1095   Your race, the interest of your authority.
    Were I rejected, I would be too hated.
QUEEN: Yes, just now I gave you grounds for hope, but from
    Confirming it the people now dispense me.
    I came to tell you there is too much danger
1100   In angering these haughty souls against me.
    In wishing for my crown, and perhaps my heart,
    You have your reasons, and these I forgive you.
    But when you think of them, I must think of myself.
SOSTRATE: You have your reasons, madam; that I see.
1105   This speech reveals your heart's innermost secret;
    Reasons of state are not all you consider.
QUEEN: Have you forgotten, Prince, to whom you're speaking?
SOSTRATE: When you overwhelm me, suffer my despair.
    I rouse your anger, sure of the indifference

1110   That a lover fears when he has lost all hope.
              Why poison me just now with a false hope?
              Heaven! what do your contrasting moods reveal?
              Spite, change of heart.
              QUEEN: What do you dare to tell me?
              SOSTRATE: Gelon's too lucky; he knows he's belov'd.
1115   Yet, madam, if I judge by his proud words,
              It is not sure he'll deign to accept your favor.
              I see my arguments start to displease you.
              I'll leave. I'd make your anger fall on me.
              Your hate today would punish me—despised,
1120   Unhappy one—even for another's crime.
                      Exit Sostrate; enter Phoenix.
              QUEEN: When you pressed me just now to favor Gelon,
              I did not take offense at your zeal. But
              I have other plans and other wishes, Phoenix,
              And I forbid him to be mentioned ever.
1125   PHOENIX: May I speak again without displeasing you?
              I saw Sostrate leave, all inflamed with anger,
              And, dare I say, he's prejudicing you.
              Sostrate is vexing you by his deception;
              Filled with dark anger, he arouses yours.
1130   He fears to see another wield the sceptre.
              He dreads above all a glorious prince, who
              Alone deserves to reign and win your love.
              Just now you were not prejudiced against him.
              You've changed your mind; Sostrate has been with you.
1135   Ah, madam, may your happy subjects see
              Today the effects of your concern for them.
              May reasons of state be paramount with you.
              On a day so crucial act solely as a queen.
              Procure for us peace, glory, tranquillity,
1140   By giving us as king the greatest of heroes.
              But I'll drop a subject where my zeal offends you.

My reason for coming is of great importance.
Deputies from the army have arrived here;
Their plan is to implore your kindness, madam.
1145   The favor which they ask is not yet known.
QUEEN: Let's go then, Phoenix, to learn what they expect.

Exeunt.

ACT V

Enter Phoenix and Gelon.

PHOENIX: The news is all too certain, sir; Sostrate
    Is angered by the Queen's refusal. His friends,
    Whom he gathers in secret, his unease,
1150   Too clearly show he ponders a deadly plan.
    There's even a suspicion, which seems likely,
    That of Attale's death he may be found guilty.
    The friends whom we see he'd won to his side
    Reveal he'd long been aiming at the throne.
1155   The Queen in horror orders his arrest,
    And the scepter is yours, if your hand is ready.
    Since Heaven offers it, you must receive it.
GELON: Heaven does not offer me the sovereign power,
    Since the offer has injustice as its price.
1160 PHOENIX: Thus love leads you by its whims and caprice.
    Why make a name with your illustrious exploits,
    If for you glory yields to no other laws?
    Choose between the faithful lover and the hero.
    The throne for heroes is the natural place.
1165   Their lofty soul is never crushed by love.
    Love is their weakness; it is not their virtue.
GELON: Phoenix, in me love's not at all a weakness,
    But, as all know, I was to wed the Princess.
    There could occur no changes great enough
1170   To cause me to forget my troth, my oaths.
    I'd act the same even were I not in love.
    The Princess has for me the most sincere
    Passion that ever engaged a lover's troth.
    To place me on the throne she gives me up;
1175   She's set to choose a life of sad seclusion;
    And, far from acknowledging a love so perfect,
    Could I, profiting from this desperate act,
    Reign thanks to her misfortunes, perhaps her death?

In Phaedra's arms she swoons, seems close to dying.
1180 Her whole heart's frightened of the plan she made.
I see her tears flow; they ask for my troth.
And I believe them, rather than her words.
If I abandoned her to overwhelming torment,
Phoenix, I'd think myself a horrid monster.

1185 PHOENIX: What! Epirus shows its love for you in vain?
Today all the people loudly clamor for you.
Besides, sir, do you know that our army, once
So charmed by your famed exploits, makes its wishes
Known at the moment I am speaking through
1190 Its deputies who've just come to the palace?
They're begging the Queen, for the common interest,
To stabilize the state's uncertain fortune,
To give us a king who can calm all factions;
To sum it up in a word, sir, to name you.
1195 The people, who've already shown their zeal for you,
Follow their example and send deputies.
After such a demonstration can you hesitate?
The entire state wished to place you on the throne.
The subjects have dared to ask for you as master.
1200 It would be dangerous for you not to be.
Another king, alarmed with reason, would
Ever hold you criminal for having been named.

GELON: Fear does not hold much sway over my heart.
You might have spared me this embarrassing remark.
1205 These perils, if I'm truly threatened by them,
Would simply make me finish what I started.

PHOENIX: Oh, sir, could it be . . . But the Queen advances.
Enter Queen; exit Phoenix.

QUEEN: For your sake people cast off the respect due me.
You know the army has sent me deputies,
1210 And dares to ask that I name you as king.
This care in subjects contains too much boldness.

He who comes to beg is threatening in secret.
So rash a step offends authority.
GELON: Madam, you know whether I've engaged in plotting.
1215   I can't be implicated in the people's crime.
QUEEN: It is not time yet, Prince, to answer me.
I've not rejected what they press with zeal;
I did not dare to in my present state.
Again I make my answer depend on your choice.
1220   But listen next to what I announce to you.
A king is needed; you must surely see that.
The war with which we still are threatened can
Be prosecuted only by a king.
Only a king can calm the excited rabble.
1225   If you are not king, you must leave this land.
Your person, Prince, attracts too much attention.
After what my subjects dare to do for you,
After they've shown you such audacious fondness,
Another king would certainly not let you
1230   Live in his kingdom in tranquillity.
Your very valor, which would serve us well,
If you won't reign, forces me to exile you.
My subjects would always tend to favor you.
Evasion would be vain: rule, or depart.
1235 GELON: Yes, madam, your authority's too offended
By the choice which a senseless mob proposes,
And you must punish with a just refusal
An insolent pride that shows you no respect.
Deference to it is shameful in a sovereign.
1240   Refuse your subjects, since you are a queen.
QUEEN: You take the side of my authority.
No doubt you should; your loyalty pleases me.
I had neglected it where you're concerned,
And on this point perhaps I risk my glory;
1245   But glory in such cases may perhaps

Be simply to seek out my subjects' good.
A scepter flourishes in well-loved hands.
Thus I've not blushed to offer it again
To you.

GELON: Think, madam, whether I could accept it.

1250   QUEEN: A useless love makes you resist then your
Own glory and the wishes of Epirus?
You should have grasped and followed my example.
Love ought to have no power on such as we.
I loved, I told you so, and you perceived it.

1255   But I hate still more and wish to let you know it,
For in the end I won't let my heart rule me.
I loved you, yet could give you to my sister.
My hand was offered elsewhere while you had my heart.
A victim in fact to the rank of queen,

1260   I sacrificed to the state my love and hate.
Now that Attale is dead, the state has asked
That you be offered the throne; I have complied.
For the same reason I'd have wed Attale,
I made you this offer which your heart abhors.

1265   Your love rebels and you could not betray it.
You rejected me, and I must hate you. Thus
I hate you to the extent justice requires.
But now I sacrifice my hate, as well.
The state comes first; I want to make you king,

1270   Despite feelings which are only for myself.

GELON: I must leave, madam. Exile is legitimate.
Hate me, but may I not lose your esteem.
My heart is bound by loyalty and honor.
I can't be yours without offending justice.

1275   'Tis to another fate that glory calls me,
And in pursuing it I refuse a throne.

Exit Gelon.

QUEEN (*alone*): Speechless, confused, I loathe my destiny.

Is there another cure than death for my ills?
My heart despairing feels them all together,
1280   I complain about an ingrate, I exile him,
And tremble! I feel all his slights that come
To vex me! I cannot forgive, but cannot hate!
Enter Phaedra.

PHAEDRA: Are you informed of the princess' fate?
As soon as she found out the army's wishes,
1285   She set out for the temple of Diana.

QUEEN: Just Heaven!

PHAEDRA: She wishes there to end her days.
The Prince of Sicily learns of this news;
He'd just left you, he rushes after her,
But vainly, madam, does he run to stop her.
1290   If you don't help him, what might he attempt?
You lose a sister, a lovable princess.
Please, madam, call her back; the time is pressing.
Diana's temple is quite close to here.

QUEEN: Let her return and come into my presence.
1295   Let my guard bring her.
Exit Phaedra.
(*alone*) O too fatal honor!
To call my happy rival back to my side!
That's the painful endeavor, sign of love,
Which in this cruel moment I've just achieved.
Why, Heaven, did you not give me a common soul?
1300   Have I fortitude only for my misfortune?
Alas! must I myself provide assistance
To content an ingrate who always offends me?
What! even at the instant he learns I love him
He runs after my sister, filled with extreme passion.
1305   Yet far from following my too just anger,
I respect my sister in my jealous fury.
He loves her, finds her a magnanimous lover,

But how easy, with requited love, it is to be so!
How anguished I feel! O day full of torment!
1310 Attale's death turns, alas, into misfortune for me.
Is it enough, cruel gods? What care devours me?
If I trust my fears, what must I still expect?

Enter Argira.

ARGIRA: Ah, Madam, what woes must I announce to you![69]
Order, your sacred rights, all will be overthrown.
1315 The Princess was approaching Diana's temple
When Gelon stops her, he attests the goddess,
Invokes all the gods who guard the plighted word,
Falls at her feet, which he moistens with tears,
Threatens, implores, and shows a mortal sadness.
1320 To vanquish him she uses cruel skill.
They alternately show their pain, their virtue.
The people all are touched by a love so perfect.
Then your order's received, your guards arrive.
They bear away from us the despairing Princess.
1325 Gelon, his spirit calmed, wants to leave at once.
But the people are displeased with his just exile.
They surround this prince in the midst of the square.
Some have the audacity to proclaim him
King. At that moment the Princess is named.
1330 You must stop this disorder at its outset.
Though Gelon is still willing to disclaim
An honor he cannot expect without you,
Who knows . . .

Enter Princess.

PRINCESS: Why this opposition to my plans?
Madam, my retreat would have calmed everything.
1335 I've learned what daring steps are taken in my name.
My life is in your hands, and I come to surrender.
QUEEN: Let's go and show ourselves to ungrateful subjects.

Princess, stay here. You, do not follow me.
                    Exit Queen.
PRINCESS: Great gods, who shower me with disgrace today,
1340   Are not your hands weary of striking me?
        Have I not exhausted your most dreadful blows?
        And what's my crime but an unhappy love?
        But why do I hide from this faithless people?
        Let's go denounce in public their false zeal.
1345   If need be, to check the course of their madness,
        Let's give up our life and avenge a sister.
ARGIRA: The Queen does not want such cruel proof of loyalty,
        Madam, and you are not allowed to leave this place.
        But she'll make every soul return to duty,
1350   And you'll see this confirmed in a few moments.
PRINCESS: I wish it, but, O gods! my fear increases.
        A dark foreboding worries and upsets me.
        Is it the truth that speaks thus in my heart,
        Or is it only fear and anguish?
                    Enter Phaedra.
                            Phaedra,
1355   Tell us, if you know, what is happening.
PHAEDRA: As soon as the Queen came into the square,
        The natural respect which all hearts owe her
        Dispelled the storm and calmed the murmuring.
        This awe which just Heaven inspires in us
1360   For those it sets in power by legal right
        Imposes silence on the most seditious.
        On seeing her, Gelon gave thanks to the gods.
        Detained until then by the unjust crowd,
        He sees them slip away on seeing the Queen.
1365   He approaches, speaks to her, falls on his knees,
        Shows his respect, displays it to us all;
        Vows that, rather than see her rights assaulted,

He'd plunge his sword into his breast before us.
The Queen speaks to the people, gets their attention.
1370 A few at last approach to kneel before her.
And when order seemed about to be restored,
We saw Sostrate appear with his friends. He
Was seen escorted by an odious rabble.
PRINCESS: Sostrate! What, was this traitor not arrested?
1375 PHAEDRA: The guards sent to seize the perfidious man
Found him supported by a daring band.
They were defeated, madam, and the traitors
Now dare to turn their weapons against us.
A thousand arrows were shot in this wild riot.
1380 They've no respect even for the Queen herself.
PRINCESS: Gods! Will the Queen and Gelon, now exposed
To their arms, find the death which you refuse me?

Enter Phoenix.

PHOENIX: Madam, forgive my sorrow and distress
When I come here to acknowledge you as queen.
1385 The Queen is dead.
PRINCESS: Heaven! Hold me up, Argira.
PHOENIX: Sostrate may have believed Gelon was king.
The order of arrest that threatened his life,
The Queen who kept crying out that he be seized,
All this stirs up his rage, disturbs his mind.
1390 Nothing can save us from his cruel onset.
Mass shooting into the crowd marked his fury.
Even the boldest tremble for their life.
The Queen disdains to care about her peril.
It's only for Gelon that she fears danger.
1395 Far from avoiding death aimed only at him,
She stays near to the Prince, risking her life.
She thinks the sight of her will stop the fighting
And that her presence will inspire respect.

Nothing can stop Sostrate; he clears a path
1400 And cries: "You're going to reign, Gelon; receive then
My homage." But he himself goes to his death.
Gelon advances toward him and with a swift
Stroke bathes the villain's insult in his blood.
Sostrate dies. Milo wishes to take vengeance.
1405 He shoots a fatal arrow, guided by some demon.
It strikes the Queen; he runs away at once.
She takes a few steps to go toward the temple,
Leaving a glorious example of her zeal.[70]
Some try to help her, but the wound is fatal.
1410 She invokes Diana and dies on her altar.
We furiously pursue Milo and overcome him.
We ripped apart the abominable monster.[71]
One sees a hateful slaughter rather than a battle.
Gelon to the enemies seems like a god,
1415 But an angered god, of crime the just avenger.
Each blow he strikes destroys a victim. Flight
Is the sole means that can save them from ruin,
Which they contrived to bring upon themselves.
PRINCESS: I remain speechless. In my supreme misfortune
1420 I hardly feel and recognize myself.
Let's go embrace a sister one last time.
May we with this embrace expire with grief.
Enter Gelon.
GELON: Madam, I join you only to lament.
Your woes are greater than you could have feared.
1425 I know you. A throne and its charms will not
Console you for a sister's death, I know.
At least, if vengeance lessens your sense of loss,
This sad delight is offered to your wish.
The criminals are dead; the few who've fled
1430 Will soon be wiped out by the angry crowd.

PRINCESS: Have full assurance of my gratitude,
But sorrow keeps me from displaying it.
Yet, if I live, to you I'll keep my troth.
You'll have the favor of queen and people both.
Exeunt.

END.

Marie-Anne Barbier

Arria and Paetus
(Arrie et Pétus)

The Author

We know next to nothing about the life of Marie-Anne Barbier.[72] According to her biographer Michau, she was born in Orléans in 1670, into a highly respected family of comfortable means, and received a solid education. She began to write light verse at an early age, and received much encouragement from family and friends. By around 1700 she had moved to Paris, where the venerable playwright Edme Boursault became her literary mentor. Between 1702 and 1719 she had five plays (four tragedies and a one-act comedy) staged at the Comédie-Française, and three opera-ballets at the Académie Royale. She dedicated her first three tragedies to royalty, and her fourth to the minister d'Argenson, at whose insistence she allegedly wrote the play. In addition, she published several volumes of literary miscellany, consisting of poems, novellas, and drama criticism. Her death seems to have attracted no attention from the world of letters. Nineteenth-century biographical sources placed that event in 1742, but Michau, followed by the *Dictionnaire de biographie française* (1951), states that she died in Paris in 1745.[73] It seems that she never married. Her private life, as well as her whereabouts and activities after 1719, remain a mystery. From the prefaces to her published works we learn only that she was a conscientious artist, and a staunch defender of the rights and abilities of her sex.

The Play

Significance

Of all the tragedies written by French women authors, *Arria and Paetus* is, in my judgment, the most effective and most readable. It also presents with unusual forcefulness the two forms of female heroism (good and loving versus evil and unfeeling), in sharp contrast to the failure of male heroism, both good and evil.

Because Barbier was so explicit in proclaiming her desire to exalt the noblest representatives of her sex, the language and behavior of her female characters are especially revealing. The play's climax would necessarily feature Arria's suicide (the gesture for which she earned her renown), but this one action could not suffice for an idealized portrait of female heroism. That a noble character would not fear death, especially when honor is at stake, was taken for granted in French tragedy. By turning Arria into a very young woman who has much to gain if she renounces her principles, and much to lose if she stands firm, the playwright has consciously shifted the emphasis from the accounts of the Latin historians. In her play Arria wins our esteem with a wide variety of noble qualities: her devotion to her murdered father and her determination to avenge him; her skill in coordinating the conspiracy led by Vinician and Scribonian; her self-reliance, demonstrated by her unwillingness to bring Paetus into the plot until the situation becomes desperate; her hatred for tyranny and desire to reestablish a republican form of government; her refusal to cower before the two mightiest people in Rome. But at the same time she must not lack the crucial feminine qualities: unshakable constancy in love; solicitude for her beloved's life, even though she never fears for herself; concern for womanly honor and reputation; belief in the sanctity of marriage (despite Claudius' reminder that in Rome divorce was legal). She is stoical, but only up to a point; when the safety of Paetus is at stake, she can show temporary hesitation, even weep. She is a model of heroic firmness and dedication, yet not devoid of human feeling.

Agrippina is likewise a model of Roman fortitude, but utterly lacking in love, compassion, and respect for traditional moral and religious values. Ruthless and single-minded in her quest for the supreme power, she impresses us by her boundless energy, her indomitable will, and her consummate skill in manipulating people and in governing. She frequently speaks of love, vengeance, and devotion to the gods, but these are merely masks to hide her self-serving ambition, and no other character in the play is deceived by her hypocrisy.

Barbier's critics have repeatedly accused her of magnifying the heroism of her female protagonists by debasing the male characters. Even if the charge may have some validity in regard to her third play, *Thomyris*, it cannot possibly apply to *Arria and Paetus* or to her other tragedies. It is hard to see how anyone could conceive of the Emperor Claudius or Caecina Paetus as models of Roman fortitude. As Barbier herself noted in the preface, she went to great lengths to rehabilitate those two men. Even so, Claudius emerges as weak, irresolute, easily manipulated, unwilling to respond to a crisis situation, and unable to appreciate Arria's heroic firmness. Paetus is gallant and valiant, but lacking in shrewdness and leadership ability.

The other remarkable feature of this play is the dialogue in which it engages with the tragic masterpieces of Corneille and Racine. To condemn Barbier for lack of originality, as some critics have done, is unjust. In addition to the fact that her mentor, Edme Boursault, had been a protégé of Corneille, she was writing a tragedy, the genre to which the strictest rules applied, and she was submitting her play to the Comédie-Française, which then held an absolute theatrical monopoly in Paris. Ever since that troupe was formed in 1680, it had perceived its mission as twofold: to keep in its permanent repertory the acknowledged masterpieces of the past and to accept only those new plays which conformed to the official dramatic models. The young dramatists, aware that their audiences knew Corneille and Racine by heart, aimed to create new effects by reshaping and recombining elements drawn from familiar material.

No single element is new in *Arria and Paetus*. There had been previous plays that featured heroic women; in some of them, notably by the brothers Corneille, the women were far

more heroic than the men. Yet no single play had ever contrast-
ed the two forms of female heroism, both with one another and
with male weakness. It is no accident that the play's central
scene is the confrontation between Arria and Agrippina. A slight
tinge of mutual admiration adds spice to what is basically a ver-
bal duel, for each lady understands that the other is the single
most dangerous threat to her own plans.

The tragedy contains deliberate echoes of earlier plays,
which acquire ironic force when the audience draws the appropriate parallels, especially Corneille's *Cinna* (which also centers
around a plot, led by a group of Roman patricians, to assassinate an emperor with a criminal past), and Racine's *Britannicus*
(which also features Agrippina and Narcissus). But whereas
Corneille had emphasized the conflicts *within* the characters
and allowed them to evolve and mature, Barbier concentrates
on the conflicts *between* the characters, who undergo no real
change in the course of the play. Likewise, Barbier, who aimed
to create exemplary characters in her plays, was hardly intent
on competing with Racine in the creation of characters with
great psychological depth, or in the presentation of a funda-
mentally unheroic world where the good characters are so weak
and fragile that they never pose any serious threat to the diabol-
ical villains.

Perhaps even more remarkable than the play is the preface,
in which Barbier openly displays her feminist views and proudly
calls attention to the existence of a significant tradition of previous women writers in France. In addition, she directly addresses
one of the most annoying (and most persistent) problems facing
women writers: the accusation that, if their work is good, they
must have had a male collaborator. Barbier combats this prejudice by citing a number of notable women authors who wrote
without male assistance and by logical argument (how is male
glory enhanced by stealing honors that rightfully belong to
women?). It is sadly ironic that the author of one of the boldest
feminist declarations to emerge in the age of Louis XIV should

have been repeatedly accused of the charge she most resented: using male collaborators.[74]

Historical Background

There are three main sources in Latin literature for the story of Arria and Paetus. The epigram of Martial (I. 13) to which Barbier refers in her preface would probably have been familiar to many in her audience:

> When chaste Arria was offering to her Paetus that sword which with her own hand she had drawn from out her breast: "If thou believest me," she said, "the wound I have inflicted has no smart; but the wound thou shalt inflict—this for me, Paetus, has the smart."[75]

The account in Cassius Dio's *Roman History* (LX. 16) is quite similar. He explains that Arria,

> who was the wife of Caecina Paetus, refused to live after he had been put to death, although, being on very intimate terms with Messalina, she might have occupied a position of some honour. Moreover, when her husband displayed cowardice, she strengthened his resolution; for she took the sword and wounded herself, then handed it to him, saying: "See, Paetus, I feel no pain." . . . Matters had now come to such a pass that excellence no longer meant anything else than dying nobly.[76]

Pliny the Younger, who knew Arria's granddaughter personally, recounts in his letters (III. 16) some equally heroic episodes in the famous lady's life, and gives a more detailed account of the events leading up to Arria's suicide. Paetus joined the revolt led by Scribonianus in Illyricum, and after the latter's death he was arrested and brought to Rome as a prisoner. Arria begged the soldiers to take her with him, even offering to perform the services of a slave for her husband, but they refused. She then chartered a small fishing boat and followed him to Rome. She came before Claudius and in his presence denounced the wife of Scribonianus, who was trying to save her own life by volunteering to give evidence of the revolt. Pliny writes, "This proves that her determination to die a glorious death was not a sudden impulse." Moreover, Arria's family made repeated efforts to dissuade her from dying with Paetus, which left her unmoved. Asked by her son-in-law Thrasea whether, if he ever had to die, she would want her daughter to join him in death, she replied, "If she lives as long and happily with you as I have with Paetus—yes."[77]

Gaius Appius Silanus, who in the play becomes the heroine's father, was the first in a series of men wrongfully killed by the Emperor Claudius. The tale that Dio relates is so unedifying that it is easy to understand why Barbier eliminated most of the details from her play:

> [Claudius] had sent for this man, who was of very noble family, and governor of Spain at the time, pretending that he required a service of him, had married him to Messalina's mother, and had for some time held him in honour among those nearest and dearest to him. Then he suddenly killed him. The reason was that Silanus had offended Messalina, the most abandoned and lustful of women, in refusing to lie with her, and by this slight shown to her had alienated Narcissus, the emperor's freedman. As they had no true or even plausible charge to bring against him, Narcissus invented a dream in which he declared he had seen Claudius murdered by the hand of Silanus; then at early dawn, while the emperor was still in bed, trembling all over he related to him the dream, and Messalina, taking up the matter, exaggerated its significance. (Dio, LX. 14)

As the murder of Silanus occurred in A.D. 42, only one year after the emperor's accession, the leading Romans found themselves disillusioned with a man who, it had been hoped, would bring stability to the state after the excesses of Caligula. Two of the men who had been named the preceding year as possible choices for the throne, Annius Vinicianus and Furius Camillus Scribonianus, each plotted a revolt at this juncture. But Vinicianus, realizing that he had no military backing, whereas Scribonianus, as governor of Dalmatia, had a large body of Roman and foreign troops under his command, decided to form an alliance with his rival. Many senators and knights flocked to him. However, Scribonianus never arrived in Rome,

> for the soldiers, when Camillus held out to them the hope of seeing the republic restored and promised to give back to them their ancient freedom, suspected that they should have trouble and strife once more, and would therefore no longer listen to him. At this he became frightened and fled from them, and coming to the island of Issa he there took his life. Claudius for a time had been in great terror, and had been ready to abdicate his power voluntarily in Camillus' favour; but he now recovered courage. He first rewarded the soldiers in various ways. . . . Then he sought out those who had plotted against him, and on this charge put many to death. Several, indeed, including Vinicianus, committed suicide. (Dio, LX. 15)

Suetonius gives a different explanation for the soldiers' change of heart: at the moment of receiving the order to march toward Rome, they were unable to adorn one of the eagles and move the banners. Seized by superstitious fear, they deserted Scribonianus in large numbers, and the rebellion was crushed in five days (*The Twelve Caesars*, "Claudius," 13). Tacitus provides a differing account of Scribonianus' death: he was assassinated by a common soldier named Volaginus, who was then promoted from the lowest to the highest rank (*Histories* II. 75). In the play, none of the principal conspirators appears on stage, and the revolt is little more than a backdrop for the heroic behavior of the title characters.

By the standards of her day, Barbier followed Roman history quite faithfully. Of course, the conventions of French tragedy and the demands of popular taste necessitated certain types of modifications. It is highly significant, however, that all of the principal alterations of history in *Arria and Paetus* contribute to the author's explicitly stated goal for the play: the presentation of ideal feminine heroism.

Perhaps the most obvious departure from historical chronology is the absence of Messalina, who actually died in 48, some six years after the suicide of Arria. Messalina, known for her public debauchery, would have seemed especially inappropriate in a play devoted to heroic womanhood. Moreover, Dio's statement that the two women were "on very intimate terms" would have seemed to tarnish the heroine's purity. In addition, Barbier must have realized that it would be far more dramatic to show two ladies of genuine heroic stature and to make them enemies, rather than friends. By juxtaposing the death of Arria with the day scheduled for the coronation of Agrippina, Barbier could make two interlocked romantic triangles central to the plot; in other words, Claudius and Paetus are each a direct threat to the other, and the same applies to Arria and Agrippina. The latter's presence in the play also makes possible several telling references to future events: her murder of Claudius, and Nero's murder of his mother.

Arria herself has been considerably altered in the play. Barbier has made her much younger (according to Pliny, she had a married daughter at the time of her death), unmarried when the tragedy begins, the daughter of Silanus, and living in Rome. The reasons for some of these changes are stated in the author's preface. It is also true that from the standpoint of a theatre audience of the time, Arria would have much more to lose by her suicide if she were very young and beautiful, if she were still unwed and very much in love, and if she had the opportunity to become empress of Rome. By making Silanus the heroine's father, Barbier allowed Arria to become one of the main organizers of the conspiracy against Claudius, instead of a mere bystander, as in Dio's account. Arria can thus display such noble qualities as filial piety and the ability to help direct a normally all-male enterprise. Even the rehabilitation of Paetus, whom Dio brands as a coward, contributes to the idealization of Arria. Barbier, who adopted Corneille's conception of heroic love based largely on esteem, could not have allowed Arria to love a man capable of fearing death.

Performance History

The play was first performed at the Comédie-Française on June 3, 1702. According to Joannidès, it had an initial run of twenty-one performances; according to Lancaster, only sixteen. There was also a performance at Fontainebleau before the court on September 21 of that year. Because it was unusual to present new tragedies in the summer, the actors decided to give an afterpiece with it starting with the first performance, instead of waiting until the receipts from the main play started to drop, as was the normal practice. Press coverage was favorable; the *Gazette de Rotterdam* even declared in 1703 that *Arria* and Barbier's next tragedy, *Cornélie mère des Gracques*, were on a par with Corneille and Racine! *Arria* was revived in 1711 and given seven performances according to Joannidès, six according to Lancaster. Either way, it was by far Barbier's most successful play, and it ranks as the third most popular tragedy by a woman in the annals of the Comédie-Française.

Arria and Paetus

(Arrie et Pétus)
Tragedy

Marie-Anne Barbier

Actors

CLAUDIUS, Emperor of Rome.
AGRIPPINA, widow of Domitius, betrothed to Claudius.
PAETUS, Roman Consul.
ARRIA, daughter of Silanus.
NARCISSUS, freed slave and advisor to Claudius.
ALBINUS, confidant of Paetus.
JULIA, confidante of Agrippina.
FLAVIA, confidante of Arria.
PROCULUS, assistant Captain of the Guards.
GUARDS.

The scene is in Rome, in the palace of Claudius.

. . . . .

To Her Highness, the Duchess of Bouillon.[78]

What is my fate? What happy auspices
For my Muse to show her first fruits on the stage!
An illustrious Lady, to whom I dare offer
It, listens to its verses and is moved.
5   She accepts the homage of its timid wishes,
And as crowning honor gives it her endorsement.
Ah, Princess, 'tis too much! After such great
Kindness I place no limits on my rashness.
Yes, without fear I dare defy all critics.
10   Let them aim their shafts; your name reassures me.
You have absolute sway over all hearts.
Having pleased you, I could not be displeasing;
And since with your kind aid I am no longer
Powerless, I'll give my gratitude full scope.
15   What do I say? Your name flatters my heart in vain;
As soon as I must laud you, my fear returns.
Vainly do you uphold my zeal in this.
I feel I stagger, though I have your full support.
I fear a task so full of charms for me;
20   And the fear of falling stops me at my first step.
When I see with what gifts nature adorned you,
I hardly dare begin to sketch a picture.
Without trembling, I can't trace for posterity
A heart so generous, a wit so brilliant,
25   A soul that rises far above itself
To carve itself a path to supreme glory.
No, seeing the rich assortment of so many
Virtues reduces me to a just amazement.
You see what powers such a subject demands.
30   At every step I find more miracles,
Princess, and since I cannot bear their sight,
I keep silent from respect as well as prudence.

Preface

There are few subjects in Roman history better known than that of Arria and Paetus,[79] which I have arranged for the theatre with more success than I had hoped. The main action to which all the others are related is of the simplest kind, and I chose it thus in order to avoid the predicament in which the majority of authors fall; by cramming too much action into their plays, they do not take care to make pathos dominate, because the concern of unraveling the plot takes their full attention. Although the public has pronounced in favor of this first attempt, I will nevertheless reply to some objections that have been made to me, even were it merely to justify the applause that has been lavished in my favor.

The late Mr. Boursault,[80] who was a friend of mine, after seeing several elegies composed by me, which he pronounced to be full of clever ideas and pathos, persuaded me that I could successfully write a play, if I undertook to do so. Besides, he knew that I enjoyed the theatre and that I had studiously read all the authors who have written about it. With this intention, he proposed to me the subject of Arria and Paetus. This was to attack me by my weak side. The action of this incomparable Roman lady is so glorious to our sex that I felt a strong urge to present it in the most favorable light I possibly could. I accepted this subject without hesitation, but before beginning I made a preliminary sketch which I submitted to his judgment. He approved it with one exception: I planned to make Arria and Paetus lovers; he wanted them married, as they are in history. It was no use my telling him that conjugal love would be dull on the stage, and would not be to many people's taste. He did not change his views, and I myself, after some consideration, indeed felt that he was right and that history would be too distorted. Thus I decided to make them lovers for the first three acts and a married couple in the last two. Another friend whom I consulted at the same time wanted Narcissus to be eliminated. He said that this freed slave of Claudius had been completely opposed to Agrippina; but I pointed out to him that according to my plan, since Arria was the daughter to Silanus, who had taken Messalina's mother as his second wife, Narcissus, who had convinced Claudius to put him to death, would have had to take Agrippina's side against Arria, all the more so because if the latter had been made empress, she would not have failed to destroy him in order to avenge her father's death. Some time later people objected to me that Claudius was not properly characterized, and that I made him speak with too much intelligence for a man whom history represented as an imbecile. To that I replied that his imbecility came more from his poor health than from mental deficiency. This comes out especially in the testimony of Suetonius, who relates that this ruler had done extensive study of literature in his youth and had composed several histories. The same author, as well as Tacitus, makes him in addition the inventor of several new letters of the alphabet, which were in use during his reign. To this I added that I believed it to be the duty of an author of tragedies to correct the manners of her heroes and to be more assiduous in depicting their hearts than their minds. Moreover, if I had made Claudius speak as a dull-witted man, all the faulty things he would have said would have been blamed on me; and besides, he is quite well depicted in his actions, since he is the dupe of Agrippina, of Arria, of Paetus, and even of Narcissus. As for the other characters, I do not think they need justifying. They seem to me quite accurately rendered, except Paetus, whom I improved, not wanting to make my hero a coward; and that is what led me to attribute to an effect of his love the fear that in reality he had of death and for which his wife set him an example.

These are, if I am not mistaken, the principal difficulties that have been raised and to which I thought I was obliged to reply. Concerning the rest, it was found to be quite good, and perhaps better than I should have wished, since certain people took the occasion to say that a woman was not capable of succeeding so fully. In truth, I would never have imagined that what people like in my work should have been prejudicial to me, or that persons of our sex would be denied the merit of producing good things. I well know that one could not praise a play more highly than by finding it above a woman's capability, and that my vanity ought to be flattered. However, I admit that I was not insensitive to this injustice, and that I could not see without a little irritation that people had wanted to take away from me the most precious fruit of my work. Truthfully, I do not doubt that the limited capability that men grant to women has given rise to the report that several people have pretended to spread. However, without looking for examples in antiquity, our century has furnished enough learned ladies to destroy this prejudice, and I could cite an infinity of them to authorize what I am claiming. But I content myself to speak here of the excellent works in prose and in verse of the illustrious Mademoiselle de Scudéry, of the beautiful poems of the Countess de la Suze, of Madame Deshoulières and of her witty daughter who is following so well in her footsteps.[81] The Academy prizes, which have, so to speak, become the prerogative of the ladies since two of those whom I have just named opened the path to them, are incontestable proofs of the merit of our sex. And if I must add something on the subject of dramatic poetry, the tragedies of Mademoiselle Bernard are too recent to be erased from the memory of those who envy our glory. They will doubtless say that we do but lend our names to all the works that are attributed to us. But how would men yield to us a glory that is not ours, since they contest even the one that does belong to us?

ACT I

Enter Agrippina and Julia.

JULIA: O what a somber sadness clouds your brow!
Whence, madam, can so prompt a change arise?
You were content with your lot yesterday.
Today I see you nonplussed and uneasy.
5   Today, however, by giving you his hand,
Claudius sets the Roman Empire at your feet.
He loves you and, easily forgetting Messalina,
All his ardent feelings are for Agrippina.
AGRIPPINA: It's true; I thought to see my finest day:
10   Claudius at my feet, and Messalina dead.[82]
All things seemed to confirm me in my hopes.
But O too vain semblance of too glad a fate!
My luck will change, and this great change becomes
(Would you have believed it?) the work of one moment.
15   In vain I hear the adoring people's wishes.
Not yet am I upon the Caesars' throne,
And the fate that calls me to that charming rank
Awaits me at the final step to cast me down.
JULIA: Heaven! What do you tell me?
AGRIPPINA: It's to you alone
20   I want to reveal that the Emperor forgets me,
That a proud rival dares to contend with me
For this throne to which Claudius was to raise me.
JULIA: Think, madam, with more justice of his love.
AGRIPPINA: No, there's no doubt; I've learned all from Narcissus.
25   JULIA: What! Narcissus . . .
AGRIPPINA: He is less the Emperor's than mine
And betrays him out of loyalty to me.
But why conceal my rival from you longer?
I feel unequaled horror as I name her.
It's Arria. At that name your mind's confused.
30   The daughter, as you know, of proscribed Silanus,

Whose blood was shed by Claudius himself,
She ought to hate him more than he loves her.
But love, bestowing our hearts at his whim,
Rejoins what hatred has most separated.

35 JULIA: In vain does Claudius love. Have no fear, madam,
That the proud Arria will approve this passion,
Or that, rather than fight an odious victor,
She'll give her heart at the expense of claims of blood.

AGRIPPINA: How little do you know the empire's value,
40 When it's offered to us by a heart that sighs!
At that point nature speaks to us in vain.
Haughty ambition speaks quite differently.
One can't resist the rank it promises,
And that's the sole voice great hearts ought to hear.
45 But if to that rank Arria dares to climb,
Let her know what price she must pay for it.
I will destroy her, and the Emperor himself
Won't snatch her, Julia, from my utmost fury.
For now, I am content to defer my wrath
50 And hide from her the arm the blows will come from.
My power is still uncertain in this place,
And I must show more love than hate here. But
I see the Emperor; let's hide our feelings.

Enter Claudius and Narcissus.

I cannot show you by too great a rapture
55 How much, on this great day when your love shines,
The glory of being yours fills and delights me.
Yes, sire, all Rome—its dearest wish fulfilled—
Already counts our wedding among its happy feasts,
And seeing the union on the same throne of
60 A race that always was its dearest hope,[83]
It asks the gods, who witness our betrothal,
To shower prosperity on both you and me.
Respond with speed to the ardor of its zeal;

Complete the forming of so fair a bond.
65   They wait only for you; people and senate
Long for a match that fortifies the state.
The feast is heralded by myriad echoed cries.
Already incense smokes and the rites are ready.
      CLAUDIUS: With common voice the people and the senate
70   Have done you justice by approving my choice,
And the honors which are destined for you here
Are worthy of my love and of Agrippina.
All things seem to conspire for my coming joy.
I see a thousand hearts who love you with me,
75   And Rome in my sight offers sincere homage
When it adores in you Germanicus my brother.[84]
But various rebels, jealous of so fair a fate,
Postpone the moment that is to unite us.
Two of them, arrested through Narcissus' care,
80   Will name their leader at the sight of torture.
You see, I must give full attention to this matter.
      AGRIPPINA: The matter of our love, sire, is it not
Paramount? Ought various rebels, stirred by envy,
To decide the happiness of my life? Don't
85   You have those tender feelings for me any more,
That harmonized so well with my great fondness?
What! Does the slightest danger chill, alarm you,
And keep me from the throne where your love places me?
Don't think, however, that this glorious rank
90   Dazzles my eyes with its accompanying splendor.
High rank is often just a pompous bondage.
To rule a tender heart is a sweeter portion.
That's my sole aspiration, and you know, sire,
That I love Claudius, not the Emperor.
95   CLAUDIUS: I love these feelings, but permit me, madam,
To respond to your affection in my turn.
A love so perfect joined to so many virtues

Deserves the Emperor and not Claudius.
My power is under enemy attack.
100 Ought I to raise you, when I fear my downfall?
Shall I have no fruit from my tender care,
Except to see my work destroyed in just one day?
To shelter you from so sad a disaster
I must dispel the onslaught of the rebels,
105 And must, by calming the recent agitation,
Bolster the throne to which I elevate you.
AGRIPPINA: Then, sire, my coming to complain was wrong.
But those who love well have cause to fear all things.
Enough, I yield at last, and on this day
110 Your love reassures me in my tender fears.
Go then, and through faithful Narcissus' care
Thwart the injustice of all my enemies.
I'm their real target; jealous of my good luck,
They seek to take the gift of your hand from me.
115 Do not waste time; I run, at your example,
To the temple to ask, with redoubled prayers,
That heaven avert a blow that makes me shudder,
And save you in your turn from all your foes.
                    Exeunt Agrippina and Julia.
CLAUDIUS: Of all my foes 'tis she alone I fear.
120 Narcissus, I expect her utmost fury
As soon as she learns that my new love makes
Her lose the empire and my heart together.
I've no illusions. I know Agrippina.
Her sole aim is the rank my hand destines to her.
125 And when I seize from her what she most craves,
I foresee an outburst dangerous for Arria.
NARCISSUS: Sire, I admit, you should fear Agrippina,
And her angry heart will know no self-restraint.
Germanicus her father was dear to
130 The Romans, and the empire would have gone to him

Had not his foes, in their persistent fury
And treachery, cut short his life by poison.
When one is so close to the highest rank, sire,
One can't stifle desires sanctioned by blood.
135   For greatness only Agrippina longs.
You were yourself planning to make her empress;
The promised empire has become her property.
To keep it for herself she'll stop at nothing.
Besides, when your heart is smitten by Arria,
140   Do you think hers is not inflexible?
Your orders sent her father to his death,
And her anger is a barrier to your love.
CLAUDIUS: Narcissus, I know too well that stern Arria
Will think marriage to me would blight her honor,
145   And that a father's blood shed by my orders
Too loudly speaks against my love. I must
Surmount an insuperable obstacle.
But offer of empire can work this miracle,
And I hope to assure my peace of mind today.
150   You, go discover the conspirators' plots.
To punish their boldness and find out their leaders,
Use promises and threats at the same time.
Observe above all Agrippina's movements.
I'm going to find Arria, and don't doubt
155   That her soul . . .
NARCISSUS: Sire, I see her coming forth.
CLAUDIUS: Go, hurry, manifest your zeal and prudence.
          Exit Narcissus; enter Arria, who starts to withdraw
                    upon seeing Claudius.
Why do you flee this place on seeing me?
What, madam, do you always want to hide from
Our eyes and, wholly wrapped up in anxiety,
160   To seek out solitude amid my court?
ARRIA: Sire, in the misery my life's reduced to,

It is for solitude to hide my anguish,
Above all on the day planned for your wedding.
My unwelcome sadness would disturb that feast.

165 CLAUDIUS: That feast, without you, would be sad for me.
My happiness is linked to seeing you.
Such talk surprises you; I well know, madam,
That if I must base my feelings on your heart,
Which I see daily strengthened in its hatred,
170 I ought to have just hostile eyes for you.
But despite this law your heart imposes on me,
A stronger destiny ordains otherwise,
And when yours tries to stir me up to hate you,
I feel too well *my* heart can only love you.

175 ARRIA: Me!

CLAUDIUS: Don't bring up my passion for Agrippina.
I withdraw a hand which love destines for you.
I didn't yet know the power of your eyes
When I promised a glorious throne to her.
It's for you to ascend. Reign, madam; reign
180 Over the Romans as over my heart.
Were there on earth a more exalted rank,
The gods and my love would have reserved it for you.
But finally I set at your feet earth and sea.
The spouse I offer you is master of the world.
185 You see, however, great though he may be,
That this world master's subject to your laws.

ARRIA: Whatever splendor, sire, your love flatters me with,
You'd waste your too great bounty on an ingrate.
Retain your presents to excuse my heart
190 For not being touched that I'm an emperor's choice.
In the state I'm in, contrary to myself,
I hate, I flee all things, even the daylight.
Agrippina will be more responsive to your love.
Return your love to her, keep your engagement.

195   I've already told you, I like solitude;
       I've made it a sweet habit in my woes.
       Alas! By loving me, don't take from me
       My sole remaining asset, which can soothe me.
       CLAUDIUS: And you, by a refusal fatal to my hope,
200   Don't take from me *my* sole remaining asset.
       No, I set the value of the Roman Empire
       On the sole pleasure of giving you my hand.
       Consent, madam; think that the destiny
       Of one who loves you all depends on you.
205   ARRIA: What, sire! You love me, yet you want to draw
       A flashing storm upon my head! If I
       Perish, must it be that your love orders it,
       And that your hand crowns me to immolate me?
       For I know all too well that an ambitious
210   Heart nears the thunderbolt by nearing the gods.
       I've learned at my expense fortune's reverses
       And know all the misfortunes it drags with it;
       And to avoid the useless task of looking further,
       I've an example in my family.
215   CLAUDIUS: Forget misfortunes whose end is so fair.
       Think only of the throne my choice summons you to.
       ARRIA: Happy the man who flees the storm and stays in port.
       I contemplate the fate of Silanus my father;
       I see him marry into Messalina's race.
220   Nearing the throne, he hastens to his ruin.
       He digs a dreadful precipice for himself.
       A less high rank would have brought him more luck.
       I've the same fate in store; your love prepares it for me.
       Grant that I may save my head from this danger.
225   I know Agrippina and all her fury.
       I foresee results that chill and horrify me.
       And when you offer me the highest power,
       I must not doom myself, and doom you, too.

CLAUDIUS: I don't much fear this danger, and, sole master here,
230   I see only the gods exceed my station.
      But vainly do I strive to reassure you.
      A stronger obstacle makes my love desperate.
      When you reject the empire and my troth,
      I read your hate for me in your refusals.
235   I see what return I must expect for my
      Love. You reply only to shield yourself,
      And you cherish a sad memory too much.
ARRIA: Sire, I do what I can to banish it.
CLAUDIUS: You'd easily forget such an offense,
240   If you let gratitude have its effect.
ARRIA: Sire, this great effort is not in my power,
      And in my sad heart all things yield to duty.
CLAUDIUS: Whatever that duty is, its hold is too great.
ARRIA: Whatever that duty is, virtue inspires it.
245 CLAUDIUS: I can guess all the cares that are inspired to you.
      You hide still more of them than you are showing.
ARRIA: Well, since I must, I will keep nothing from you.
      I saw the executioner strike down my father.
      You know that, sire, and that inhuman blow
250   Was an unjust decree that came from you.
      What! could I, heedless of my honor, blight
      My sad existence with so black a stain?
      Could I allow the man who caused his death
      To lead me into such a guilty marriage?
255   Would I bring shame upon his ghost in Hades?
      Would I augment the number of his killers?
      Ah, sire, do you want me to murder him
      A second time after his woeful end?
      What a dreadful image comes before my eyes!
260   Allow me to be innocent in my woes;
      At least let my heart, persecuted by the gods,
      Experience but not deserve their anger.

CLAUDIUS: If Silanus your father was condemned,
His death was necessary for my safety.
265 We must fear all from a too-powerful subject,
And once he's suspect, he is innocent no longer.
The weight of his honors drags him to destruction.
But I'll concede the order was unjust
That with too cruel a blow struck Silanus.
270 Can I avenge him better than by marrying you?
What triumph for you! An eternal bond
Will make you sovereign ruler of my heart.
This hand, whose blow still forces you to grieve,
Has caused your woes and wants to make amends.
275 This hand, uplifting a proscribed man's family,
Slew the father, puts the daughter on the throne.
And this hand elevates you to a rank
Paid for a hundred times with people's purest blood.
But vainly do I show you its attendant splendor;
280 This rank, when I'm the giver, horrifies you.
I'll say just one more word. You know my love,
And I in turn see your hatred too well.
I speak to you as lover, but perhaps
You'll force me finally to speak to you as master.
285 It's for you to decide between master and lover.
I leave you, madam; think it over well.
Exit Claudius.
ARRIA (*alone*): My choice is made. I find the most abject bondage
Less awful than a marriage that offends me.
Cruel man, reign as a tyrant, load me down with chains,
290 But fear the just gods who avenge the universe.[85]
From their justice I expect before day's end
A bloody sacrifice to my father's spirit.
Dear shade, who hear'st me from the realm of darkness,
Support by thy wrath this heroic plan,

295 And when so many take arms to avenge thee,
Strike, if 'tis possible, in concert with them.
In my present state I have no other hope.
Thy blood showed me my duty, I recall.
I hear thy voice cry out against thy slayer.
300 Make haste, unfortunate Arria, to respond.
Let's go seek Paetus, let him lend his hand;
Let him avenge, as consul, all the empire.
Let's go reveal to him a plan he does not know.
I've hidden it from him and would still do so;
305 But on this sad day I must serve him better.
At stake is his treasure that they seek to take
From him; and we must both dispel this storm
Or die, if need be, in a common shipwreck.

Exit.

ACT II

Enter Arria and Flavia.

ARRIA: At last the long-awaited day has come,
310   When to my heart calm ought to be restored.
        Yet all things worry me, and as you see,
        Flavia, this day must decide the rest of my life.
        It makes my sad heart ever more upset,
        And I fear it as much as I've wished for it.
315 FLAVIA: Cast these unfounded worries far from you.
        The blood soon to be shed should dry your tears.
        Your fate's confided to most trusty hands.
        The tyrant will die: you have Paetus' promise,
        And to fulfil your wish, this very day
320   Must in one blow avenge Rome and your father.
    ARRIA: It's true, I have to faithful hands confided
        The vengeance for a father and the Romans.
        Paetus will do his utmost to avenge me.
        Yes, I've his love and courage as my surety.
325   But how dearly I pay for his fatal aid,
        When I think how I put his life in danger.
        Rome, father, passion, honor, hatred, vengeance,
        Who act in concert to tear me apart,
        Why do you share this hapless heart of mine?
330   Was it condemned to suffer too slight anguish?
        Does not Silanus' blood, shed by a traitor,
        Suffice to arm the rage that's guiding me?
        Do I need to be helped? May I this day
        Bring love into a project of hatred? For
335   In fact if Paetus serves the cause of my just wrath,
        You see how I expose a life so dear.
        I love and hate equally, and can't this day
        Follow my stern duty without betraying my love.
        If the blood soon to be shed should dry my tears,
340   It must also cause me mortal worries, and

I've reason to tremble when I reach the moment
That must avenge my father or doom my lover.

FLAVIA: Madam, hope for better; banish thoughts that with
So dark a cloud cover so fair a day;

345 And since your cause is heaven's cause as well,
Think that to them your doubting is offensive.
They've suffered tyranny only too long;
Ever more insolent, it's still unpunished.
If they are just, they owe their aid above all

350 To one avenging the death of a progenitor.

ARRIA: Heaven seems to wink at crimes of tyrants; it
Forgets its justice or at least defers it.
A thousand more before me, whom it dared not
Protect, had both homeland and father to avenge.

355 But I'd resort less to their supreme goodness
If I had to fear only for myself here.
What have I done? If my blood asks for an avenger,
Why satisfy it at my heart's expense?
And, blindly following deadly despair,

360 Pay for my loss with all that I have left?
No, Flavia, I can't think that without terror.
This barbarous law I must revoke at once.
Go, hurry, tell Paetus I'm satisfied,
That I agree to leave my vengeance incomplete.

365 That I spare a tyrant, that on this sad day
I overcome hatred to favor love.

FLAVIA: This belated pity is a little risky.
Ah, madam, is it time to be so noble?
And if Paetus turns back, once he has started,

370 Aren't you destroying, rather than saving him?
Besides, aren't you forgetting Claudius' passion?
You know what orders he prescribes for you.
If he doesn't die today, tomorrow you'll
See him as tyrant force you to the altar.

375 ARRIA: What? I? Could I wed my father's assassin?
    My hand would be the prize . . . No, he hopes in vain.
    I'd give him my hand just to plunge a knife in him
    And pull it out, all smoking with his blood.
    No more deliberation; I'm resolved
380   That he'll fall by the sword I destine for him.
    Silence, my love, and let my fury act.
    My guilty pity makes me quake with horror.
    I hear my murdered father's blood cry out,
    And not to heed it is too barbarous.
385   Yes, moaning spirit, you'll be satisfied.
    Seeing him I hate, I stop seeing him I love.
    Let's follow through; my heart complains in vain.
    Love must respect the voice of nature.
    But I see Paetus. Leave us for a moment,
390   And let nobody enter this apartment.
                 Exit Flavia; enter Paetus.
    Well, Paetus, will heaven be propitious for us?
    Has the time at last come for the tyrant's death?
PAETUS: Have no doubts, madam, he cannot escape.
    I've just left our friends who burn to strike him, and
395   Tomorrow at the latest their great zeal
    Will make this great victim fall at your feet.
    A thousand men are ready with Vinician.
    Scribonian himself takes up our cause.
    Returning from Dalmatia with his army,
400   He sees his forces swell with every step.
    Both to doom a tyrant and avenge the state,
    The senators will all enter his camp.
    He is not far from Rome. A trusty freedman
    Has just announced to us this happy news.
405   His unforeseen approach disturbed the Emperor
    And has spread terror even to his guard.
    At last the lightning's poised to strike his head.

He dares not stay here to await the storm.
Tomorrow he must leave, leading with him
410   New enemies whom he does not suspect.
We'll follow him, and heaven, that favors us,
Lets him give himself up into our hands.
ARRIA: May the gods until the end show us their favor!
PAETUS: When all goes as we wish, what can alarm you?
415   ARRIA: Those very gods whose favor flatters us,
Those gods whose injustice shows forth every moment,
Who a hundred times betrayed our friends, our parents,
And who've become protectors of the tyrants.
Forgive this secret fear, dear Paetus, at
420   The sight of the peril my love throws you into.
I'd have no fear to see the storm break, if
It spared your life, engulfing only me.
But I can't view it without utmost horror
If I must see my loved one die with me.
425   PAETUS: Ah, madam, this is too much kindness in one day.
Can all my blood requite a love so great?
After such favors, dying is too little.
I see you give up an empire just for me;
And to preserve your faithful ardor for me,
430   My love replaces all ambition for you.
O certain proofs of my crowning happiness!
You give me means, using my noble anger,
To free my country and avenge your father.
You set me on a path to glory, which I follow;
435   And, even more, you tremble for my safety.
How I'm indebted to your sovereign orders!
Nothing must stop me; my fate is too sweet
When for Rome and for you I risk my life.
ARRIA: I expected no less from this noble soul,
440   Inflamed by such great love and so much glory.
But when you face a fate so grim, if I

Tremble for you, is it too much for my heart?
Alas! Would that I'd spared myself this anguish!
I know that Paetus finds danger attractive,
445 And that, when a path to glory is cut for him,
Death cannot shake this truly Roman heart.
But when on my account you're armed and risk your life,
You would not perish were I not the cause.
I'll tell you, though, and you've seen it yourself,
450 My love leads me to this as much as my duty.
I kept a glorious plot secret, as long
As only vengeance for my father was involved.
But is it time to hide things from you now,
When I see a vile man coveting your treasure
455 And daring to employ his unjust power
To block a match formed by my noble parent?
Yes, I'm your treasure; I've a duty toward you.
The dying Silanus named you my husband,
Confiding to your care his wretched daughter.
460 He, falling, made you his family's support,
And his death, source of eternal miseries
To me, left me your hand to dry my tears.
However, a cruel tyrant whom I loathe
Wants to deprive me yet of my sole asset
465 And by abolishing a match so sacred,
He's hounding Silanus even in the grave.
Let's avenge ourselves and stop his barbarous crime.
Paetus, let's not allow him to separate us.
But as you rescue me from the direst fate,
470 Remember, my life is bound up with yours;
And if in this great peril you are killed,
Duty and love bid me to follow you.
PAETUS: Yes, I rush to avenge you and to show you
What power duty and love have over me.
475 And since the fates are linking to the death of

One man my happiness and that of Rome,
I'm eager to respond to their supreme law
By blows worthy of it and you and me.
But if heaven finally betrays our cause,
480   Live on to keep so fair a love alive;
Live for my vengeance, and let my proud victor
Ever find me at the bottom of your heart.

Enter Flavia.

FLAVIA: The Emperor comes here, madam, to surprise you.
ARRIA: O heavens! Farewell. Go, Paetus, don't delay;
485   And to restore calm to my worried spirit,
Think, I love you as much as you love me.

Exit Paetus; enter Claudius.

CLAUDIUS: You triumph, madam, and I can't hide from you
That you are arming heaven's wrath against me.
Yes, heaven, favoring your fervent wishes,
490   Wants me to pay in blood for the tears you shed.
Scribonian is conspiring, and that rebel
Betrays his duty only for your cause.
His guilty secrets have just reached me. If
He's coming, it's to avenge Silanus' death.
495   But when this faithless man conspires against me,
When he wants to take both life and empire from me,
Will you arm all your rigor still? Shall I
See you today working to pierce my heart
And in collusion with my enemies?
500 ARRIA: Sire, I do not wish any bloody vengeance.
You fear me little in my present state.
I weep for Silanus; that's all I can do.
CLAUDIUS: And that is just what causes my alarm.
I have no foes more powerful than your tears.
505   Shed no more, madam, and I'll cease to fear;
I'll see Scribonian fall at my feet.
His plan for my demise and ruin will fail.

One word from your mouth, and the storm is quelled.
Indeed, you only have to mount the throne
510   To end all pretexts for my overthrow.
Fair Arria, give in to my just desires.
If you don't value me, the whole state begs you.
ARRIA: May the Roman Empire die a thousand deaths
    If I, to save it, have to marry you!
515   I hate a remedy filled with so much horror.
My pity for the state would be a crime,
And I prefer death to the foremost rank,
If I must betray my family to gain it.
CLAUDIUS: Ah, madam, that's too much, and my just anger
520   Must replace the care I take in pleasing you.
What! Rome, kneeling before you with your emperor,
Instead of touching you, provokes more horror!
Well, since I ask and plead with you in vain,
    I see it's time at last that I command.
525   It's for me to save all the Roman Empire.
Madam, be ready to wed me tomorrow.
ARRIA: What! You use tyranny even on my heart!
CLAUDIUS: I've left your hate unpunished too long. But
    What does Narcissus want?

Enter Narcissus.

                        Have you done as ordered?
530 NARCISSUS: I've just discovered the most heinous crime.
Our prisoners have broken silence, sire.
They couldn't withstand the violence of torture.
Both of them named Vinician as their leader.
    It's he who arms Scribonian against you.
535 CLAUDIUS: That traitor! He'll feel the full weight of my vengeance.
NARCISSUS: His own hand has already punished his offense.
CLAUDIUS: Who are the plotters?
NARCISSUS: Sire, in this attempted
Murder nearly all the senate is involved.

But Arria should have slightly better information.

540 CLAUDIUS: Gods! What do I hear? Arria!

NARCISSUS: She's been named.

ARRIA (*aside*): O heaven, I'm betrayed!

CLAUDIUS: I cease to wonder

   Why my amorous declarations have been futile,

   Why the offer of my empire couldn't content you.

   Doubtless you expected it from one you love.

545 ARRIA: What, sire!

CLAUDIUS: Enough, but I am much deceived,

   Or else you'll see not mine, but his blood flow.

   Scribonian plots as vengeance for your father;

   The traitor destines my head and the empire

   For you. I doubt no longer that your hand

550   Will be the worthy prize of this cruel blow.

   Ingrate, I made this gift legitimate;

   But you wouldn't have it other than by crime.

   And this barbarous heart, athirst for my blood, wants

   My death to serve as her step to the throne.

555   I'll have revenge for so perfidious a plot!

ARRIA: Do you think death intimidates me, tyrant?

   Or believe your threat's entitled to drag from me

   Complaints that would be viewed as lack of courage?

   If I complain here that the gods betrayed me,

560   It's that I see my death assures your life.

   But what do I say? Assures? Have no illusions.

   My blood will arm a thousand men against you.

   Thus you can't shed it soon enough. Give orders

   For my death. Farewell, I leave to wait for it.

               Exeunt Arria and Flavia.

565 CLAUDIUS: Guards, put her under arrest. Heaven! What fury!

NARCISSUS: From now on view her as inspiring horror.

CLAUDIUS: Narcissus, do you think that one can easily

   Convert one's love to hatred in a moment?

NARCISSUS: She hates you, sire.

CLAUDIUS: And I love her always.

NARCISSUS: Let

570   A noble indignation come to help you.

CLAUDIUS: Yes, I must have revenge, and I'm prepared,
      Narcissus.
      But by prolonging let's increase her punishment.
      Let her live and ever have before her eyes
      An odious lover, an unwelcome love.

575   That's the sole punishment my heart destines for her.

NARCISSUS: Restrain your emotions; I see Agrippina.

Enter Agrippina.[86]

CLAUDIUS: Do you know whose hand betrays me, madam?

AGRIPPINA: Yes,
      I know all, sire; I have been told already.
      The crime, however, comes as no surprise.

580   What should you have expected from the daughter
      Of Silanus? Her father's hate passed to her heart,
      And makes her share his madness and his crime.
      Destroy this guilty woman; let your justice
      Give equal felonies an equal sentence.

585   CLAUDIUS: Let us defer the effects of such just wrath.
      Arria's a criminal worthy of death.
      But since all things conspire here toward my ruin,
      I must use artifice, not open force.
      If I'm severe, they might overwhelm me, madam.

590   AGRIPPINA: Then the rebels make you tremble thus already?
      But to think of pardon when you have to punish
      Is to revive their boldness, far from quelling it.
      Since an unlucky race makes you its foe,
      Show it was guilty, and still is today.

595   The revolt will know no limits, sire, if you
      Don't dare hand over the girl after her father.

CLAUDIUS: All right, since her crime is a crime of state,

I must convoke the senate to pass judgment.
AGRIPPINA: You'll shield the guilty one from execution
600   By making her accomplices her judges.
Sire, don't you know who are your enemies?
CLAUDIUS: I know that at certain times people are lawless,
And that in this great peril feigning is important,
To force those who've stopped fearing me to love me.
605 AGRIPPINA: Is that the road that your ancestors took?
Unseasonable love degenerates to scorn.
Rome, ever an ingrate toward her emperors,
Is never haughtier than when she's flattered.
CLAUDIUS: She's brought back to her duty even less
610   When too much rigor drives her to despair.
AGRIPPINA: But when you lavish kindnesses on Arria,
Will she at least stop being your enemy?
CLAUDIUS: Time that destroys all things can tame her pride.
AGRIPPINA: Time rather will give her more recklessness.
615 CLAUDIUS: We'll see whether her heart will be stubborn always.
I leave to clarify this point with her.
                Exeunt Claudius and Narcissus.
AGRIPPINA (*alone*): Go make the most with her of this odious
triumph.
Go reveal to her the power of her eyes.
If need be, show her Agrippina's shame.
620   But as you protect her, tremble for her ruin,
And know that my hand, guided by my fury,
Will penetrate her heart better than you.
                Exit.

ACT III
Enter Paetus and Albinus.

ALBINUS: Where are you running, sir? Alone, defenseless,
You dare defy the power of Caesar? What
625 Are you coming to seek in this hostile place?
Please save yourself, while it is still allowed.
PAETUS: No, don't think I am hastening to my ruin.
In vain is the conspiracy discovered.
I am not named, but even if in this place
630 They set the cruelest death before my eyes,
I'd sacrifice all to save the one I love;
And I want to involve Agrippina herself.
ALBINUS: What, Agrippina!
PAETUS: Her ambitious heart
Aspires only to rise to her ancestors' rank,
635 And I've already told you Arria is her rival.
She must send that fatal beauty far away.
It's in her interest, and it's her own hand
That must prepare the way for our escape.
ALBINUS: You're quite demanding of that haughty creature.
640 To stoop so low Agrippina is too proud.
To send her rival off in this pressing danger
Would show that she is feared and not protect her.
But you yourself fear bringing down her vengeance
When you dare take up Arria's defense.
645 PAETUS: No matter what it costs, Albinus, I must help her,
And I come here to save her or to perish.
Too happy if I share the fate destined for her.
Say nothing more. But I see Agrippina.
Enter Agrippina and Julia.
AGRIPPINA: Thanks be to heaven who leads you toward me,
Paetus.
650 I know your loyalty to the Emperor.
You see what peril has threatened his life.

The gods have turned away the tempest's fury,
And the care their hand takes in protecting him
Shows with what zeal Rome must seek vengeance for him.
655 You know the crime; order the executions.
Punish the leaders, track down the accomplices.
But remember, Arria is in this first group,
And you must start by putting her to death.
I know the Emperor must speak on her behalf
660 To you. He wants to test your zeal, don't doubt it.
Scribonian, they say, and his vile plot
Have found supporters even in the senate.
Stamp out this false report; prove you aren't guilty,
Consul. All will depend on the choice of victim.
665 Sacrifice Arria; show us plainly that
You can confute a scandalous report.

PAETUS: Our loyalty, madam, recognized till now,
Was always backed up with the deepest respect.
Must Rome today show to the Emperor that
670 She claims to absolve or punish despite him?
She must obey as soon as her master orders.
From this sacred duty no one is excluded,
And we can hardly prove our zeal to him
By usurping power that he received from heaven.
675 Let him enjoy to the full a right so lawful.
The crime's acknowledged. Let him name the victim.

AGRIPPINA: I admire your deference in this clever speech.
But the deeper it is, the more I suspect it;
And if I must tell what I think, between us,
680 I see your treason through your obedience.
Yes, I see the light at last; too long I've doubted
A rumor that's been spread and I've discounted.
The senate is involved in the blackest crime,
And despite his artifice I know its author.
685 Tremble for him, Consul; but consider that

Our blows, before they crush him, will strike you.
PAETUS: May you hurl the thunderbolt on me alone.
Let it explode and pulverize me, madam.
I won't complain of heaven's severity,
690   Provided it takes care of a more precious life.
But why conceal what I fear any longer?
A noble heart was ever opposed to pretense.
I love Arria. At these words you understand
Enough that, seeing her life so sorely threatened,
695   It's not for Paetus to make opposition
To an imperial order saving his beloved.
AGRIPPINA: What, you love Arria and you dare admit it!
On such a reef you could well founder. But
I'm willing to respond to what you have confided.
700   You love; what recompense does your passion have?
When you love Arria, are you loved by her?
The Emperor is enchanted by the same eyes
As you, and can you think one would reject
A heart offered by the master of the world?
705   Join forces with me in my just revenge.
They are betraying us both and breaking faith with us.
Let's satisfy ourselves and slay an ingrate.
PAETUS: What, madam, could I plot against her life?
I, who would die a hundred times to save her?
710   No, you yourself should rather deign to help her.
Allow me, at your feet, to plead with you.
Her loyalty to me is still inviolate.
Her recent efforts to destroy the Emperor
Show too well whether she's your rival for his heart.
715   No, of this new crime she's not capable,
But do not force her into turning guilty.
If up till now her heart has never wavered,
It might be shaken by the sight of danger.
To see on one side death, and on the other empire

720 One would suffice against more constancy.
Yes, madam, she might well consent to reign,
And we must keep her from being forced to choose.
To shield her from that I see only flight.
Confide to me the care of escorting her.
725 Give your consent, and with no more hesitation
Assure your rank against possible dispute.
AGRIPPINA: I can assure it without losing my vengeance,
But I want to show indulgence to your passion
And not take steps when I could do anything.
730 Go then, I shall prepare her for her exile.
It's through me Maximus gives orders in this palace.
Guards, listen. Summon Arria to my presence.
I'll offer her the chance to save her life,
But the least refusal is her sentence of death.
Exeunt Paetus and Albinus; enter Arria and Flavia.
735 ARRIA: Madam, when your order calls me to your presence,
Is it to triumph over my mortal grief?
And don't you feel a rather gentle pleasure
To see that your lover has escaped my wrath?
Must I join my misfortune to this gladness?
740 Must you still crush me with an unwelcome joy?
But rather have you not summoned me here
To make me feel the horror of my death?
Pronounce the sentence; I accept my doom.
AGRIPPINA: No, mercy's what I offer you today.
745 It's for you to respond to my eager offer,
And you've but one moment to deliberate.
Make up your mind. To punish your crime, there
Is no severity that's not legitimate;
And I've no need to make you tremble, to
750 Waste many words reminding you of this.
Impose a voluntary exile on yourself.
But the speediest flight is necessary, madam.

Paetus will escort you; I know of his love.
Flee, and far from this court and far from Rome,
755   Enjoy a happiness beyond your expectations.
    ARRIA: I have to thank you for your kindness, madam,
    But hostile heaven has brought me so low that
    My honor lies in not profiting from it.
    The gods have raised a storm over my head;
760   Let's not prevent them from finishing their work.
    Let them thunder at will; I fearlessly await it.
    I'll make them blush for taking arms against me.
    Let the tyrant crush a wretched family;
    Let him massacre the daughter, like the father.
765   I'll see his kindness shine forth in his rage.
    My death is the most wished for of his presents.
    AGRIPPINA: Either I'm much deceived, or I've an inkling,
        madam,
    That by other presents he knows how to charm your soul.
    I know that he adores you, and in your eyes
770   Empire is more attractive than a tedious exile.
    That hope seduces you, and through your ruin
    You might be taught to reckon with Agrippina.
    If you dared aspire to the rank I've been promised,
    In my just fury I would stop at nothing.
775   Remember, too great pomp would be more fatal
    To you than this obscure exile which you detest;
    Despite the Emperor, all things should alarm you,
    And I'm better at hating than he is at loving.
    ARRIA: So then, retracting your initial kindness,
780   You show your genuine feelings in my sight,
    And in spite of your pride my example serves
    To allow you to speak openly for once.
    To this sincere avowal I must respond.
    Madam, Claudius gives commands to the whole world.
785   He wants to share with me the honors he

Receives. They're great, but my heart's greater still.
No, the Emperor in his love persists in vain.
He's made me pay too dearly for the honor he
Plans for me, and my father, struck dead at his feet,
790 Has put between us an eternal barrier.
Shall I, ungrateful daughter, forgetting my
Wrath, sacrifice a father to the desire to rule?
That crime would outrage nature and the gods,
Madam, and your suspicions are insulting.
795 To love him Claudius could not compel me.
Don't expect either that he'll force me to fear him.
No, people won't see my dejected heart
Belie my virtue in its final breaths;
And to preserve my life from his pursuit,
800 I won't call to my aid a shameful flight.
AGRIPPINA: In your words I see intrepidity,
But you had promised me sincerity,
Madam, and you surpass me in the art of pretense.
It's fitting, when you've naught to fear, to be defiant;
805 One hardly fears the wrath of an ill-treated lover,
When deep within his heart love speaks for us.
But this assurance might prove fatal to you.
You may defy a lover; fear a rival!
The blow I keep for you is the most dangerous,
810 And you're alive only as long as I want.
ARRIA: If I still had any more love for life,
I could forestall this barbarous desire;
And if my dying satisfies your wishes,
You'll owe that, madam, to my scorn for death.
815 You have total control over my life,
But to reverse it I have but to say one word,
And despite your plans this blow so full of danger
Can fall on me only as long as I want.
AGRIPPINA: Freely enjoy this illusory happiness,

820   And while Agrippina engineers your doom,
        Display the power of one word, of a single glance.
        But, madam, fear that you'll use it too late.
     ARRIA: I understand; my death's already settled.
        Already you usurp absolute power,
825   And the Emperor already has put in your hands
        Both the lives of Romans and the empire's fate.
        But unless just heaven sends me a vain portent,
        Claudius himself, experiencing your rage,
        Will find the fate that he evades today,
830   And your audacity will one day reach him.[87]
    AGRIPPINA: Don't burden your soul with matters of the future.
        The present more than anything concerns you;
        And since heaven puts your fate in my hands, madam,
        Nothing is left for you but death or exile.
835   The time has come; choose.
     ARRIA: Let them lead me back.
    AGRIPPINA: What, you have no fear of your certain doom?
       (*to guards*) Have Paetus called. (*to Arria*) Make good use of
          the moments
       That my pity steals away from my resentment.
                     Enter Paetus.
       (*to Paetus*) Come, and if possible, rescue a victim
840   Who, to reward her crime, wants only death.
        But if you see her steadfast in her choice,
        Receive her parting words for the last time.
       Exeunt Agrippina and Julia; Flavia goes to keep watch.
    PAETUS: For the last time I'd see the one I love?
        Have I heard aright? But, madam, what of you?
845   Could you consent to this cruel farewell?
        What! When I come to rescue you from death,
        You, heedless of the fears of a heart that
        Adores you, hesitate between death and me?
        You don't reply! Explain yourself, please. What

850   Does Agrippina mean? Whence comes her anger?

ARRIA: Is it you I hear? O heaven! Can I believe it?

      What, Paetus! You yourself attack my honor!

      At least my enemies only seek my death;

      But if I accept the aid that you advise,

855   I cast an eternal stain over my life.

      Yes, Paetus, my exile would make me criminal.

      The vengeance for a father, for the state

      Would henceforth pass for a vile heinous plot.

      Let the tyrant sacrifice his victims as he pleases.

860   Let's all defy his wrath and leave flight for crimes.

      But no, let me confront death by myself.

      I only am accused; you are not named;

      And hostile heaven's no longer so adverse,

      Since, as I die, I leave an avenger for my father.

865 PAETUS: No, don't delude yourself with that unjust hope.

      I know how great a power you have over my heart,

      But there's no power that would force me to live

      As soon as your death bids me follow you.

      Even if you armed yourself with unjust rigor,

870   It is my fate to live or die for you.

      Don't believe either, madam, that I hope

      To change your feelings through the peril *I* face.

      I see it all too well: you've never loved.

      Till now I've wasted all my protestations.

875   Your wishes were confined to vengeance for your father;

      Ceasing to have the power, I cease to please you.

      To serve you vainly means not serving you,

      And you're punishing me for fate's mistakes.

      If need be, I'll forget this extreme injustice;

880   But punish me alone, and not yourself as well.

      May I, in dying, know your life is safe;

      And my fidelity is amply paid.

      Rescue your life from the intended blow.

Accept the exile Agrippina offers you.
885   I want only the honor of escorting you,
And I return to seek a fair death here.
Scribonian advances to avenge your father.
I owe you this great vengeance more than he,
And through my death or feats of bravery
890   I want to show that Paetus was worthy of you.
     ARRIA: No, Paetus, I well know how far your zeal goes;
There's no need for this further cruel proof.
Live, and allow that our courageous friends may
Keep to the full their promises to us.
895   If I flee from this place, you see my flight
Could slow them in pursuing Claudius.
My example gives them a most powerful aid;
I must maintain it, though it costs my life.
However, my doom's not inevitable.
900   Claudius still loves me, innocent or guilty.
He'd suffer more than I from my death blow.
     PAETUS: And that hope, madam, makes my fear increase.
Your hold over his heart is too supreme.
Perhaps you view his love for you with pleasure.
905   One hardly can resist an emperor's passion,
And I fear his love as much as all his fury.
     ARRIA: Stop; you're too cruelly insulting me.
Since when, you ingrate, do you speak this way?
What, you suspect me of betraying my duty?
910   PAETUS: Ah, pity a love reduced to desperation,
Fair Arria. O misfortune! Cruel necessity!
Must I either see her die or see her faithless?
No, I must free myself from a fate so barbarous.
You loathe your life, and I run off to death.
915   I'll go reveal all my crimes to the Emperor.
Because you wish it, he shall take two victims,
And I must show you the path to the altar.

ARRIA: Ah, Paetus, stay! What an inhuman plan!
　　I yield; my heart ceases to be inflexible.
920　You've struck it in its most vulnerable spot.
　　My own impending death could not upset me;
　　But your death is enough to make me tremble.
　　My duty speaks in vain. My tenderness is stronger.
　　Your interest wins out over all of mine.
925　Let's flee, since we must, and leave this place behind.
　　But in departing let us choose a glorious exile.
　　Scribonian approaches; let's go to his camp
　　To share his peril as well as his renown.
　　Let my father marshal for his cause a daughter,
930　A consul, my tears and your fasces together.[88]
　　Let's seek death or victory on this great day.
　　But while doing my duty, let's safeguard my honor;
　　And since fate henceforth binds me to you, let's
　　Show that the man I've followed is my husband.
935　Let a mutual troth exchanged before the altars
　　Unite us as we leave with an eternal bond.[89]
PAETUS: Ah, madam, let me at your feet . . .
ARRIA: 　　　　　　　　　　　　　　　　No, Paetus,
　　Let's not waste time in useless deference.
　　Let's run to Agrippina, and doing as she hoped,
940　Accept the aid that her hand offers to us.
　　　　　　　　　　　　Exeunt.

ACT IV
Enter Claudius and Narcissus.

CLAUDIUS: I cannot hide my fear and pain from you,
Narcissus. My uncertain gait, my sighs,
My unease—despite myself these all betray me.
I take each thing I see as an enemy.
945 I hear from all sides, I hear thunder roaring.
It strikes, and yet I can't make a decision.
NARCISSUS: Be reassured, sire. You see that the gods
Have lavished their obliging care upon you.
Their powerful aid sufficiently reveals
950 That Rome must bow under her master's laws.
When she betrays you, they are your protectors;
But do not force them, by unworthy fears,
To withdraw the helping hand they kindly offer.
Avenge yourself; you must; let nothing stop you.
955 Destroy those ingrates who dare to defy you.
The gods have started; it's for you to finish.
CLAUDIUS: In these urging words I recognize your zeal.
I see in my woes how loyal you are to me.
I even know that when one has to reign
960 There's hardly any life that one must spare.
Arria has earned the death she's asking for.
But, Narcissus, what blood do you want me to
Shed? I'd let my own flow a hundred times for hers!
To stop me it has all too loud a voice.
965 I want to punish the ingrate, yet feel I love her,
And my deferred blows fall back on myself.
NARCISSUS: Why this persistence in a fatal love?
See what abyss it's going to drag you into,
Sire. Arria is impervious to your kindness.
970 The more you flatter her, the more unyielding
Her heart is; she still aims at vengeance for her father.
By aiding her against you, are you not

Yourself planning to arm this haughty foe
And let her have control over your life?
975 You will repent for being so generous.
An unpunished felon is more dangerous still.
CLAUDIUS: Her hate for me's the greatest of her crimes.
You fail to arouse my wrath against another plot.
Narcissus, I'd forget all; one glance from her eyes
980 Would blot out her mad project in my heart;
And if I must make a sincere admission,
She's armed herself only to avenge her father.
Be it weakness or reason, I'm aware that
My heart will be a lenient judge for her crime.
985 But when, instead of treating her as rebel subject,
I summon her myself to the highest rank,
And, daring to protect her from her rival,
I seek by many gifts to avenge myself,
For the ingrate, seeing such great love, to hate me,
990 That's a new crime that I *must* punish. Yes,
I've wavered too long; I can and I must.
Narcissus, let's see her for the last time.
And if the proud girl is persistent in refusing,
Let's abandon her to Agrippina's fury.
995 But what does Proculus want? Whence comes his fear?
What blow have you in store for me, cruel gods?
Enter Proculus.
PROCULUS: Ah, sire,
Arria has fled.
CLAUDIUS: O heaven!
PROCULUS: It's Maximus
Who has committed such a crime despite our care.
CLAUDIUS: What, the head of my guard? Ah, have him pursued.
1000 Proculus, your head today will answer for this.
Exit Proculus.
To steal away my loved one from amid my court!

Whom should I suspect of this audacity?
Who could deal my heart a blow so terrible?
But might it not be some secret rival? Have
1005   You not found out anything, Narcissus?
NARCISSUS: I
Can't start to guess the author of such insolence.
I hardly can get over my amazement,
Sire.
CLAUDIUS: Ah, just heaven, what will become of me?
I see all things conspire to drive me to despair.
1010   To wrest from me both life and empire is trivial.
Narcissus, this last blow's far more severe.
They want my loved one as well as my throne.
At least, would that I knew who is the traitor!
But let's neglect no means of finding him;
1015   And as my final effort strikes him countless times,
Let him fall beneath the weight of my just anger.
NARCISSUS: Sire, Agrippina enters.
Enter Agrippina and Julia.
CLAUDIUS: Come here, madam;
Exult over the troubles that rend my soul.
They're taking Arria from me, and as final horror
1020   The hand that wounds my heart is hidden from me.
AGRIPPINA: And who better than you should exult in her
Flight, sire? If you fear that the senate will pursue her,
She's shielded from the rigor of the laws.
Far from betraying you, her abductor serves you.
1025   CLAUDIUS: That traitor serves me!
AGRIPPINA: What makes you upset?
CLAUDIUS: What a dread abyss this blow plunges me into!
AGRIPPINA: Explain yourself, sire.
CLAUDIUS: For the gods' sake, madam,
Let me conceal my weakness from your sight.
AGRIPPINA: I read the depths of your soul all too well.

1030 You fail to hide from me your newest passion.
Arria's my rival; she prevails against me.
She alone has caused your agitated state.
No, don't delude yourself; you can't deceive me further.
I know you love her.

CLAUDIUS: It's true, I adore her.

1035 However much she scorns my vows and homage,
I can't be happy unless I possess her,
And my heart, that sighs for her and is her slave,
Attaches the empire's whole worth to her only.

AGRIPPINA: What, you love Arria, faithless man, and it's

1040 To me that you admit this newest passion!
Ah, blush at least for words so cowardly!
If you can't break out of an unworthy bondage,
Cease to prefer the shame of your chains to
The dazzling homage which the whole world brings you.

1045 I'll speak no more to you of Agrippina's.
I kiss the hand that murders me with respect;
And seeing how far you dare go to insult me,
I leave it to your conscience to avenge me.

CLAUDIUS: You have your wish, and as for your revenge,

1050 My heart works all too well in concert with you.
I love without being loved, with no hope of being happy.
Could you select a torment that's more dreadful?
I know that I'm cruelly insulting you,
That I'm an ingrate, perjurer and traitor.

1055 Yes, I know that my heart ought not to have betrayed you.
But is it up to us to love or hate?
Lay the blame on the gods whose sovereign law
Instills both love and hatred in all hearts.
Accuse them; they have caused my agitation.

1060 And far from crushing me, pity me, madam.

AGRIPPINA: Yes, pity touches me for your lot, but
More than your misfortunes I pity your weakness.

Your deadliest blows come from yourself alone.
What, when your fate depends only on you,
1065   A condemned man's daughter holds your soul in bondage,
And you dare not stamp out so vile a passion!
At least if your love had managed to touch her,
I'd pity your choice, but would not reproach you.
But is her hatred, sire, any less strong?
1070   You've just experienced how she tries to strike you.
Not content to hate you, she aims at your death.
The gods, the just gods lend you their assistance;
And you lay blame upon their sovereign law
Which in all hearts instills both love and hatred!
1075   Ah, be more grateful for their heavenly kindness!
Could it have been displayed more opportunely?
What have you obtained from Arria, your ingrate?
The fire you burn with reignites her fury.
Heaven, by opposing her hate to your love,
1080   Has just declared its will, and by instilling
In turn hate in her heart and love in yours,
It wants, don't doubt it, each to destroy the other.
I do not want here to recall your oaths,
Confirmed so often with such eagerness;
1085   And since your heart persists in its crime, I
End a complaint unworthy of Agrippina.
But, sire, can you yourself without remorse
Act so unjustly to the heroes of my race?
To stamp out a too deadly passion, you
1090   Have but to see who I am, who my rival is.
You'd take your hand from me to offer it to her!
And what would the whole Roman people think of you?
Ah, far from condemning Maximus' misdeed,
Think that you owe your honor to his crime.
1095   His hand, snatching you from a shameful bond,
Has with one blow avenged your ancestors and mine.

His zeal for the state has made him reckless. In
A word, he did what I ought to have done.

CLAUDIUS: What, his vile crime finds in you a supporter!
1100 He wounds my heart, and you speak for him! But
At last I see the light; the more I view the crime,
The more I see Maximus' real motive.
That traitor was your hand-picked choice; he could
Betray me solely to follow your orders.
1105 No, I've no further doubts; *you* are behind this.
It's you who in your fury steal my loved one from me.
But if she's not returned to me, think that my wrath
In my disordered state may even reach you.

Exeunt Claudius and Narcissus.

JULIA: You heard him, madam; you must fear the worst.
1110 His desperate heart has thrown off all restraint.
This respectful suitor speaks to you as emperor,
And his initial deference gives way to his fury.

AGRIPPINA: I know better than you this ingrate who insults me,
And I've long enough experience of his heart
1115 To know how to bring him back to me when I want.
My rival's presence was causing all my fear.
At last she's gone; that's why I'm optimistic.
It's time to let my joy break forth in your sight.
I triumph, Julia, and I can at will
1120 Place myself with assurance on a wished-for throne.
I saw the fatal day that would make me step down,
And though I would have stopped at nothing in my fury,
Perhaps my efforts would have had no power.
But I have just removed the strongest obstacle.
1125 Heaven, with what pleasure did I see my foe,
Ever more confirmed in her first rapture, in
The presence of the gods, of Maximus and me,
Pledge to her lover an eternal troth!

JULIA: Ah, hide that secret in the night of silence!

1130 Beware the violence of an angry lover.
If the Emperor learns that, madam, he'll destroy you,
And in his desperation naught will stop him.
AGRIPPINA: And do you think, whatever fate heaven plans for me,
That fear can enter Agrippina's heart?
1135 Do you think my pride today will be belied?
Let the Emperor do his worst, and the gods, too;
Nothing can shake me. Though I saw their thunderbolt
Ready to fall on me and pulverize me,
Though they forgot all they have promised me,
1140 I'll fulfil the destiny of my son without them.
Yes, Nero must one day be master of the world.⁹⁰
Heaven made me this prediction; I must comply.
This important secret is known just to you,
Julia, and you well know that without fear I learned
1145 That this son whose greatness is so dear to me
Would plunge a knife into his mother's breast.
What do I say? Without fear? I was ecstatic.
My joy was visible immediately.
"No," I exclaimed then, "there is naught I fear.
1150 If my son must reign, let him kill me and reign."
And you could still presume that my heart would
So far forget itself as to fear Claudius?
Let him seek vengeance; let him storm and threaten;
Indeed, let danger from all sides surround me.
1155 I've told you once before, nothing can shake me.
You'll see me fall rather than vacillate.
Yet Claudius is not so formidable.
The violence that you fear from him I think unlikely.
My power's as great as his; we are of the same race.
1160 The splendor of his rank alone sets him above me.
And if he dared indeed stir up a storm,
Perhaps he'd see its fury strike his own head.
I'd make him tremble here amid his court.

Enter Narcissus.

NARCISSUS: Madam, Proculus has just arrived back here,
1165   Leading Arria and Paetus with him. I
        Saw it with my own eyes.

AGRIPPINA: O fatal news!

NARCISSUS: They say that hardly had these lovers left
        This dangerous place, their dearest wish fulfilled,
        When Proculus, followed by a mighty escort,
1170   Appears before them on the road to Ostia.[91]
        On seeing him, Maximus in desperation,
        Knowing it meant death to fall into his power,
        Abandons himself to his own violence.
        He dies. Paetus draws up to Arria's side.
1175   To keep her for himself he shows fresh vigor
        And makes a rampart for her with the dead and wounded.
        The most reckless fall a sacrifice to his rage;
        None dares to clear a path directly to him.
        In valor he excels our bravest Romans.[92]
1180   But when at last his sword breaks, he's delivered
        Defenseless into the hands of trembling Proculus.

AGRIPPINA: Say rather, heaven delivers them to my vengeance.
        Great gods, you so ordain. They both shall perish.
        Your just anger breaks out against them. Yes,
1185   The wrath of heaven doubtless shows forth clearly:
        It ties the public safety to their death.
        In vain have I saved them from the mortal blow.
        The fate that dogs them brings them back to the altar.
        Let's waste no time. Come, follow me, Narcissus.
1190   Let's make all ready for this great sacrifice.
        They'll give me satisfaction for my agitation.
        Let's use, if need be, steel or poison.

NARCISSUS: Heaven!
        Where are you running? What will you undertake?
        You'll see the Emperor arm for their defense.

1195   You have all to fear.

AGRIPPINA: And naught to hold me back.

NARCISSUS: And what do you intend, madam?

AGRIPPINA: My vengeance.

What! Could I allow my haughty rival to

Attain a glory fatal to my own?

Vile reject of an ingrate who dares scorn me,

1200   I'd be a subject when I ought to reign!

No, let's mount opposition to Arria's triumph.

My glory is at stake; your life is, too,

Narcissus; let's save ourselves from the deadliest

Fate. Agrippina's downfall means your death.

1205   Your soul must be thrown into mortal fear.

Your hands are still stained with Silanus' blood;

And if his daughter rises to the highest rank,

Her first duty is vengeance for her father.

Perhaps her hand, given only at that price,

1210   Will sign that dreadful marriage in your blood.

NARCISSUS: I see what storm is on the verge of forming,

Madam, and more than you, it must alarm me.

A subject who's responsible for his master's crimes

Must bear sole blame to make him innocent.

1215   But there are perils one must not confront.

We'll ruin ourselves, madam, thinking to save ourselves.

Let's seize a more propitious time to avenge ourselves.

A downfall, a reversal would make us too guilty.

The people, who follow only false appearance,

1220   Always judge a criminal plot by its result.

As soon as it succeeds, they call it justice;

But fruitless crimes deserve an execution.

Prudence supports a project, of whatever kind.

What is your plan? Today do you want a passion

1225   For vengeance, fatal to yourself alone,

To sacrifice you at a rival's feet?

As I said before, let's choose another time.
Our blows, if less visible, will strike more surely.
You see the people's and the senate's fury;
1230 All things will be against us and for Arria.
Scribonian himself, zealous to avenge her,
Will back up Claudius, if he wants to protect her.
Shall we cause division in our trembling forces
When the common foe, already at our doors,
1235 Can without dividing us make us all tremble?
The storm is strong enough; why double its force?
Let us use artifice against your rival,
Madam.

AGRIPPINA: But what if he at last weds her, Narcissus?

NARCISSUS: The wedding's not as ready as you think.
1240 Her horror of it is your guarantee.
But to avert this fatal match more surely,
Let's fortify her hate by a new crime.
Let's go incense the Emperor against Paetus.
May he himself sacrifice him to his just
1245 Rage. May a husband's blood joined to a father's
Make Arria ever more opposed to his wishes.
I dare still take renewed hope in this blow.
She loves Paetus enough to follow him in death;
And using her own hand to strike our victim,
1250 We shall enjoy in peace the fruit of our crime.

AGRIPPINA: You prevail, Narcissus; you dictate my choice.
I recognize the weight of your wise counsel.
Let's go see Claudius; both working together,
Let's spur him to revenge against a happy rival.
1255 But if this stratagem has too little power,
I'll take advice only from my desperation.

Exeunt.

ACT V

Enter Claudius and Agrippina.

CLAUDIUS: This news of yours, is it possible, madam?
Ah, if he is my rival, his doom is assured.

AGRIPPINA: You soon will be informed from his own mouth.

1260 He is your rival, but one who is loved,
Sire. Maybe you will learn still more from him.
But meanwhile steel your heart against Arria.
Her tears for her lover might move you to pity;
And if you spare him, he will cause your death.

1265 I know how weak a heart in love is, and
In this great struggle I fear only you.

CLAUDIUS: Me! Could I, so long deceived by a false hope,
Still heed the voice of a rejected love!
No, no, too great a fury grips my soul.

1270 The cruel maid teaches me to turn barbaric,
And I don't guarantee that my just wrath
Won't sacrifice even her to my wild jealousy.

AGRIPPINA: It's no use her deserving all your anger;
She'll surely find the secret of how to please you.

1275 One word, a single glance will be able to
Disarm you, sire; your heart can't help loving her.
I stop opposing this most fatal passion.
I love you always; time will do the rest.
My rival has won out; perhaps the gods

1280 Will open your eyes about her and me.
That's all I am expecting from their lofty kindness.
I implore it for you, far more than for me.
And you see, sire, that all my prayers are ready
To sacrifice my dearest interests to you.

1285 When I incense you against a happy rival,
I become the initial victim of your blows.
As Paetus plunges into death's endless night,
He brings about a marriage fatal to me.

Arria, while losing him, can easily forget him;
1290 By burying her love, she'll bury her hate.
I work for you, for her, and against myself.
But I must save you; that's all I consider.
Then secure your life by slaying a guilty man
And avert his blow before it crushes you.
1295 He's coming; I withdraw and let you finish.
Sire, once again, give thought to your own safety.

Exit Agrippina; enter Paetus.

CLAUDIUS: Approach, and if you can, not blushing for your
crime,
Tell me what motive sets you against my life.
For I don't doubt that with Scribonian
1300 You are betraying Rome as a cowardly citizen;
And your care in protecting Arria shows
Sufficiently that your heart shares her madness.
At least a father's blood authorizes her act.
That blood can absolve her from the crime of ingrates.
1305 Her hand is noble, and yours is perfidious.
One's an avenger; the other, a heinous felon.
Reply, if you are able; tell me what
Fury leads you to conspire against your Emperor.

PAETUS: Depict this murder plot in the blackest colors.
1310 I need only recall a thousand dreadful stories
To dare admit to it in your sight without blushing.
What! Shall Rome's people under a hateful yoke
Have seen just a tyrant till now in their master?
And shall their liberator pass for a traitor?
1315 Shall I see Rome prey to the cruelest woes,
Not daring to shed tears for her children's blood,
And flattering tyranny with trembling voice,
She must moan secretly to see it unpunished?
Shall I hear her sighs, and to avenge my country
1320 I, cowardly citizen, would take no action!

But you yourself, sire, who call me perfidious,
Yet turn your holiest duty into brutal murder,
Can you, without blushing for our disgraceful
Chains, run through all the evils we have suffered?
1325 What! Your bloody orders have sent to their death
Thousands on whom Rome based its noblest conquests,
And ever more athirst for the purest blood,
You still are asking why I have conspired?
CLAUDIUS: In the wake of great crimes always comes despair.
1330 You worsen the evil, seeing that it's hopeless.
But your death sentence shortly will avenge me.
I shall pronounce, and Rome will ratify it.
PAETUS: Slave to a tyrant who compels its silence,
Rome may endorse this act of violence,
1335 And with a dry eye see a consul fall
By your decree, dying solely for her interests.
But you would know what blood she aspires to shed,
If she dared make her wishes known to you.
CLAUDIUS: I grant that Rome aspires to shed my blood;
1340 But are your crime and hers in the same rank?
This barbarous blow of which I've just complained,
Was it from Paetus that I had to fear it?
Could I suspect him after treating him so kindly?
Did I make you consul just so you could murder
1345 Me? Ingrate, see what cost my fury brings.
I showered you with honors; you want to slay me!
PAETUS: True, I received the purple toga from your hands;[93]
But since I must speak as consul of the Romans,
Learn that as soon as the Emperor names them, consuls
1350 Consider nothing other than Rome's interest.
This slave, formerly queen of all the world,
Reserved this right when falling into bondage;[94]
And having just the semblance of her freedom,
1355 Awaits deliverance from an empty name that's left her.

Caligula's death had made her ecstatic.[95]
You only, fatal remnant of a race so wretched,
You've plunged her back into captivity.
She still bemoans this and wants to be avenged.
That, sire, that is the motive for my actions.

1360   Behold my crime; judge whether I should blush.
I'm willing to conceal a blacker picture
Of evils I deplore and which are your work.
The deaths of Chereas and of Sabinus . . .[96]

CLAUDIUS: Continue, add the death of Silanus.

1365   That name makes you turn pale! I know your final crime:
Your love for his daughter drives you to avenge him.
Reply, happy rival, be less disconcerted.

PAETUS: Sire, Agrippina has not told you all.
My lot is happier than my rival thinks.

1370   But it's not up to me to break the silence.
And if I've said enough to earn my death,
I leave you to settle my fate at your leisure.

Exit Paetus.

CLAUDIUS (*alone*): You'll have your wish; yes, traitor, you shall
die.
Let's blindly follow where my fury leads me.

1375   Let's sacrifice a rival to my jealous rage.
He's done only too much to earn his death.
What ho, guards, come! (*to guards*) Have Arria brought here.
Let
Her in her turn feel how far my fury goes.
Let this lover so dear, expiring in her sight,

1380   Avenge me on her and by his death kill her.
Cruel man, what shall you do? What wildness drives you?
To earn her hatred, is one crime too little?
What! You're sometimes her foe, at others jealous lover.
The man she holds most dear will fall beneath your blow!

1385   You'll sacrifice the lover after the father!

What other harm is left for you to cause her?
And always treating her with more severity,
Do you think to win her while you pierce her heart?
No, no, let's not conclude this dreadful sacrifice.
1390   Let's save the one I love from this new torture.
But what's my plan? What, should I go today
To prove my love to her at the expense of my heart?
No, no, I have too long deferred my anger.
Let my rival die since he makes me despair.
1395   His loved one approaches; let's summon our fury,
And see her henceforth just to horrify her.

Enter Arria and Flavia.

ARRIA: Why do you call me? Do you think that my disgrace
So humbles my bold spirit as to plead with you?
And must it be that your cruel power still,
1400   To add to my woes, forces me to see you?
CLAUDIUS: Your woes will finish, madam, have no doubts.
My love has gone forever from my soul.
Fury takes its place, and I am grateful to
The gods whose just wrath brings you back to this place.
1405   Those gods, you see, have thwarted your escape.
Their fairness hands you over to my pursuit.
They can't endure that, after your evil plot,
You dare affront the orders of the senate.
ARRIA: You think then that the death prepared for me
1410   Could have made my hapless soul turn cold with fear?
And giving an unworthy pretext for my flight,
To suit you, you attribute it to my fear.
Be undeceived, begin to do me justice.
I was fleeing the tyrant, not the execution;
1415   If I could banish myself from this horrid place,
I planned to come back here to take your life.
But since at last the gods betrayed my anger,
I limit my wishes to joining my father.

And I'll complain of destiny's rigors less

1420   If you love me enough to take my life.

CLAUDIUS: Yes, I love you enough, implacable foe,
To go even much further than you wish.
Your lover cannot hope to escape my blows,
Ingrate, and it's through him that I shall strike you.

1425   This makes you tremble! I at last find, madam,
The secret to strike fear into your soul.
You're justly frightened that Paetus is near
Death. I know all; your love has reached my ears.
It increases my hate for this happy rival;

1430   And since you love him, his death is assured.

ARRIA: Ah, cruel man, how long will your fatal wrath
Make me feel its most terrifying blows?
Does it not suffice that I rush to my death?
To avenge you, is my heart required to moan?

1435   And with your sword in hand to sacrifice me,
To crown your fury, do you come to envy
Me, at the foot of the altar where I'm summoned,
The deadly pleasure of being the only victim?
I do not want to justify Paetus here.

1440   I see too well my trying would all be futile.
Agrippina accuses him, and *I* destroy him.
It's I, sire, I'm the one who made him guilty.
If he could betray you, it was by obeying
Me; he'd be innocent, did he not love me.

1445   Ah, must it be that I myself kill him today?
Spare my distracted soul from this regret.
Don't hand him over to the axe that awaits me.
I shall receive its stroke without a murmur;
And my heart, renouncing all its anger, will

1450   Forgive you for my death and for my father's.

CLAUDIUS: Too happy rival! If he makes your tears flow,
Would at that price I were weighed down with misfortunes!

But hoping to save him, madam, you destroy him,
And I shall quench your passion in his blood.

1455 ARRIA: All right! This wretched lover then shall die,
And I'm the one who makes him fall to your resentment!
I can't possibly doubt it; heaven's anger
Attaches misery to my fatal love.
Ah, since it's thus, to satisfy my wishes,

1460 Would I could love you as much as I hate you!

CLAUDIUS: Stop irking me when I want to show mercy,
And as you hear the threat, avert the blow.
I feel my fury gives way to my pity,
And I can't reconcile the lover and the avenger.

1465 My rival must die, but indeed I love you;
And since to strike him means to strike yourself,
I cannot view his death without horror, and
I want to save him so as not to lose you.

ARRIA: What, sire, your kindness . . .

CLAUDIUS: I implore yours here.

1470 I make a sacrifice and ask another.
Deign to consent, madam, and on the morrow
Banish your lover and become my wife.

ARRIA: O heaven!

CLAUDIUS: You hesitate!

ARRIA: The gods . . . my father, sire . . .
But let's hide nothing. I've been too long silent.

1475 I see that Agrippina hid our marriage
From your jealous gaze, to doom the lover better.
You ask for my hand, I've already given
It. Yes, I'm joined to him in holy wedlock;
And if you disbelieve two lovers' word,

1480 Agrippina is witness to our sacred vows.

CLAUDIUS: What have I heard, great gods! It's too much,
    madam;
This last crime finally makes me resolved.

What, you bestow yourself despite my power?
What, you in spite of my love take a husband?
1485   He'll die for this, madam, and my just anger . . .
This reckless rival still dares to defy me!
Just now, in my sight . . . I misunderstood,
But I'll make him pay dear for this intended joy.
ARRIA: Ah, show yourself magnanimous through self-control!
1490   What, must I, eternal victim of your vengeance,
Always lament, and must I by your blows
Lose first a father and a husband later?
CLAUDIUS: And what do you intend? Do you think that,
A hapless witness to his crowning happiness,
1495   Favoring his wishes at my heart's expense,
I would myself confirm a match that kills me?
No, don't hope for it. If you hold him dear,
Requite my passion, madam, to save his life.
And as you take my hand before the gods,
1500   Arrange for him to leave this place forever.
That's what his pardon costs.
ARRIA: What madness drives you?
You want to make the gods witnesses to your crime!
Their laws . . .
CLAUDIUS: An emperor follows only those
He chooses. Mortals like us are above laws.
1505   Come follow me to the temple for this marriage.
My ancestor Augustus set the example.[97]
ARRIA: Seek finer examples in your forebears' lives.
Imitate their virtues, not their faults. But, tyrant,
It is in vain that I have told you this.
1510   I give advice you're unable to follow.
Your heart no longer knows remorse or virtues.
To save my husband my attempts are vain.
I see too well that his last hour has come.
Then don't postpone this dreadful sacrifice.

1515   Since you must slay him, strike; your avenging arm
        Can't miss him at the bottom of my heart.
        CLAUDIUS: Just gods!
        ARRIA: You shudder at your own madness. Do
        You think you'll strike Paetus without slaying Arria?
        No, don't deny your fatal blows their scope.
1520   Join daughter to her father, wife to husband.
        You dare not, cruel man! Love stops you in vain.
        If your hand should refuse, mine is all ready.
        CLAUDIUS: I'll listen to no more. Decide his fate,
        Madam, and choose between the throne and his death.
1525   ARRIA: I've no hesitation in a choice so dreadful,
        And viewing him I love and him I loathe,
        I prefer to free myself forever from your power
        And die with him, rather than reign with you.
        CLAUDIUS: So that is all your answer, madam. If
1530   I pronounce a single word, he's doomed.
        ARRIA: Pronounce it.
        CLAUDIUS: All right. Guards!
        ARRIA: What, alas, will you pronounce?
        What is the blood, sire, that you're going to shed?
        (aside) To what test, Heaven, do you subject my constancy?
        (aloud) Sire, you prevail, in spite of my resistance.
        Order that Paetus be brought to my presence
1535   And that no one disturb our farewells here.
        CLAUDIUS: Obey her, Guards.
                      Exit Claudius.
        FLAVIA: At last propitious heaven
        Places you on the throne and snatches him from death.
        You save yourself, madam, saving your husband.
1540   How I have trembled for him and for you!
        ARRIA: Tremble more than ever, Flavia! What, could I
        Tarnish my whole life's reputation in one moment?
        But our discussion here might be overheard.

You'll know me better after I've seen Paetus.

1545 He comes, withdraw.

Exit Flavia; enter Paetus.[98]

PAETUS: What favorable fate

Permits me to see you in my crushing anguish?

I'm seized with horror for your precious life.

What happens to our love? What does the Emperor say?

Madam, might I have lost you forever?

1550 ARRIA: Ah, please stop speaking words that kill me.

Strengthen my heart, instead of softening it.

The sentence is pronounced; you must die, Paetus.

I'm asked, and I can't repeat it without trembling,

At the cost of my troth, to accept the throne;

1555 They want your wife, working with your tormentors,

To preserve your life while giving you a death blow.

What, I could lose you and live for another?

No, I must defend my honor and yours better.

You see me Paetus, for the last time. But

1560 Since you must needs die, choose your means of dying

And be sole arbiter of your destiny.

Contend with the tyrant for so proud a title.

What a disgrace for you, if he drags you to

The altar to deal the mortal blow as he likes.

1565 Dear Paetus, save yourself from this great shame,

And defy tyranny even as you expire.

Cut short the sad course of your wretched life.

I give you such a fatal aid with regret.

I have deceived our enemies' vigilance,

1570 And always wary of fortune's reversals,

I've managed to hide on me the means to defy

Its blows; I did not think to use it against you.

But you turn pale!

PAETUS: Madam, if I turn pale,

Love only is the source of my soul's worry.

1575 As you well know, the approach of death
Has never caused a heart like mine to tremble.
But close to handing you over to Agrippina's
Fury, I shudder at the fate in store for you.
ARRIA: Do you think, Paetus, that my chief endeavor
1580 Is limited merely to causing *your* death?
Would I set you on a path where I'd not follow you?
No, no, I can't survive you for a single moment.
For me life has no charms when yours is lost.
Our bond is too fine ever to be broken.
1585 Then banish fear from your soul, my dear husband,
And don't reject the example of a woman.
> *She draws a dagger and stabs herself.*
PAETUS: What are you doing, madam? O misfortune!
Fatal despair!
ARRIA (*pulling out the dagger and handing it to him*):
Here, Paetus, it does not hurt.
PAETUS (*taking the dagger*): It hurts me only too much when I
see you dying.
1590 I can't fulfil your expectations soon enough.
> *He stabs himself. Enter Claudius and Narcissus.*
CLAUDIUS: Yes, she'll accede, Narcissus, to my wishes.
My rival must depart from here forever.
I've reached the moment . . . But what ghastly spectacle!
ARRIA: Don't come near me, monster whom I detest!
1595 At least spare my indignant heart the sight
Of you and let me enjoy my final moments.
My husband's dying, cruel man; see your handiwork!
Satiate yourself; enough blood flows to please your rage.
But his and my blood seem to join forces to
1600 Accuse the gods of being too slow to punish you.
Our cries are heard, barbarian, have no doubt.
Already I see what fate heaven prepares for you.
It destines for this illustrious task a hand

Too unworthy of us, but too worthy of you.
1605 Tyrant, you didn't deserve a glorious death.
Agrippina . . . at that name I die contented.
CLAUDIUS: She's dead. Ah, cruel man, what an outcome for
Your love! It's you who stole the sun's light from her.
Barbarian, die, forestall her threat's fulfillment,
1610 And cruel to all, show no mercy on yourself.
Exeunt.[99]

END.

Françoise d'Issembourg d'Happoncourt de Graffigny

Cenia

(Cénie)

The Author

We know considerably more about Mme de Graffigny than about any of the other playwrights in this volume, both because she achieved far greater fame in her own time and because she left a detailed and voluminous record of her activities in her correspondence.[100] Her letters to her closest friend, François Devaux (nicknamed Panpan), written almost daily from 1738 until her death, read practically like a diary. Graffigny was so esteemed as a letter-writer by her contemporaries that Devaux promised, upon her death, to edit and publish her collected correspondence. However, being a very lazy man, he never even began work on this imposing task, and it was not until the 1980s that a team of scholars undertook to produce a complete edition.

Mme de Graffigny was born as Françoise d'Issembourg du Buisson d'Happoncourt in Nancy on February 11, 1695. Her parents were both from the Lorraine nobility (though their families had been ennobled only within the past century), and neither family was very wealthy. Little is known of her childhood, but her education seems to have been rudimentary, and it would not be until her meeting with Voltaire many years later that she would develop an interest in literature. At age seventeen she married François Huguet de Graffigny, whose family had been ennobled only in 1704. She bore him three children, all of whom died in infancy. The marriage quickly ran into trouble: François was ill-tempered, jealous, and a spendthrift, and he frequently insulted and beat his wife. By 1718 they were living apart, and a legal separation was obtained in 1723. In 1725 the husband was arrested for robbery and assault, although he was eventually released owing to very poor health. His brothers-in-law took him to Neufchâteau, where he died several months later.

With no money and no occupation, Françoise went to the ducal court in Lunéville, where many ruined noblemen lived as parasites of the ruling family. At the court she became very friendly with a group of young intellectuals, including Panpan and Léopold Desmarets, who would be her lover for many years. It seems that she preferred the company of young men, to whom she could pour out her heart as a friend. In 1735 she first met Voltaire, who took refuge at the court of Lorraine in the wake of the scandal caused by his subversive poem *La Pucelle.* One of his reasons for choosing Lunéville was to see his friend the Duchess de Richelieu, whose marriage he had arranged. He took an immediate liking to Panpan and to Mme de Graffigny, and later corresponded with them on occasion.

The Treaty of Vienna, signed that same year, spelled an end to Graffigny's comfortable life in Lunéville. The Duke of Lorraine was to yield his state to Stanislas Leczinski (father-in-law of Louis XV), upon whose death Lorraine would become joined to the French crown; Duke François would receive in compensation the duchy of Tuscany. When the Duke and his family departed from Lorraine in 1737, Graffigny solicited an invitation to Cirey, where Voltaire was staying in the chateau of his close friend (and mistress) Emilie du Châtelet. She arrived to an enthusiastic reception on December 4, 1738, and began at once to relate in letters to Panpan all the details of the exciting intellectual activity, as well as the (not always edifying) private life of the great master and their hostess. However, things turned sour at the end of the month, when Mme du Châtelet accused her guest of stealing a manuscript of *La Pucelle* and sending it on to Panpan—a charge which, had it been true, could have landed Voltaire in serious trouble. As it turns out, the accusation was unfounded: Emilie, who regularly monitored her guests' mail, had simply misconstrued a statement in one of Panpan's letters. Despite a belated and half-hearted reconciliation between Graffigny and her hostess, the former felt humiliated and unwanted. Nevertheless, with no money to go elsewhere, she had no choice but to wait over a month for the arrival of Desmarets, who was to take her to Paris.

In April of 1739 Mme de Richelieu returned to the capital and opened her sumptuous residence to Graffigny. Life seemed stable again until August of 1740 when the duchess died of tuberculosis, her condition being further weakened by a painful childbirth. A falling out with the duke obliged Graffigny to seek other lodgings; she even spent a short interval at a convent. Only the arrival of la Clairon, an actress from her circle of friends in Lunéville, saved her from starvation. It is not clear how she managed to live for the next few years, but her decision to take up writing was directly related to her ongoing financial worries.

In the salon of the retired actress Jeanne-Françoise Quinault, she came to meet some of the leading writers of the age, such as Diderot and d'Alembert, as well as aspiring young poets, some of whom became her protégés. Surrounded by writers, Graffigny was encouraged to attempt a short story, which she published in 1745. Not long after, she moved into a more elegant apartment and set up her own salon. In 1747 she published an epistolary novel, *Lettres d'une Péruvienne* (*Letters of a Peruvian Princess*), which became an instant best seller and established Graffigny as an eminent woman of letters. This, combined with the presence of her beautiful and witty niece, Catherine ("Minette") de Ligniville, who came to live with her early in 1749, made the Graffigny salon one of the most brilliant in Paris. Visitors would include such distinguished names as Diderot, d'Alembert, Rousseau, Helvétius, Duclos, Turgot, and d'Argenson.

Her fame as an author led to a lucrative commission from the Emperor of Austria (formerly the Duke of Lorraine, her original protector) and his family: she was to supply them with plays, preferably of an edifying nature, to be given private performances by the children of the imperial family. (One of those children, by the way, was Marie-Antoinette, future queen of France.) Two of the plays, *Phaza* and *Ziman et Zénise*, a pair of fairy tale comedies, were published posthumously in 1770; the pseudo-historical *Les Saturnales*, a work for which she solicited assistance from several male friends, including Rousseau, was printed only in 1978; the other plays have disappeared. It seems likewise to have been for financial reasons that Graffigny (who never learned how to manage money) tried her hand at full-length sentimental comedies. *Cenia*, performed in 1750, was a triumphant success with public and critics alike, winning praise from such luminaries as Rousseau, Baron Grimm, Gottsched, and Lessing. Diderot is reported to have called it the first and most perfect model of bourgeois drama.[101] Unfortunately, the fiasco of her next play, *La Fille d'Aristide* (*The Daughter of Aristides*), composed in a similar mold in 1758, was more than her delicate nerves and fragile health could stand. She worked feverishly to prepare the play for publication, and her death occurred on the very day when she finished correcting the proofs, December 12, 1758.

Graffigny did not manage to escape the fate of most successful women authors: she was accused of using a male ghost writer. A scandalmonger named Chévrier claimed that her novel had been written by Abbé Pérau, one of the frequent visitors to her salon, and that she had simply bought the rights to the novel. Later Chévrier announced that *Cenia* had originally been composed in verse by Abbé Voisenon, another regular at the salon, and that Graffigny's contribution consisted of nothing more than reworking the play in prose. Both charges are absurd, and no one at the time took them seriously. Voisenon, by the way, had already published several comedies under his own name and could hardly have been fearful for his reputation. The story of Chévrier's libels had an ironic sequel: an obscure poet named Des Longschamps, inspired by the success of *Cenia*, recast the work in verse and published his own version in 1751, giving credit to Graffigny.

Georges Noël, in his biography of Graffigny, gives a rather mixed assessment of her character, viewing her as a gentle, kindhearted, sentimental soul. Although disappointed that she was not a more coherent and original thinker, he admits that it cannot have been easy for her to absorb the barrage of new ideas surrounding her or to make sense of her own experiences. The frivolous society in which she lived, together with the breakup of her family, her precarious finances, her loss of faith in Catholicism and in the existing social order must have contributed to her sense of alienation and rootlessness.[102] In Noël's estimation her literary works served primarily to give expression to the pain and frustration in her heart, and the happy ending of *Cenia* was basically wish fulfillment. It is just possible, however, that the play's conclusion is a summation of the values which the author upheld: compassion, total sincerity in love and in friendship, personal integrity, philanthropy, relaxation of outdated social restrictions, and, most of all, women's quiet heroism.

The Play

Significance

During the second quarter of the eighteenth century, French authors began to experiment with a dramatic genre intermediate between tragedy and comedy. The term *drame*, which had not been commonly used in the French language until that point, came to be associated with the new genre, although such labels as bourgeois tragedy and tearful comedy were found as well. One of the two principal pioneers of the *drame* in France was Pierre Nivelle de La Chaussée, whose "comedies" introduced the tone (sustained intensity of pathos, combined with constant moralizing) and many of the principal situations (the plight of the poor, the status of illegitimate children, discord and reconciliation between family members, and the nefarious effect of society's "prejudices" and inequities). The other was Denis Diderot, who championed the intermediate genre's autonomy and legitimacy, and whose remarkable treatises on dramatic theory advocate a realism in style, situation, and gesture so absolute that an audience could be induced to mistake the performance of a play for real life. Historians of French drama, in the search for the single greatest innovator, have exalted either La Chaussée or Diderot at the expense of each other and of all their contemporaries. Thus it is that the pivotal role of Françoise de Graffigny has tended to receive scant attention at best.[103]

Cenia, produced in 1750, appeared between the major plays of La Chaussée (whose first success came in 1733 and whose last in 1747) and the publication of Diderot's *Le Fils naturel* (1757), and provides an important transition between them. Unlike her predecessor, who clung to the label "comedy," Graffigny called *Cenia* "pièce nouvelle," which could mean either "new play," or "dramatic novelty." She substituted prose for La Chaussée's mediocre verse. Perhaps the most remarkable feature is the portrait of a villain who does not convert in the final scene. As the play's most energetic character, Mericourt provides an element of fear and revulsion that had been lacking in tearful comedy and anticipates the melodramas of the early nineteenth century. Graffigny improved on La Chaussée in numerous ways (see following section) and managed to compose a play that is far more readable than any of La Chaussée's or Diderot's dramatic works. (Since several of those plays have been reprinted in this century, readers can draw their own conclusions.) Moreover, Graffigny's contemporaries received *Cenia* with great enthusiasm: in a single year (1751) it went through three editions, and it received more performances than any other play by a woman author at the Comédie-Française prior to the Revolution. That the acclaim given to *Cenia* helped prepare the Parisian public to accept the *drames* of the following decades cannot be doubted.

To be sure, the eighteenth-century *drames* are spoiled for the modern reader by two of the very components that assured their original popularity: the dominance of sensibility and of overt moralizing. Both can be explained in historical terms, but we are entitled to fault the playwrights for making these devices overly intrusive and often gratuitous. The ostentatious displays of philosophical precepts were in fact closely related to the goals of the *philosophes*. The theatre, like the *Encyclopédie*, was to function as a pulpit for the promulgation and dissemination of enlightened thinking. Their views on such subjects as natural law, natural morality, social and political rights and responsibilities, and the triumph of reason over "prejudice" and error could not help filtering into literary works, especially in the genres (the *drame* and the novel) that they considered the most realistic. Graffigny, as a friend (for a time, at least) of men like Voltaire and Rousseau, accepted many of the new ideas and wished to promote certain social reforms with her plays.

The cult of sensibility, based on the philosophical views that people are born naturally good and that virtuous conduct can, or should, be grounded in "natural" emotions, was to mark a sizable percentage of eighteenth-century literature in France, and in neighboring countries, as well. Dramatic characters endowed with that sensibility have a number of distinctive characteristics, including: the propensity to weep at the slightest provocation; the ability to feel emotions with an intensity that leads to frenzy of word and gesture; the belief in the inherent rightness of their feelings and ideas, even if opposed to those of society; a willingness to become excited over abstract principles and to accept great sacrifices in order to uphold them; and the conviction that sensibility and virtue are, if not synonymous, at least inseparable. However unpalatable these ideas seem today, they were undeniably in vogue in 1750, and Graffigny, as an aspiring playwright hoping to have her work accepted by the leading company in France, could hardly have avoided using them.[104] Moreover, the sensibility of the age was in accord with her personality, as her letters make abundantly clear.

If *Cenia* were nothing more than a historical curiosity embodying popular taste at the midpoint of the eighteenth century, it would be of interest only to a handful of scholars.

However, I find in the play an incipient feminist consciousness and a concern for presenting female characters in a more favorable light. Unlike the heroines of La Chaussée, who are lifeless and interchangeable (one could describe them as passive, insipid, timid, weepy, and overly willing to accept their role as victims and martyrs), Graffigny presents women who are active, capable, thoughtful, and dignified. In addition, her heroines have all devoted considerable reflection to the role of women, especially married women, in a male-dominated society.

Cenia, although young, is not really an ingénue. Unafraid to speak her mind, she boldly confronts the villain in the play's central scene. She chooses a life of poverty in a convent rather than submitting to his blackmail demands. In other moments of great emotional stress, she is more successful than the men in keeping her self-control and in making decisions. She is clearly not the stereotypical heroine of melodrama, who lets herself be tied to the railroad tracks. Orphise, another figure of quiet dignity, whose noble bearing impresses all the other characters (except, of course, the villain), has managed for some fifteen years to survive as a member of the working class, deprived of her name, her husband, her relations, and her fortune. Yet she has never once uttered a word of complaint to anyone, not even confiding her woes to Cenia. She preaches a doctrine of resignation to fate and to society's dictates, however much she may disapprove of the latter, and she never falters in setting an example to others. Lisette, who disappears after the second act and whose primary function is to lend credibility to the villain's schemes, is a highly intelligent, observant, and efficient servant. At times she appears good-hearted, but she can also be spiteful and malicious, and her fondness for Mericourt quickly alienates the audience's sympathies. Her rather ordinary character serves as a foil to the extraordinary nobility of spirit displayed by Cenia and Orphise.

The closest Graffigny comes to depicting an evil woman is Melissa, the recently deceased wife of Dorimond who falsely claimed Cenia as her daughter and who in her final years made the villainous Mericourt her confidant. Yet, from the letters which she wrote on her deathbed and which are read at strategic moments in the play, one can deduce a motivation for her actions that is more touching than sinister. Melissa explains that Dorimond rescued her from abject poverty by marrying her and that she was much younger than he. She presumably suspected that charity played a larger part than love in Dorimond's decision and realized, knowing his delight in the joys of domesticity, that it might be difficult to keep his affection unless she could produce a child. Although Melissa never admits this in so many words, it is probable either that she found herself unable to conceive, or else that her husband was impotent and unaware of the fact. That is the probable reason for her desperate decision to adopt the infant daughter of a destitute woman and to pass the child off as her own.

The play also suggests, but does not address directly, the question of working women. How was a woman of noble birth but only modest education to earn a living, especially in a society where the nobility was expected not to engage in business activity, and where opportunities for women (of all classes) in the work force were severely limited? Convents often served as a refuge for single women, but, as the author knew from personal experience, they expected their boarders to pay rent and did not welcome the indigent. In the play, as in the France of the eighteenth century, fortunes could be made or lost with amazing rapidity and frequency, but the author makes no attempt to propose a solution. The obligatory happy ending requires that sooner or later riches will come into the possession of saintly, philanthropic men who will relieve the plight of the oppressed. Graffigny must have understood that it would take more than the largesse of a few kindhearted men to cure the social and economic ills of her day, but she also realized that the Parisian public demanded a more optimistic stance in the theatre. If neither she nor her audience were ready for a play with explicitly feminist ideology, she at least succeeded in creating more dignified and lifelike heroines for the *drame*: women capable of serious thought and decisive action, who inspire admiration as well as sympathy.

Source

While the play's female characters have certain parallels with the lives of Mme de Graffigny and her niece, the principal source was incontestably La Chaussée's *La Gouvernante*, which opened at the Comédie-Française on January 18, 1747, and had an initial run of seventeen performances. The plot has two interlocked components, only one of which was utilized by Graffigny. Angélique, believed to be the niece of a wealthy baroness, has a domineering and prudish governess (the title character has no name and is referred to throughout as The Governess) who pressures her to break her engagement to Sainville, even though the young people love one another. Revealing that Angélique is really a penniless orphan, whom the baroness adopted out of charity, she urges the girl to send back Sainville's letters and portrait. Angélique, who has received no word from him in a long time and suspects him of infidelity, finally agrees. But the young man, a *philosophe* of austere principles who has been sent to the capital to learn the ways of the world, returns more convinced than ever of the corruption of society and of the rightness of his desire to lead a secluded life in the country. He is quickly reconciled to Angélique, and they sign a promise of marriage. But when the governess learns of this act, she forces the girl to turn over the paper, which she gives to Sainville's father, the Président (presiding judge). Then she demands that Angélique break with Sainville definitively and go away with her. Angélique is so exasperated by the governess' behavior and by her masochistic philosophy (which at times seems to be "If a course of action makes you miserable, it must be virtuous"), that she refuses outright. The governess has no choice but to reveal, very belatedly, that she is Angélique's mother.

The other portion of the plot concerns the moral dilemma of The Président, a judge of impeccable integrity. He has just learned that, owing to his secretary's deliberate suppression of some crucial evidence in a lawsuit many years earlier, he issued an unjust verdict and caused the ruin of an innocent family. The husband of that family is dead, and the wife and daughter have disappeared, but the baroness has at length discovered that the governess and Angélique are the persons in question. The Président decides to reimburse the victims out of his own funds, even though this would consume most of his fortune. But first he puts the situation to his son as a hypothetical case. Sainville unhesitatingly replies that the judge should make restitution; but when his father offers to arrange a marriage for him with a rich heiress in order to compensate him for the financial sacrifice involved, he refuses to marry without love. Meanwhile, the governess refuses to accept the Président's offer of restitution, preferring to go off into a life of obscurity and poverty with her daughter. In the last act the baroness, having learned of the mutual love of Angélique and Sainville, convinces both parents that the marriage of the young people would be the best way to make amends for the past injustice.

The only scenes in La Chaussée's play that still hold our interest are those involving the Président and his dilemma. The female characters are unconvincingly drawn. The governess, arguably the most insufferable of his "virtuous" women, alienates our sympathies at every turn. It is hard to understand why she has deliberately avoided telling Angélique the truth about her identity, why she refuses to accept even a small portion of the Président's restitution, and why she persists until the final scene in opposing the match that will assure her daughter's romantic and financial happiness.

If Graffigny probably found it difficult to empathize with the Président, she must have considered the character of the female leads insipid, if not offensive. I submit that *Cenia*, far from being a pale imitation of *La Gouvernante*, as Lanson charges, is a reply to the earlier play, showing how truly virtuous and heroic ladies would behave in an analogous situation. The role of Dorimond also involves a measure of social criticism, suggesting that male philanthropists, however pure their motives, are still susceptible to outbursts of childish and irrational behavior and are still bound to social and sexual prejudices. It is likewise significant that Graffigny decided, unlike La Chaussée, to keep the father alive; Dorsainville serves as a reminder of how those prejudices can harm men, as well as women.

Performance History

The premiere took place at the Comédie-Française on June 25, 1750. Any first-time playwright was bound to experience difficulties with the troupe, but Graffigny's influential friends provided valuable assistance. The play, well served by an excellent cast, had a respectable success, running for twenty-five performances during its first year, and was frequently revived. By the time it left the repertory in 1762, it had enjoyed sixty-five performances, far more than any other work by a woman author prior to the Revolution.

Because of its widespread acclaim, *Cenia* must have been performed in private theatricals in aristocratic houses and by provincial companies. We know from Lessing that it received several performances in Hamburg in the months of May and July 1767, in the German translation by Luise Gottsched. It is likely that there were additional performances in Hamburg and in other German cities. Given the publication of *Cenia* in Dutch, English, and Italian translations, it is not impossible that the work was mounted in some of those countries, although I have not found any evidence to confirm this. There have been no known revivals since the eighteenth century.

Cenia

(Cénie)

New Play in Five Acts

Françoise d'Issembourg d'Happoncourt de Graffigny

Actors[105]

DORIMOND, a rich old man.

MERICOURT,
CLERVAL, his nephews.

CENIA, supposed daughter of Dorimond.

ORPHISE, governess of Cenia.

LISETTE, maid to Cenia.

DORSAINVILLE, friend of Clerval.

The scene is in the gallery of Dorimond's house.

· · · · ·

To My Lord the Count of Clermont, Prince of the royal blood.[106]

My Lord,

In dedicating *Cenia* to Your Serene Highness, I pay you homage with your own kindness. You know, my Lord, that it was only the desire to contribute to your entertainment that made me return to a work that I had abandoned for several years. You deigned to note its defects; it became less ill-formed. You took upon yourself the danger of making it public; the name of Your Serene Highness made its success.

It is not without extreme pain, my Lord, that I force myself to suppress the tribute of praise that my gratitude would inspire. But if people find it difficult to pardon women for thinking and for writing about matters that are within their grasp, how would people receive the sketchy picture that I could make of the eminent qualities which make all Europe admire the greatness of your soul? Would it be suitable for me to speak of cities captured by your courage and your ingenuity, of battles won by a valor that is hereditary in heroes of your race, the memory and image of which you constantly recall? No, my Lord, I must restrict myself to admiration, and to the profound respect with which I am,

My Lord,
Of Your Serene Highness,

The most humble and most obedient servant,
D'Happoncourt de Grafigny.

ACT I

Enter Lisette.

LISETTE: Can Mericourt have got away from me again? I thought I saw him walking toward this gallery. Yes, I wasn't mistaken. Sir, sir . . .

Enter Mericourt.

MERICOURT: What! Is it the attractive Lisette whom I find here?

LISETTE: Yes, sir, it's Lisette, always faithful to your interests, who for the last hour has been watching for the moment to converse with you.

MERICOURT: My dear child, we have to postpone this conversation till a later time. My uncle has monopolized me since I got out of my sedan-chair. I haven't seen anyone yet.

LISETTE: I want to be the first to speak to you. Except for your uncle, everyone is still sleeping in the house, and I will have the time to have words with you. Tell me, has anyone ever stayed away so long when everything should have been calling you back here?

MERICOURT: I couldn't come back sooner. You know that my uncle sent me word, by the same courier whom I dispatched to him at Melissa's death, not to leave the province without completing the trial that was in progress.

LISETTE: I had given you good advice. You shouldn't have sent me back here; you should have given me charge of the funeral and come yourself to announce his wife's death to him.

MERICOURT: The advice was very bad. Dorimond has a naive mind that does not let him see things except as they naturally ought to be. Not to wait for his orders, not to pay the final duties to so dear a wife, would have meant offending him in his most sensitive spot. But tell me, has the period of mourning ceased?

LISETTE: Yes, our six months came to an end yesterday. As for your uncle, he'll remain in mourning all his life, I think.

MERICOURT: I found him even more grieved than I was expecting.

How could he bring himself to keep you here? You who constantly remind him of the one he has lost?

LISETTE: Really now! Has he ever sent anyone away? At my arrival, the good man told me, sobbing all the while, that I should not think of leaving his house. I saw that it was in your interest for me to remain; I remained.

MERICOURT: In my interest? You are then attached to Cenia?

LISETTE: I am, but not really, for the governess, in her polite but imperious manner, keeps me away from her charge as much as possible. But if she, by doing so, prevents me from serving you as much as I would like, I am at least in a position to warn you about what is going on.

MERICOURT: Well, Lisette?

LISETTE: Your business is going badly.

MERICOURT: How's that?

LISETTE: Very badly, I tell you.

MERICOURT: So speak.

LISETTE: Patience. Before I speak I must know your secret. See if you can bring yourself to confide it to me.

MERICOURT: Why, you need only speak. All my secrets belong to you.

LISETTE: Someone who didn't know you would think he already had them.

MERICOURT: How do you expect me to satisfy you if you don't tell me what you want to know?

LISETTE: Were you in love with Melissa?

MERICOURT: Are you crazy, Lisette?

LISETTE: She's dead. There's nothing more to hide.

MERICOURT: You can't mean it! What, the adored wife of an uncle to whom I owe everything!

LISETTE: As for scruples, let's leave them aside. I don't know you to have many.

MERICOURT: I am not a monster, and Lisette would be, if she were speaking in earnest.

LISETTE: Let's see then whether my theory is so implausible. Melissa, a woman of odious character, seduces through her false virtues an old man of scrupulous integrity, supremely good, a devotee of honor, an enemy of suspicion, and who, because of his fear of being unjust, is easy to deceive. She monopolizes him to the exclusion of everyone else; she gives him a child, ruins your fortune. You are ambitious; you ought to hate her, and you grovel before her. You are either the falsest of men or the most in love.

MERICOURT: A few words can clear up this mystery. Dorimond saw only through Melissa's eyes; so it was only through her that I could keep myself in his favor. She had ruined my fortune, as you say; she could reestablish it by giving me her daughter; I was treating her tactfully. It's quite simple.

LISETTE: Dash it all! What simplicity!

MERICOURT: Dissimulation is no vice, and too much sincerity is often a fault.

LISETTE: Ah! That fault will never make you blush. But couldn't your friendship with Melissa have been carried on openly? Why so much whispering during her life, and such secret discussions at the approach of her death?

MERICOURT: Lisette, don't go any further, and moderate your curiosity.

LISETTE: All right. Besides, it's not a match between equals. It remains for me then to warn you, first of all, to distrust Orphise. She doesn't like you.

MERICOURT: I won't trouble myself over Madam Orphise's ill will. Let's move on. How is my brother thought of by my uncle?

LISETTE: Splendidly. Ever since his return, Dorimond has increased his affection for him. He thinks he can't do enough to compensate him for making his useless trip.

MERICOURT: How's that? Clerval . . .

LISETTE: Clerval brought back nothing from overseas except the cruel certainty that there is no earthly fortune for either of you. But for all this, I wouldn't pity you, were he not more in love than he is self-seeking.

MERICOURT: What! My brother could be in love with Cenia?

LISETTE: Even more. He is beloved.

MERICOURT: Beloved! That's saying a lot. Is my uncle informed of this intrigue?

LISETTE: No, indeed. Given the mood he's in, he would have married them off already.

MERICOURT: Perhaps. That depends on the manner in which he would learn of it. Clerval rob me of Cenia! Him! That is what we will have to see. But are you quite sure of what you're saying?

LISETTE: Quite sure. I'm a good judge.

MERICOURT: That Cenia received with indifference attentions that should have persuaded her . . .

LISETTE: Of a love which you didn't feel.

MERICOURT: I was attributing that to her extreme youth.

LISETTE: Youth sometimes has an instinct surer than experience.

MERICOURT: But that she should love my worthy brother! She will most kindly have to be separated from him.

LISETTE: That will not be easy, I warn you. Clerval is attractive, and, young though he is, he has acquired a reputation in the wars that has placed him in good repute at court. That can't fail to be an advantage in the eyes of a young person.

MERICOURT: We will find weapons to fight him.

LISETTE: For my part, I see no resource for you except in the affection that Melissa had for you. Her memory is dearer than ever to your uncle. Profit by this circumstance. Here he is; I leave him with you.

Exit Lisette; enter Dorimond.

DORIMOND: I simply can't do without seeing you, my dear nephew. I left you in order to get over the excitement caused by our first conversation. I seek you at present, alas! who knows why? Perhaps to distress myself anew.

MERICOURT: It is natural, sir, that my return has renewed your grief. It is so justified!

DORIMOND: You know better than anyone whether I ought to weep over this virtuous spouse all my life. You must excuse my weakness; it is only with you that I can give free rein to my sorrow. Yet I wouldn't like to overwhelm you with it.

MERICOURT: I share it so sincerely . . .

DORIMOND: That is what ought to restrain me. Let's try to suspend it for a moment and speak of your interests. I have a thousand obligations to you, my dear Mericourt; you managed my business better than I could have done myself. But I feel even more keenly the attention you gave to Melissa up until her final hour. I want to reward your zeal, and I would like to reward it in a way that suits your taste, for no one succeeds in doing good unless he acts to the liking of the people obliged.

MERICOURT: If I have deserved anything, sir, it can only be through my loyal affection.

DORIMOND: I was awaiting your return with impatience in order to carry out a project formed long ago. You once showed romantic interest in Clarice. She's a mature girl of suitable age for you; her parents are my friends and won't refuse her to me. I intend her for you with a quarter of my fortune. My daughter will be for your brother; they are better matched in age. Does this arrangement please you?

MERICOURT: Why make any, sir? Why despoil yourself? Enjoy your riches; they have cost you so much peril and labor!

DORIMOND: I will enjoy them; I'll make you all happy.

MERICOURT: Why, sir, what haven't you done for us? Haven't your nephews found in your house the kindness of a father, an education, an abundance . . .

DORIMOND: I count that as naught; it was a duty.

MERICOURT: A duty!

DORIMOND: Yes, a duty. I had contributed to my sister's marriage. I intended to make her happy; it turned out just the reverse. She could not survive the ruin of her fortunes, the loss of her husband. Wasn't it only right for me to take charge of her children?

MERICOURT: Well, sir, your alleged duties are fulfilled by everything you've done. It is for us at present to work toward our own fortune.

DORIMOND: Why should I leave you that trouble, if I can save you from it? Is the marriage I'm proposing to your liking?

MERICOURT: Sir . . . my obedience . . .

DORIMOND: Let's not speak of obedience; that's a constraint. I don't want to impose on anyone.

MERICOURT: One can obey without constraint.

DORIMOND: True, but, when someone accepts my offers, I want to notice on his face a certain joy that assures me that he has as much satisfaction as I intend to give him.

MERICOURT: You ought to see, sir . . .

DORIMOND: I don't see anything that pleases me. You know I cherish sincerity just as much as I hate deviousness.

MERICOURT: Ah! As for sincerity, I think I've proven myself.

DORIMOND: Not always. In the past I suspected you of having a bit too much of that dissimulation that people more distrustful than I might have taken for falseness. But a long time ago Melissa made me change my mind on that score.

MERICOURT: Ah, sir, if I owe your improved opinion only to Melissa, she is dead. Who can guarantee that in the future . . .

DORIMOND: My heart. Besides the fact that it is sweet for me to love my nephew, I find suspicions annoy me; and of all the evils necessary to society, mistrust is, to my taste, the most unbearable.

MERICOURT: All your kindness barely suffices to reassure me that I won't have the misfortune of losing your esteem——I who make it my sole pursuit to deserve everyone's.

DORIMOND: And you are quite right: take my word for it. If you are generally esteemed you can never be completely unhappy. That esteem is what supported me in my setbacks; to it I owe my riches, and the satisfaction of having lost none of the rights of my birth in a commercial career which my integrity made honorable.[107] Besides, don't worry about the past. If I didn't esteem you, I might be generous to you, but I wouldn't live with you. Let's get back to our business. Speak with sincerity.

MERICOURT: You want me to, sir? Well, I was counting on your kindness enough to flatter myself that I could become your son-in-law.

DORIMOND: You love Cenia?

MERICOURT: Yes, sir; my fondness for her, the desire to be more closely bound to you—all these combined to make this union my dearest wish.

DORIMOND: I am grateful to you. Although Cenia is rather young for you, I'd be delighted . . . Does she love you?

MERICOURT: I don't know, sir; it wasn't becoming for me to take any steps in the matter without your approval.

DORIMOND: No one could behave with more discretion and decorum. You don't know the satisfaction you are giving me, my dear nephew. I would have proposed my daughter to you a long time ago, had I not feared to trouble your romantic interest in Clarice.

MERICOURT: Could you doubt my feelings?

DORIMOND: Come on, I am going to propose you to Cenia at once.

MERICOURT: I think, sir, that it wouldn't be advisable to speak to her in front of her governess.

DORIMOND: Why?

MERICOURT: It is always prudent not to confide one's plans to a servant.

DORIMOND: You don't know Orphise. She is a woman of superi-
or merit, with nothing of the baseness of her station.

MERICOURT: That's true, but, as this confiding isn't necessary,
you can dispense with it as something useless.

DORIMOND: All right, I'm going to find out whether my daughter is awake and communicate our project to her.

Exit.

MERICOURT (*alone*): Thank god, my affairs are going smoothly.
But Dorimond is so pliable . . . His daughter's refusal could
make him change his decision in a moment . . . Ah, Cenia,
tremble for your future, if you love Clerval enough to defy
my ambition! I won't let fifteen years of constraint go for
nothing. I have the means to be avenged on your contempt.

Enter Lisette.

LISETTE: Well, sir, I saw Dorimond leave. How are your affairs
going?

MERICOURT: Quite well. My uncle is going to recommend my
suit to Cenia.

LISETTE: That's fine. But what if she refuses you?

MERICOURT: She wouldn't dare. At her age, one knows only obedience.

LISETTE: She is young, sir, but her mind . . .

MERICOURT: I'm not a fool, Lisette.

LISETTE: Granted. But she loves Clerval.

MERICOURT: And Dorimond loves me.

LISETTE: Let's not flatter ourselves. What you have with the old
man is only a friendship acquired through artifice. He loves
Clerval quite naturally; the difference is great.

MERICOURT: I'm prepared for anything; I can ward off anything.

LISETTE: In that case, my little warnings are useless to you. Let's
forget that I said anything.

MERICOURT: You're getting angry, Lisette?

LISETTE: Yes, I'm angry. You must be really in the habit of lying
to do so with me.

MERICOURT: Me, a liar?

LISETTE: Yes. Whatever look you put on, you are not at ease. I had thought of a helpful hint to give you, but . . .

MERICOURT: Say it all the same.

LISETTE: I take an interest in you, I can't help it; and I utterly hate Madam Orphise. If Dorimond could be informed of certain of your brother's intrigues, he would lower his opinion of the young man. I have a feeling that she is on Clerval's side. What a pleasure to oppose her! It would be a great thing.

MERICOURT: What, Lisette! Could there be some irregularity in Clerval's conduct? Ah, speak quickly!

LISETTE: I don't really know what it's all about. I only see wandering around here a kind of soldier, with whom your brother has very mysterious conversations.

MERICOURT: Well! That soldier . . .

LISETTE: Be patient. He's a man he brought back from the Indies.

MERICOURT: So?

LISETTE: I hardly know anything more. Until now they have taken so many precautions in speaking to each other that I have only been able to catch a few words like "pardon" . . . "minister" . . .

MERICOURT: We must get to the bottom of this mystery. Clerval is an imprudent young man; he might have got himself embroiled in an awkward affair . . .

LISETTE: From which you'd like to free him, no doubt? How good-hearted!

MERICOURT: Lisette!

LISETTE: What the deuce, why do you want to take me in? Well now, here's our man hiding himself. Withdraw, I want to question him.

MERICOURT: Use all your skill to unravel this intrigue, my dear Lisette, I beseech you.

LISETTE: You are truthful in certain moments. Go now.

Exit Mericourt; enter Dorsainville.

Come forward, I'm alone now.

DORSAINVILLE: Do you know, miss, if Clerval is here?

LISETTE: Clerval! You are then on quite familiar terms with one another?

DORSAINVILLE: I'm in the wrong. But is he alone? Can I go up to his room?

LISETTE: You're in quite a hurry. Let's chat a moment. What's the matter? I find you look sad.

DORSAINVILLE: Rarely am I cheerful.

LISETTE: You are quite unhappy then? Listen, I've a good heart, and I take an interest in you. You are involved in an intrigue; so am I. Confide in me; I'll be able to do you a good turn.

DORSAINVILLE: I'll come back at another moment.

LISETTE (*aside*): I'll never get anything out of that devilish man. (*aloud*) Wait! Clerval has company. I'll go inform him; you can wait for him here.

Exit.

DORSAINVILLE (*alone*): How misfortune brings petty cares that are known only by the unhappy! One bears a spectacular reverse with steadfastness; one's courage collapses under the contempt of those very people one feels contempt for.

Enter Clerval.

CLERVAL: I had you summoned with the greatest eagerness. Last night I saw the minister; your pardon is assured.

DORSAINVILLE: O worthy friend of the unhappy! I owe you too much.

CLERVAL: You owe me nothing. The court felt, as I do, that when an affair of honor has reduced a man of your birth to the profession of simple soldier, and when he has demonstrated his valor, to restore him to his country is an act of justice, and not a favor bestowed upon him.[108]

DORSAINVILLE: Alas! What good will this turn of fortune do for me, if I can't share it with a wife so worthy of being loved?

CLERVAL: What news have you learned of her?

DORSAINVILLE: Still the same. She disappeared almost at the same time I did, after giving birth to a baby girl who died at once. And in the last fifteen years none of our acquaintances knows what has become of her.

CLERVAL: You mustn't despair yet. When you have resumed your real name, when you can act openly, you'll make better progress in your search.

DORSAINVILLE: It's too long I have searched in vain. I'll never see her again.

CLERVAL: What! Your courage abandons you when you are reaching the end of your sufferings?

DORSAINVILLE: Pardon me, dear friend, if I don't feel the value of your kindness enough. My wife meant everything to me. Without her there is no happiness for me.

CLERVAL: You'll find her again.

DORSAINVILLE: But how could she not have succumbed to the horrible condition I left her in? As she is about to give birth to the first fruit of our tender union, I tear myself from her arms, I leave her without money, without assistance. In such desperate straits, what could become of her?

CLERVAL: There are shelters for women of her rank when pursued by misfortune.

DORSAINVILLE: Convents are more the shelter of the reasonably well-off than of the destitute. Extreme indigence is not welcomed there, and that is the condition in which I left my wife. However, I haven't neglected anything; I have gone through all the convents in vain.[109]

CLERVAL: Perhaps she changed her name, just as you did?

DORSAINVILLE: But even if that were so, why hasn't she written to me?

CLERVAL: The war, as you know, had interrupted mail service. Your letters and hers may well have got lost. I myself received no news from my family during the whole time I spent in the Indies.

DORSAINVILLE: What power a friend's care has over a soul in despair! Your reasoning delights me; you are rekindling my hope.

CLERVAL: I will promote it. Let me conclude your business, then we will work together for the interest of your loved one. Your letters of pardon will be sent off tonight. A few formalities remain to be completed; the minister is still demanding that you not appear in public today. For additional security, spend this day in my apartment; let's not leave one another's side; I'll enjoy the pleasure of seeing you there. Suffer this constraint for my own peace of mind.

DORSAINVILLE: How sweet it is to be obligated to you! Ah, dear friend! The gratitude you inspire is not burdensome; it doesn't crush a delicate heart under the weight of kindnesses. It removes everything that the fear of importunity makes irksome. You will never create ingrates.

CLERVAL: Friend, I haven't seen Cenia today. As we have nothing left to say to one another, allow me to leave you.

DORSAINVILLE: Go then; if your attractive ladylove knows the value of your heart as I do, you are as happy as you deserve to be.

CLERVAL: Aren't you coming upstairs to my room?

DORSAINVILLE: Please don't mind if first I go to speak again with a person who might have more definite news of my wife. After this errand I'll be back to join you.

Exeunt.

ACT II

Enter Cenia and Orphise.

ORPHISE: What's the matter, Cenia? You just left your father with tears in your eyes. Might you have had the misfortune of displeasing him?

CENIA: No, my dear. Never has he shown me so much kindness. It is his tenderness that distresses me.

ORPHISE: How is that?

CENIA: He just declared to me that he wants to marry me off to Mericourt. He believes he is making me happy.

ORPHISE: Why wouldn't you be? Mericourt has wit and is courteous. That's as much as it takes to make him likable.

CENIA: However, I'm quite sure I'll never love him.

ORPHISE: There is perhaps a bit of prejudice in your aversion. That's a fault of judgment that reason will correct.

CENIA: No, madam. On the contrary, it seems to me that reason plays a large part in my repugnance. I'm sure that in my place you would think like me.

ORPHISE: My feelings are not involved.

CENIA: Forgive me, my dear. I take pleasure in valuing people whom you esteem. And surely my cousin isn't one of those.

ORPHISE: Why? If you judged him by his scornful manners with me, you might be mistaken. This is an annoyance linked to my station and not to his character.

CENIA: But, madam, if it is true that falsity is a contemptible vice, how can you esteem Mericourt?

ORPHISE: I barely know him. Confined within the limits of my duty, I haven't been around him sufficiently to get to know him. But even if he had the falsity you accuse him of, that is often the vice of society more than of the heart. Your sincerity will give him an appreciation of truth; you will reform him.

CENIA: If the misfortune I fear came to pass, I would take care not to reform him. Once his falsity was removed, he wouldn't have even the appearance of virtues left.

ORPHISE: At your age one doesn't make such profound reflections.

CENIA: Forgive me, madam, when a lively interest brings us to do so. For a long time I have foreseen my father's intentions. I thought I couldn't do enough to probe Mericourt's character. Alas! I have found nothing there that isn't opposed to my happiness.

ORPHISE: Happiness is not always where one believes one sees it, and virtue has a firm point of view. Follow virtue; obey your father. You'll find in yourself the reward for your sacrifice.

CENIA: What a reward! Madam, as you give me this advice, are you thinking of the horror of getting married to a man one cannot love?

ORPHISE: Alas! It is sometimes fortunate to have for one's husband only a moderate tenderness.

CENIA: I have formed a different idea about marriage. A husband who isn't beloved seems to me nothing but a formidable tyrant. Our virtues, duties, obligingness—nothing is of our choice. Everything becomes tyrannical; we bend beneath the yoke; our merit is only that of an obedient slave. But if we find in a husband the object of our true love, I think that the desire to please him makes virtuous acts easy; we perform them out of feeling. General esteem is the result of it; we acquire without violent distaste the only glory we are permitted to aspire to.

ORPHISE: Alas! Your error is quite natural. Experience alone can reveal to us the pains that are inseparable from too tender an affection. But this felicity whose image leads you astray depends too much on the life, the feelings, even on the good fortune of the beloved, for it to be lasting. Tenderness doubles our natural sensitivity; it multiplies the trifling pains whose repetition overwhelms us. The true misfortunes are those of the heart.[110]

CENIA: You are deeply moved. Ah, my dear, might you have experienced some of the woes which you seem imbued with?

ORPHISE: Pardon, my dear Cenia, if there escape from me any feelings which the state you are about to enter recalls to me. I fear them for you.

CENIA: You think I still don't deserve your confidence? Yet my heart would be worthy of it.

ORPHISE: Lovable child, share instead the sweetness you often make me feel. There are moments . . .[III] Let's change the subject: your age isn't that of sadness.

CENIA: I am so unhappy that I find sweetness in pitying the unfortunate.

ORPHISE: You distress me. I wish reason could make you imagine the lot that awaits you in a different light.

CENIA: I can't.

ORPHISE: With the brilliant fortune you were born to, could you have thought that you would be mistress of your choice?

CENIA: I flattered myself that I would.

ORPHISE: Might you have made a choice?

CENIA: Yes, my dear.

ORPHISE: What, Cenia, you have bestowed your heart?

CENIA: Spare me your reproaches. I need only advice.

ORPHISE: My advice will displease you. I pity you.

CENIA: What, madam! You would refuse to guide me at a time . . .

ORPHISE: I am far from abandoning you. Your sound natural character has thus far anticipated what my counsels might have inspired in you. It is from this moment that you need me, to help you bear with courage the sacrifice that you are going to make of your preference to virtue.

CENIA: Then is there only one way to be virtuous?

ORPHISE: There are unfortunate occasions when choice is not permitted us. In the situation you are in, all that remains for you is obedience.

CENIA: Well, madam, my father is good-hearted. Perhaps, if he were informed of my feelings, he would just as easily give me for a husband either one of his nephews.

ORPHISE: It's Clerval whom you love?

CENIA: Yes, madam. Do you condemn my choice? You esteem Clerval; you know whether he deserves to be loved. What a comparison!

ORPHISE: Is he informed of your feelings?

CENIA: No, madam; at least I haven't made a declaration to him.

ORPHISE: And what did you reply to your father?

CENIA: Alas! Nothing at all. Surprise and pain kept my mouth shut. Someone entered; I withdrew to hide my tears. I think, however, that my father noticed it.

ORPHISE: I'm not sorry about that.

CENIA: Then you don't condemn my intention to declare my feelings to him?

ORPHISE: I condemn it very strongly. To a well-born girl it is permitted at most to admit her repugnance, and never her fondness.

CENIA: Ah, Clerval, what will become of you?

ORPHISE: He's the one you pity?

CENIA: Yes, madam. I can contemplate my misfortune with courage, and I can't bear the idea of the one I am going to plunge him into.[112]

ORPHISE: That's just the confidence of your age. Experience will teach you that, in a man's heart, love itself consoles him for the unhappiness it causes.

CENIA: Well, madam, speak to him yourself. If you find in him the flightiness of which you think him capable, whatever aversion I feel for the match that is proposed for me, I will blindly obey. Here he is; I leave you with him.

Exit Cenia; enter Clerval.

ORPHISE: Stay a moment, sir. I have to speak to you on behalf of Cenia.

CLERVAL: She runs away from me. Grief is all over her face; yours seems to announce a misfortune to me. Speak, madam. O heaven! What are you going to tell me!

ORPHISE: That Cenia has confided to me your feelings for her; that you must stifle them.

CLERVAL: And it is she who instructed you to tell me so?

ORPHISE: Yes, sir.

CLERVAL: Cenia despises me enough that she won't deign to speak to me herself! Madam, forgive my distrust. I can't believe I'm as unfortunate as you say.

ORPHISE: Cenia is marrying your brother. There is the truth.

CLERVAL: My brother! Ah, madam, the more you add to my misfortune, the less plausible I find it.

ORPHISE: You apparently flattered yourself that you were beloved?

CLERVAL: No, madam, but I didn't think I had a rival.

ORPHISE: If you have one, he may not be beloved. It seems to me that Cenia is obeying her father, that she is following her duty.

CLERVAL: Ah! I breathe again. My uncle won't be inflexible.

ORPHISE: What, sir! You intend to take steps?

CLERVAL: Who would stop me? I don't owe anything to my brother.

ORPHISE: No, but you owe it to yourself not to sow disorder in your family in order to satisfy an amorous fancy that the first opportunity will transfer to another.

CLERVAL: I would despise myself if I had the feelings you accuse me of. No, madam, I have always regarded with horror the cowardice that authorizes us to break our word with women. Even if one doesn't believe in loving eternally, one must feel what power a tender esteem has over a virtuous heart. Cenia's budding charms introduced me to love; the development of her character made me hers forever. It is her heart, her soul that I adore; it is only to beauty that one becomes unfaithful.

ORPHISE: Nevertheless, you must give up Cenia. The more you love her, the more you must be careful of her reputation. The person who turns us away from our duties fails us in a more essential way than one who is unfaithful.

CLERVAL: Would I be failing Cenia by throwing myself at Dorimond's feet, by declaring to him my love for his daughter, by imploring his kindness?

ORPHISE: It would at the very least mean distressing the best of men and the tenderest benefactor. Beware, sir. Gratitude and ingratitude are not incompatible. All too often one combines the behavior of the one with the feelings of the other. What does it matter to Dorimond if deep down in your heart you feel the worth of his kindness, if you appear ungrateful by thwarting his plans, by distressing his soul, by depriving him of the sole satisfaction that remains to old age, that of disposing as he pleases of his wealth and of having his own way?

CLERVAL: Ah, madam! What weapons you employ to combat my love! They are the only ones that could impose on me a silence which will result in my death.

ORPHISE: The integrity of your feelings touches me, sir. I have some influence over your uncle's decisions. I will not abuse his confidence; I will only try . . .

CLERVAL: You are restoring my life. Yes, madam, speak to Dorimond, deal gently with his heart and his kindness. I am counting on yours; don't abandon me.

ORPHISE: I am not committing myself to anything in regard to your love. I promise you only to probe your uncle's true feelings, to determine whether he has fixed his resolve. Then you will see how you must behave.

Enter Dorimond and Lisette.

LISETTE (*to Dorimond*): There he is, sir. I just knew he had to be here.

DORIMOND: I am looking for you, Clerval, to tell you that I am very dissatisfied with you.

CLERVAL: In what way, sir, might I have had the misfortune to dissatisfy you?

DORIMOND: In that my house isn't made for harboring schemers whose protector I never would have suspected you of being.

CLERVAL: Sir, I understand whom you are referring to. Such a calumny makes me shudder.

DORIMOND: Will you deny that there comes to my home an unknown man with whom as late as this morning you had a mysterious conversation?

CLERVAL: No, sir, but shortly I will reveal to you the identity of the most honorable of men and the most unfortunate of friends.

LISETTE (*aside*): All is lost. Friends, misfortunes: we can't hold our ground against all that.

DORIMOND (*to Clerval*): A friend whom one dares not acknowledge is always suspect. I know some things on that score.

CLERVAL: Someone is deceiving you, sir. If I were allowed to speak, I would easily destroy these hateful suspicions.

DORIMOND: I can't bring myself to believe you. So much mystery isn't used for honorable purposes.

CLERVAL: Well, uncle, the secret of this unfortunate man is to be publicly revealed tomorrow. In the meantime, if you want to grant me a moment's private interview, I will make known to you the error into which you have been induced, by recalling to you the name and fatal adventure of a man whose misfortune you have pitied more than once.

DORIMOND: I'll be obliged to you. Destroying a suspicion is a considerable gain. In a moment we'll move into my study. I also have to speak to you about a marriage that's very suitable for you.

CLERVAL: For me, sir?

DORIMOND: Yes, for you. It's Clarice I intend for you. She is a person of worth. You know her?

CLERVAL: I implore you, sir . . .

DORIMOND: What! Is this another refusal? I am beginning to get tired of meeting with them. I'm not surprised that the world is filled with wicked people. The inclination toward evil is always sure of success. One can make people unhappy even without knowing them; but, however great one's desire, it isn't as easy as one might think to make people happy. It's disheartening, and one gets hardened from lack of success.

LISETTE: Come, sir, don't get angry. Your nephew is not capable of disobeying you; and if you ever so slightly show him that you are firmly resolved, he will comply.

DORIMOND: Everyone, even my daughter . . . *(to Orphise)* Madam, I am sorry to be obliged to lay blame on you. I esteem you, and I thought you to be above these petty women's intrigues that constantly disrupt the tranquility of families.

ORPHISE: Is this speech addressed to me, sir?

DORIMOND: To yourself, I repeat. I am sorry to lose the high opinion I had of you, but I am not unaware of the advice you are giving to Cenia.

ORPHISE: If you know it, sir, it constitutes my justification. I have nothing to reply.

DORIMOND: Don't speak to me in that tone of voice. I myself saw on her face the impression of disgust that you are producing in her for people I like. I haven't had the time for a full explanation with her, but . . . In short, madam, for the brief time she will be needing you, I beg you not to meddle any further in our business.

CLERVAL: What a setback! O heaven!

ORPHISE: I must obey you, sir; you will be satisfied.

DORIMOND: All right, Clerval, I'm ready to hear you. Come give me the pleasure of justifying you.

Exeunt Dorimond and Clerval.

LISETTE: I can't get over my surprise caused by Dorimond's bad mood! At least, madam, I have no part in it.

ORPHISE: You came in with him; you might know the cause.

LISETTE: Me! Not at all. The master was looking for Clerval; I knew he was here; I brought him here without saying a word. You suspect me, I can see it. That is excusable after the little humiliation you have just been given.

ORPHISE: If I loved Cenia less, I would hardly be affected . . .

LISETTE: Yes, madam, you love her, and very much, as we know. But permit me to tell you that you don't love her wisely. Why prevent her from obeying her father?

ORPHISE: If I did prevent her, it would be because I had reasons for it, and I wouldn't conceal them. I am urging her to obedience, but not without disapproving Dorimond's choice deep down.

LISETTE: Might one learn what you don't like about Mericourt?

ORPHISE: His age. Although he is still relatively young, he is much older than Cenia, which ought to be an insuperable obstacle.

LISETTE: If you understood your charge's real interest, that is precisely what would make you favor him, and Mericourt would even seem too young for you. I have some knowledge of the world. A young person, upon marrying an elderly man, becomes an attractive woman. If only her behavior is correct, people pity her and admire her, she acquires merit, her charms gain in beauty from her husband's decrepit condition. He dies: even at age forty, she's considered a young widow. An old man's decay perpetuates our youth. But you aren't listening to me? Your servant.

Exit.

ORPHISE (*alone*): Then it's to crown my abasement that Dorimond is becoming unjust? Alas! I was destined to know ill-usage! Fitting result of the station ill fortune has reduced me to . . . Pardon, Dorsainville. To conserve the life of a spouse whom you hold dear, I had no recourse but to choose among the vilest of conditions. You won't blush for it; I saved your name and mine from disgrace . . . Hapless husband! Did you have to abandon me? . . . Whatever desert serves as your refuge, it's a place of honor. Shame, that tyrant of noble souls, dwells only with men. Let us flee them . . . But the more they move me away from Cenia, the more my counsels are necessary to her. Without offending Dorimond, let us give his daughter what her confidence and my affection require from me. One isn't completely wretched when good deeds remain to be done.

Exit.

ACT III

Enter Dorimond and Mericourt.

DORIMOND: I am at least as annoyed as you, but we mustn't think any more about it.

MERICOURT: I submit without complaining, sir. Am I at least allowed to ask you the grounds for Cenia's refusal? Is it hatred? Is it contempt for me?

DORIMOND: It's neither one. She didn't say a single word to me against you.

MERICOURT: You want to break the bad news gently, sir. Your kindness is visible throughout.

DORIMOND: There's no kindness in this; it's the pure truth. Cenia demonstrated only a general aversion to permanent union, which frightens her.

MERICOURT: And this aversion is undoubtedly quite natural?

DORIMOND: Ah! Don't doubt it.

MERICOURT: Cenia couldn't have a secret love?

DORIMOND: I would like her to be in love; she could only have made a good choice, and soon . . . Would you know anything about it?

MERICOURT: Take care not to think so, sir. Cenia is too well bred to have made a choice without your permission, and too artless to have had the skill of concealing a passion. You would have noticed it.

DORIMOND: I? Not at all. I would be just as easy to deceive on this score as on many others. I couldn't possibly bring myself to be cunning. Guile can hardly operate without wickedness. Be that as it may, I have given my word, and I will keep it. You can't possibly push indulgence too far when it is a question of eternal union. Perhaps at some later date Cenia will form other ideas; then I will propose your brother's name to her.

MERICOURT: My brother!

DORIMOND: He is young; he can wait.

MERICOURT: My brother! . . . I can't get over it.

DORIMOND: You amaze me. Since you can't be my son-in-law, you ought to be delighted to see me consider Clerval.

MERICOURT: I would be, if self-interest had any power over me; but I recognize only your interest, and assuredly Clerval . . .

DORIMOND: Listen. You must know that it greatly displeases me to hear bad things spoken of him. You had already given me warnings this morning, and he has fully cleared himself.

MERICOURT: I may have been mistaken, sir; it's the result of a too enthusiastic loyalty. I am overjoyed to learn that Clerval has left no dark suspicions about his behavior.

DORIMOND: That being the case, you ought to have the same reaction to the good fortune I am planning for him.

MERICOURT: The tender Melissa foresaw it. The regrets that she took with her to the grave were all too well-founded.

DORIMOND: How's that? If she spoke explicitly about her daughter's settlement, why keep it a secret from me?

MERICOURT: Am I to believe, sir, that you are unaware of her intentions, and that, if she had chosen a husband for her daughter, it wasn't in agreement with you?

DORIMOND: It is true that we had a number of conversations dealing with Cenia's settlement. That virtuous woman, out of delicacy of feeling, had resolved to give her only to one of you two; but I always found her uncertain when it came to choosing between you. If you know more about it, you are wrong to hide it from me.

MERICOURT: It is rare that a dying person doesn't give specific instructions on family arrangements.

DORIMOND: Well then, speak.

MERICOURT: No, sir. Given the state things are in, you might suspect . . .

DORIMOND: I see. So it's in your favor that she declared?

MERICOURT: Yes, sir. Melissa, as she reached the end of her life, called me near her bed. "Mericourt," she said to me in a very faint voice, "in a moment I shall be no more. Listen to my last thoughts. I adored my husband; I owe my happiness to him. You love him; be the heir of my tender feelings for him; become my daughter's husband; be Dorimond's son; be answerable to me for keeping his days peaceful; prolong their duration, and I will lose my own without regret."

DORIMOND: Stop, my dear nephew, I can't bear . . . Alas! What wouldn't I give for Cenia to . . .

MERICOURT: She is unaware of her mother's dying wishes. If you allowed me, sir, to speak privately with her?

DORIMOND: Gladly. Stay here, I'll send her to you. Remember that you will be doing me the greatest service if you can obtain her consent.

MERICOURT: I will spare no effort.

DORIMOND: However, I forbid you to intimidate her by raising the fear of displeasing me. Let us obtain everything through tenderness, and nothing through authority.

Exit.

MERICOURT (*alone*): The decisive moment has arrived. I fling aside all restraint. I foresee that Cenia's obstinacy will force me to use against her the weapons that Melissa left me. They might be cruelly turned against *me;* but can an immense fortune be acquired at too high a price?[113]

Enter Cenia.

CENIA: I had been told that my father was asking for me.

MERICOURT: Stop, Cenia; it is by his order that I await you here. Dorimond, sensitive to the scorn you are heaping upon me, is permitting me to try once again to surmount it.

CENIA: Does it mean despising you, sir, if I spare a scrupulous person like you the pain of having made someone unhappy?

MERICOURT: You are defying me, ingrate; you triumph. You believe that Dorimond's excessively obliging nature leaves you nothing more to fear. If you only knew to what excess I am pushing generosity with respect to you, this haughty sarcasm would quickly change its tone.

CENIA: I do not know, sir, the obligations I have to you. If you wished to inform me of them . . .

MERICOURT: You will learn them all too soon. You will perhaps repent in a moment of having forced me to tell you.

CENIA: You would make me tremble, if I had anything to reproach myself for.

MERICOURT: Cenia, heed my advice: consent to give me your hand. Your own interest brings me to beg you on my knees to do so. Time is running out; do not take advantage of my weakness. Speak, there is no more time for hesitation.

CENIA: I am not hesitating, sir.

MERICOURT: What is your decision?

CENIA: To break off a conversation equally distressing for both of us.

MERICOURT (*seizing her by the arm*): No, no, this moment must decide your destiny.

CENIA: What! You are bold enough . . . Mericourt, don't count so much on my father's good nature; he will deign to hear me out.

MERICOURT: No, you shall not leave; I must have a decisive answer.

CENIA: You want one? Here it is: my father gave me his word that he wouldn't force me into marriage. Nothing can make me change my resolution.

MERICOURT: Ah! You are going too far. It is time to confound so much contempt. Do you know this handwriting?

CENIA: Yes, it is my mother's.

MERICOURT: The letter is for Dorimond, but what does it matter? Listen. (*reads*) "I have deceived you, sir, and my remorse cannot be buried with me. The huge difference in our ages made me fear that I might fall back into the dire poverty from which you had rescued me. In order to assure my fortune, I claimed to have produced a child. Your last voyage made it easy for me to arrange to pass off Cenia as my daughter. Death forces me to reveal my secret. Forgive . . ."

CENIA (*falls in a faint*): I am dying!

MERICOURT: Cenia, listen to me. Learn at least in this moment how excessively I love you. There is still time. I offer you my hand; I repair the shame of your birth; I forever lock up your secret within the bonds of our marriage. Isn't that proof that I love you?

CENIA: What would I gain by deceiving everybody? Could I deceive myself? Show me that letter. (*after reading it*) My misfortune is only too certain.

MERICOURT (*takes back the letter*): Well! What are your thoughts now?

CENIA: The same.

MERICOURT: What pride! Is it for you to resist when my love surmounts the obstacles, when I ought to blush?

CENIA: You should blush, but for the imposture to which you wouldn't be ashamed to make me a party. Me, deceive the best of men! Me, usurp a family fortune! You horrify me.

MERICOURT: It is a sign of love for Dorimond to keep him in error. Melissa, by confiding your secret to me, wanted to make you happy and to restore my uncle's wealth to its legitimate possessor.

CENIA: Does one rectify a crime through another one? Each moment here makes me an accomplice in all these wicked deeds. I cannot soon enough . . .

MERICOURT: Stop. I guess your intention; you wish to destroy me. Beware of following the impulse of your hatred.

CENIA: I will follow only my duty.

MERICOURT: No, no, I know better than you think the cause of your disdain. It is not so much honor as love that guides you. You think that Clerval . . . You must give him up. Even if he were cowardly enough . . . I have weapons left . . . Keep your secret; that's the last advice I give you. I leave you to think it over. Don't push my vengeance any further, or else tremble to learn still more.

Exit.

CENIA: What can happen to me? . . . O heaven! What do I see?

Enter Clerval.

CLERVAL: Cenia, you are crying! My dear Cenia, what's the matter?

CENIA: Clerval, I am lost.

CLERVAL: My brother has just left you. Did he obtain from Dorimond . . .

CENIA: Forget me. There is no other happiness left for you.

CLERVAL: What! My brother! I'll run to Dorimond and throw myself at his feet; he will see my despair and will be touched by it.

CENIA: Ah! Take care not to speak to him.

CLERVAL: It is you, Cenia, who hold me back! I had flattered myself at least that you didn't hate me. You would have had no aversion to seeing me become your husband; you told me so!

CENIA: I was worthy of it then . . . I no longer am.

CLERVAL: You no longer are! Then you love my brother?

CENIA: Me! I could love Mericourt! You make me shudder.

CLERVAL: Well, if you don't love him, tell me that you love me. Reassure my distracted heart; let me vie with Mericourt for my uncle's kindness.

CENIA: My fate no longer depends on Dorimond.

CLERVAL: You are driving me to despair. What is this obscure language? Let me know at least the cause of my ill fortune!

CENIA: It lies in me alone; it lies in my horrible destiny. Don't force me to blush in your sight.

CLERVAL: You fear to blush? Ah! You are betraying me.[114]

CENIA: If you only knew . . . Clerval, believe me. I am not guilty . . . Farewell.

CLERVAL: Cenia, what are you going to do? If pity still has any power over your heart, clear up my fate. Let me learn it from your mouth.

CENIA: You yourself, take pity on me. See my grief, my confusion. Alas! I dare not raise my eyes to you.

CLERVAL: In the name of the tenderest love, free me from the torment I am suffering. Speak.

CENIA: No, I will not pronounce the cruel decree that separates us.

CLERVAL: You are pronouncing the decree of my death. Beware of abandoning me to my despair. I no longer answer for my life.

CENIA: What a horrible threat for a heart that would want to live only for you!

CLERVAL: You love me, Cenia; I have nothing more to fear. This admission suffices for me. Cruel one! Why postpone my happiness so long? Did you doubt my love? Ah! Judge of it by the excess of my joy.

CENIA: That's what I was most afraid of. This fatal admission crowns your woes. Clerval, remember that you forced it out of me.

Enter Dorsainville.

DORSAINVILLE: Friend, share my great joy: my wife isn't dead, and I can hope . . . What do I see? . . . I am acting rashly.

CENIA *(to Dorsainville):* Sir, you couldn't come at a more suitable time. I think I recognize in you that friend of Clerval's whose misfortunes he has recounted to me. They touched me; they ought to make you sympathetic to those of others. Don't leave your friend's side. In a moment . . . I leave you. Farewell, my dear Clerval; don't follow me.

Exit.

DORSAINVILLE: Dear friend, forgive my indiscretion. I feel nothing but your sorrow now. What is the misfortune Cenia is threatening you with?

CLERVAL: I don't know. She wants to spare herself the pain of announcing it to me. Alas! It would be far less cruel for me to learn it from her mouth. If I had to lose her! . . . No, I cannot remain in the cruel uncertainty I am in.

DORSAINVILLE: I am not leaving your side.

CLERVAL: Leave me, dear friend; I must clear up this horrible mystery. Cenia has forbidden me to follow her. I'll avoid meeting her, but someone else may be able to inform me. Friend, don't hold me back. Go wait for me, I implore you; perhaps I will need you.

Exeunt.

ACT IV
Enter Cenia and Orphise.

ORPHISE: Yes, I was waiting for you. Come, courageous Cenia, come enjoy in my arms the victory you are achieving over yourself.

CENIA: I have dealt a death blow to Dorimond. The generous old man won't survive it.

ORPHISE: By bearing witness to the truth, you make your innocence forever illustrious. Glory is the reward of virtue.

CENIA: What a glory! How humiliating it is! Ah, madam, how unhappy I am!

ORPHISE: It is at times of direst misfortune that you must revive your courage. Often lamenting softens it.

CENIA: What! Would lamenting be forbidden me when heaven snatches from me what it grants to the vilest of mortals? I will no longer pronounce the tender names of father and mother. I feel the confidence they inspire being destroyed in my heart. No more support, no more defender, no more guide for my will! My independence terrifies me; I have nothing more to hold on to, and nothing is dependent on me. Madam, will you abandon me?

ORPHISE: No, my dear Cenia. You are losing a lot, but one heart remains to you. If my life is necessary to you, it will become worthwhile to me.

CENIA: What don't I owe you? What generosity!

ORPHISE: Ah! Say rather, what a happiness for Orphise!

CENIA: Madam, you will then have pity on me?

ORPHISE: My dear Cenia, my tender compassion can find no further expression except through my tears.

CENIA: They are very dear to me; they banish from my heart the fear that had overcome it. Please protect me, lead me, be a mother to me, and may my services to you erase the shame of those you have given to me.

ORPHISE: You, serve me, Cenia! Beware of losing your

self-esteem; discouragement is the poison of virtue. Who knows who your real parents are?

CENIA: Why, madam, what sort of parents could be those of an unhappy girl whom they didn't deign to acknowledge, whom they renounced out of vile interest? What more convincing proof of my obscurity? On what foundation could I flatter myself . . .

ORPHISE: On the loftiness of your soul, on the nobility of your heart, on your feelings . . .

CENIA: They are exactly as you produced them: I am merely your handiwork. What soul, what heart would your care and your advice not have elevated? I owe you everything, and I am no longer anything.

ORPHISE: I have lost everything, my dear Cenia; you will be everything for me. But will Dorimond be able to bring himself to abandon you?

CENIA: What, madam! If his kindness extended to wishing to keep me in his house, do you think I could stay there? Could I face Mericourt without horror? Can anyone's courage withstand the humiliating looks of the servants, the insulting pity of society people? My fatal adventure would become the gossip of the day, and I would be the object of the public's curiosity. I hardly dare to raise my eyes to myself. This splendor which is no longer suitable to me fills me with horror. Let us flee, madam; may the darkest shelter bury forever the memory of what I thought I was.

Enter Dorimond.

DORIMOND: You are abandoning me to my grief, my dear Cenia! Come reassure me against the imposture. You are my daughter; I feel it in my tenderness for you.

CENIA: Alas, sir, it is only too true that I have lost the best of fathers!

DORIMOND: Your tears have overcome me; your grief has troubled my judgment. Reflection is enlightening me. Such a crime is simply not within the realm of belief. You are being deceived, my dear child; or else you yourself, deluded . . .

CENIA: Sir, I saw, I read the fatal truth written in Melissa's hand.

DORIMOND: The perfidious creature! To betray me so cruelly, me who adored her! No, I can't believe it. Who would be the accomplices in this horrible deception?

CENIA: Mericourt will be able to inform you. I already told you that he was the guardian of the secret.

DORIMOND: Mericourt! Is it possible! . . . I am having him called. He doesn't appear! No doubt he fears my presence. Ah, Cenia, did you have to reveal this deadly secret to me?

CENIA: Could I keep it? Could I deceive you?

DORIMOND: But you are taking away my life. If I lose you, everything is lost for me.

CENIA: Ah, sir, your kindness crowns my woes. From now on see in me only an unhappy victim of ambition. I am no longer worthy of your tenderness; grant me only pity. Do not make me hateful to myself by making me feel responsible for the horrid misfortune of your death.

DORIMOND: Is it you I am complaining about, my dear child? Be my daughter always, and my life is secure. Mericourt doesn't come! How this delay adds to my impatience! O heaven! Here he is. My senses are disturbed at the sight of him. (*to Cenia*) Don't leave. (*to Orphise*) Madam, stay. Heaven! What is he going to say?

Enter Mericourt.

DORIMOND: Approach. Come destroy, if possible, the suspicion of a heinous crime to which I am unable to believe you're the accomplice.

MERICOURT: Me, sir!

DORIMOND: What about this alleged letter from Melissa which would make you just as guilty as she is? If you are able to justify yourself, don't delay.

MERICOURT: In order to justify myself, I would have to know

what I am accused of.

DORIMOND: I've told you, there is talk of a letter from Melissa that contains an odious mystery. If you have any proofs to the contrary, don't hesitate to bring them to light.

MERICOURT: Who could be bold enough to bring all the way to you . . .

CENIA: I, sir. Truth will always be my law.

DORIMOND: So see what you have to counter this accusation. Speak.

MERICOURT: Yes, I will speak. I cannot punish too soon the ungrateful girl who wants to bring about your death. Learn then that she is not your daughter. Melissa, urged on by her remorse, gives authentic evidence of the truth in this letter.

DORIMOND (after reading to himself): What have I read? Can it be that so many horrors . . . Cruel Melissa! What had I done to you that you should cast me into error, or undeceive me? My death will be the price of your evil deeds.

MERICOURT: She feared to lose your affection.

DORIMOND: With what perfidy, by showering me with caresses, she was arousing in me a fatherly love that, alas, was too well-founded! . . . My heart is torn asunder at this cruel memory.

CENIA: Sir, calm your grief.

DORIMOND: And you, wretch, who have been keeping this deadly secret from me for six months, what reasons led you to do it?

MERICOURT: Revealing to you this sad truth meant—-I foresaw it—dealing you a fatal blow. Rather than bring myself to do so, you see what lengths I have gone to. I was prepared to marry an unknown girl, unacknowledged, without parents. What would I not have sacrified to conserve for you an error that was dear to you!

DORIMOND: So, then why undeceive me? Why make use of these cruel weapons to ruin Cenia or else force her into a marriage she abhors? Mericourt, your heart is revealed . . . Enough said. You won't enjoy the reward of your treachery. Cenia, I adopt you.

MERICOURT: What do I hear?

CENIA: Me! I would still be your daughter! . . . Sir . . . Ah, reduce your kindness; I am unworthy of that honor.

DORIMOND: You are worthy of my heart, you are worthy of my tenderness! My dear child, return to your rightful place.

CENIA: No, sir, your reputation is dearer to me than my happiness. Allow a convent to bury with me my ignorance of the unfortunate pair to whom I owe my life.

DORIMOND: Your parents are unfortunate people—well, they are only the more respectable for that. Let our sorrows disappear. *(to Orphise)* Madam, all of this opens my eyes to the accusations of misconduct made against you. Stay with us, take up again your position with my daughter.

CENIA: Sir . . .

DORIMOND: I'm not listening to you any further. I give you my name, my wealth, and more than all that, the love of a tender father.

CENIA: I throw myself at your feet.

MERICOURT: Wait a moment to express your gratitude. Sir, you would have just grounds to reproach me if I delayed any longer in revealing to you the worthy object of your adoption. This letter is for the young lady, but you can read it.

DORIMOND *(reading):* "It is not without pity that I reveal your birth to you, but I have arrived at the moment of truth. Your mother believes you to be dead, and her error still guaranteed my secret. You can tell her. Informed of the extreme poverty to which she was reduced, I took her out of it in order to serve you as governess. It is in her hands that I put you back."

CENIA *(in her mother's arms)*: You are my mother! My misfortunes are over!

ORPHISE: My dear daughter! What, it's you I embrace!

CENIA: My mother! How sweet that name is to me!

ORPHISE: Too unfortunate child! Alas, how you are to be pitied!

CENIA: I owe my birth to the soul of virtue. My destiny is fine enough.

DORIMOND: That's the last blow that the treacherous man was reserving for me. A fatal shock . . . *(to Cenia)* Too lovable child! . . . I can't speak . . . I feel faint . . .

CENIA *(running to Dorimond):* Ah, sir . . .

MERICOURT: Leave him alone. Your attentions can be dispensed with. You are nothing here any more.

Exeunt Dorimond and Mericourt.

CENIA: Mother, have pity on me. My courage is failing me. I am unable to withstand contempt.

ORPHISE: Summon your courage, my dear daughter.

CENIA: How I love you! I shouldn't feel anything but my tenderness. Ah, don't judge of my heart in this dreadful moment. Joy, sorrow and indignation are agitating it with such violence . . .

ORPHISE: These extremes of feeling are natural, my dear child. You have seen happiness; it has disappeared. Yet don't despair. Perhaps one day heaven, less rigorous . . .

CENIA: Ah, I regret nothing. Your kindness will take the place of everything to me. But let us leave this house, where I now breathe nothing but shame and contempt.

ORPHISE: Let us go off to seek a haven where we can be unfortunate without having to blush.

CENIA: Mother, may my respect, my tenderness, my submission take the place of what you have lost! I dare not recall to you the memory of my father.

ORPHISE: This is not the time to speak of that, my dear Cenia; the firmest soul is sometimes not strong enough to withstand so many calamities at once. One day you will learn with what courage your father sacrificed fortune to honor. What a father! What a husband!

CENIA: What do I see? It's Clerval! Ah, allow me to flee his presence.

Exit Cenia; enter Clerval.

CLERVAL: Ah, madam! I find you at just the right moment! My uncle has ordered me to look for Mericourt. In vain have I gone through the houses he normally frequents; I haven't found him. I don't know what has happened. Has he shed light on Cenia's fate? Speak.

ORPHISE: Yes, sir, her misfortune is confirmed.

CLERVAL: Ah heavens! Madam, don't hide anything from me. What course is she planning to take?

ORPHISE: That of a convent. There is no other choice for her.

CLERVAL: Well then! Yes, madam, a convent is a respectable haven for her. But won't you have the kindness to accompany her there?

ORPHISE: Could you doubt it?

CLERVAL: I know the goodness of your heart. Well! So you will follow her. But in this moment of distress, you cannot take the necessary care for this change of residence; allow me to offer my services . . . I am taking charge of everything; I will prepare everything.

ORPHISE: Stop, sir. So much eagerness to serve unfortunate people would honor the humanity in you, if it were fully devoid of self-interest. But you love Cenia. In the situation she finds herself in, your attentions from now on could only be insulting for her.

CLERVAL: Ah, madam! What are you daring to say! Yes, I adore her, and the convent where I am imploring you to accompany her ought to be a sure guarantee of my intentions. You will be a mother to her. Obedient to both your wills, I will see her only as much as you will approve. And if that isn't enough, I promise not to see her except when I offer her my hand.

ORPHISE: You, marry Cenia! Can you be serious, sir?

CLERVAL: Yes, madam. I know all the opposing arguments you could find; but all these groundless fancies adopted by men vanish from my sight as soon as they are set in comparison with virtue.[115]

ORPHISE: This generosity doesn't suffice for a man like you. He must respect himself in the choice of a partner. If Cenia's birth were found to be so lowly that it made you blush . . .

CLERVAL: No, madam, men become vile only through their own baseness. Time will teach you . . .

ORPHISE: I admire the skill with which the passions transform their desires into virtues. An excessive enthusiasm is often the quickest to contradict itself. A newly arrived misfortune kindles the imagination: heroism takes over the mind; we want to do everything in our power for the unfortunates. Little by little we get used to seeing them, we grow cold and we become like other men.

CLERVAL: Ah, madam! As you overwhelm me with grief, do not overwhelm me with contempt. I will never have any wife but Cenia; take my word of honor on it.

ORPHISE: I accept it, sir . . . Cenia is my daughter.

CLERVAL: You're her mother! All my wishes are fulfilled.

ORPHISE: No, sir. Recognize the effect of your blind passion. Let this serve as a lesson to you. I release you from your word.

CLERVAL: And as for me, I confirm it by all that is most sacred and honorable. Madam, grant me your confidence upon the paltry services I can do for you, and give me time to deserve your esteem.

ORPHISE: I honor you, sir, and I am going to give you a proof of it. The dreadful circumstance I find myself in prompts me to trust myself to your care. I accept for these first few moments the services you offer me. Seek out a convent for us; give me a guide to lead us there. Decorum does not permit you to accompany us there. Go now; I will prepare everything for my departure, and take my leave of Dorimond.

CLERVAL: And as for me, I run to carry out your orders, and I'll be back to notify you.

Exeunt.

ACT V

Enter Clerval and Dorsainville.

DORSAINVILLE: Rely on me, I'll take care of everything.

CLERVAL: Don't present them as unfortunates. Ill fortune isn't always a good recommendation.

DORSAINVILLE: I know what I have to say.

CLERVAL: Let them be well-treated. If their allowance isn't sufficient, it will be doubled.

DORSAINVILLE: You've told me all that.

CLERVAL: Urge especially that you be notified if Cenia experiences the slightest inconvenience.

DORSAINVILLE: I won't fail to do so.

CLERVAL: Make them feel that these are women of great worth. It is only by showing great consideration for them that you can make others do the same.

DORSAINVILLE: I won't forget anything.

CLERVAL: How distressing it is, in certain circumstances, not to be able to act oneself!

DORSAINVILLE: What! Do you doubt my zeal?

CLERVAL: No, dear friend. But you don't know the two persons who most deserve to have a lively interest taken in them.

DORSAINVILLE: You love them; that is enough for me.

CLERVAL: One must serve the unfortunate with so much circumspection, regard and respect!

DORSAINVILLE: Who better than I knows how to treat them gently?

CLERVAL: That's true; but a man of courage acquires a certain hardness for himself, which he might extend to others without even noticing it. There are a thousand little attentions that one can't neglect without hurting the feelings of those who have the right to expect them.

DORSAINVILLE: I won't fail in anything; I give you my word.

CLERVAL: What objection would there be if I accompanied you at this first interview? I would speak warmly. It's the first moment that's decisive. It is important . . .

DORSAINVILLE: Not to say too much. Far from serving them, your age and tone of voice might produce a bad effect. I fear already that your arrangements might harm their reputation.

CLERVAL: How?

DORSAINVILLE: By an ostentation that seems to me out of place. It is quite unlikely that word of their story won't leak out. What do you want people to think of what you are doing for them?

CLERVAL: That is not my business any more. At present I am merely carrying out my uncle's orders.

DORSAINVILLE: What does that matter? It would have been more prudent to place them from the start in a manner befitting their station.

CLERVAL: Their station! Ah! Take care not to believe that it corresponds to appearances!

DORSAINVILLE: Do you have any solid information on that matter?

CLERVAL: None is needed. Everything about them speaks and announces who they are.

DORSAINVILLE: I believe that the mother and the daughter have a thousand good qualities, but still these aren't proofs of nobility.

CLERVAL: For a long time I have suspected that Orphise is hiding her real identity. Everything I see confirms my theory: the respect I show her doesn't surprise her. She finds it natural to be addressed in the tone of voice I use with her; she doubtless guesses what I think of her, and yet she doesn't contradict me.

DORSAINVILLE: She granted you the affirmative. There aren't many people of that sort who don't have a prearranged story about the misfortunes that reduced them to servitude.

CLERVAL: Friend, in seeking to degrade a person I like, do you realize . . .

DORSAINVILLE: I'm in the wrong. Forgive my zeal that takes perhaps too many precautions. I fear that, carried away by your passion . . .

CLERVAL: I understand you; you fear I'll marry Cenia? Well, know that my mind is made up, that nothing can make me change it, that she will be my wife as soon as her mother consents.

DORSAINVILLE: Although what I say offends you, to keep silent would be to betray you.

CLERVAL: That's just what I foresaw! Since you don't have the same ideas as I do about the mother and the daughter, your care of them will lack respect, your politeness will be humiliating. O heaven! If you let escape . . .

DORSAINVILLE: Ah! Stop wronging me. I am not barbarous enough to humiliate unfortunate people. I respect those whom you love; but I am not cowardly enough not to dare fight against a love that is leading you astray.

CLERVAL: All right. You'll fight against it. But for the present don't abuse my need for your friendship; and especially don't let Cenia notice your feelings. Keep your zeal from showing. Dorimond is coming here; your presence would be unwelcome to him. Don't go very far, I implore you.

Exit Dorsainville; enter Dorimond.

DORIMOND: Clerval, she's preparing to leave! Save me, for pity's sake, from farewells which I couldn't bear. You see an unhappy old man reduced to despair!

CLERVAL: Why give way to despair, sir? Don't you have the power to keep Cenia? Who is preventing you?

DORIMOND: Her refusals, which I couldn't overcome; propriety, compassion for her and for myself.

CLERVAL: If you wanted, sir . . .

DORIMOND: No, it would be barbarous to force her to stay in a house where everything would remind her of her misfortune.

CLERVAL: Why, sir, isn't there a method to bind her to you with ties so sacred that never . . .

DORIMOND: That's what I thought at first; but by adopting Cenia I would be depriving you of my fortune. That would be an injustice that I shall never be guilty of.

CLERVAL: Why, sir, what does your fortune matter to me? Dispose of it as you like, I renounce it. I'll sign that pledge with my blood.

DORIMOND: Your selflessness cannot be an excuse for me. If I yielded to your desires, your generosity would degenerate into folly, and my obligingness into weakness . . . I will shield Cenia and her mother from the blows of fortune. You will give this wallet to Orphise; this is to cover her until I arrange for the rest. I also intend that Cenia should find in her convent not just the necessary things in abundance, but also pure amenities. I must in every way try to alleviate her misfortune.

CLERVAL: Uncle, complete your project; set no limit to your kindness.

DORIMOND: It is on you, my dear nephew, that I must now lavish it. I want to make amends for my behavior to you and create a lasting happiness for you.

CLERVAL: Yes, sir, that depends on you. With a single word you can crown all the wishes of my heart.

DORIMOND: If you love me, why don't you speak?

CLERVAL: Sir . . . (aside) How disconcerted I am! . . . (aloud) I dare not pronounce.

DORIMOND: Your embarrassment half reveals your secret. Finish it, name my niece to me.

CLERVAL: Cenia.

DORIMOND: Cenia!

CLERVAL: Yes, I cannot live without adoring her. You love her, you fear to lose her. Restore her station to her, make her virtue illustrious, and may our felicity prolong the length of our lives.

DORIMOND: It is with sadness that I learn of your passion, though I can't condemn it. Cenia is only too worthy to be loved; but she can't be your wife.

CLERVAL: What invincible obstacle . . .

DORIMOND: Her birth.

CLERVAL: You wished to adopt her?

DORIMOND: I think I told you that. When I had this thought, the deadly secret was only half revealed. Her unknown parents couldn't bring disgrace to my family. But her mother . . .

CLERVAL: Orphise was not born to the rank she now occupies, sir. Ill fortune has surely reduced her to the lowly position with which you reproach her.

DORIMOND: Come now, my dear nephew, you're fooling yourself. If she were of high birth, she would no longer make a secret of it. Humiliation is the most painful affliction. No one endures it when he can avoid it.

CLERVAL: Perhaps her original rank was so elevated that modesty itself obliges her to conceal it.

DORIMOND: All right, to prove to you how much I desire your happiness, see, try to find confirmation for your hunches. Alas! I desire even more than you what I cannot hope for.

CLERVAL: I go at once; but here she is.

Enter Cenia and Orphise.

CENIA: It is to your feet, sir, that I come to thank you for so many deeds of kindness. I will never forget that I once had the honor of being your daughter; you will not blush to have been my father.

DORIMOND: I feel torn apart by separating from you, and I am no less to be pitied.

CLERVAL (*who has whispered to Orphise*): No, madam, you are not what you wish to appear; say one word, you guarantee my happiness.

ORPHISE: If it depended on me, sir . . .

CLERVAL: It does. Confide the secret of your birth to my uncle. Do you doubt his discretion? Do you doubt his prudence? Ah, madam, speak.

ORPHISE: Courage and silence are the nobility of the unfortunate. Do not begrudge me the only glory I have left.

CLERVAL: Sir, is this the way the common people express themselves? Are there any titles more noble than lofty feelings?

DORIMOND: Madam, since you wish it, I will make no effort to drag your secret from you. But how does it happen that your daughter was snatched from you, and yet no suspicion impelled you to make inquiries which would have saved both of us a great deal of trouble?

ORPHISE: The deadliest circumstances presided over the birth of this unfortunate girl. In that dreadful moment she was removed from my sight. Death was only one step away from me; heaven in its anger restored me to life, but didn't restore my daughter to me. They announced her death to me. What reasons could have impelled me to cast suspicions on so common a mishap? You know the rest.

DORIMOND: Yes, I know enough to make up my mind. Madam, restore my daughter to me, and let Clerval's marriage reunite us.

CLERVAL: Ah, uncle!

DORIMOND: Madam, you don't answer?

ORPHISE: I hardly dare, sir, to utter a resolution which perhaps you will find strange. In any other circumstances your kindness would honor Cenia; in our present position, a convent is the only choice that remains for us.

DORIMOND: What! You are refusing me?

ORPHISE: While I admire and respect your virtues, while I acknowledge them with my tears, I cannot accept offers which I would have greatly desired at a happier time. *(to Clerval)* Sir, you promised me a guide; a longer delay would serve only to prolong regrets that we ought to spare all of us. Please cut them short.

CLERVAL *(angrily)*: Yes, madam, yes, you will be obeyed.

Exit.

ORPHISE: I see that my refusal offends you, sir. Indeed, what could you think of the course I am choosing when you ought to expect only gratitude? I am deeply touched by it; and your esteem is too precious to me for me not to buy it with a part of my secret. Be my judge, sir: can I deprive Cenia's father of the right to dispose of his daughter?

CENIA: What! My father is alive? Why isn't he here? Let us hasten to look for him.

ORPHISE: Unhappy Cenia! You will learn all your misfortunes.[116]
Enter Clerval and Dorsainville.

DORIMOND: Clerval, are you here already? My tenderness increases at this dreadful moment. Madam, don't take her away yet; I feel the value of each instant. Sir, you are doubtless that friend of Clerval's who has agreed to assist with the painful circumstance we find ourselves in? If only I could repay this service . . . If Clerval had confided to me earlier . . .

DORSAINVILLE: Sir . . .

DORIMOND: Madam, before you leave us, let's have a full explanation, I implore you. You are warning Cenia of new misfortunes. Should I not know them? Could I not prevent them?

ORPHISE: No, sir. Only the fate that has assembled them over her head can make them cease. Allow me to spare you secrets that ought to be related only to unfeeling hearts.

DORSAINVILLE: The sound of that voice! It brings to my senses a strong excitement . . .

DORIMOND: Sir, I commend them to you. Become their friend and mine.

DORSAINVILLE: Sir, gratitude and friendship have for a long time attached me to your family.

ORPHISE: What do I hear? . . . what a shock . . .

DORIMOND: My dear Cenia! . . .

CENIA: Let me expire in your arms!

ORPHISE: Calamities have changed him; but that voice so dear, is it an illusion?

CENIA: Farewell, Clerval.

CLERVAL (*taking Cenia's hand with great feeling*): Friend, give madam your hand.

DORSAINVILLE: What do I see? . . . I can't possibly doubt it.

ORPHISE: It's he! . . . I'm dying!

DORSAINVILLE: Unfortunate wife, open your eyes; recognize the happiest of men and the tenderest husband.

ORPHISE: Dorsainville! . . . Dear husband! . . . by what good fortune? . . . Cenia, embrace your father.

DORSAINVILLE: Cenia my daughter! Heaven! You shower me with favors!

DORIMOND: What, sir . . .

CLERVAL: Yes, uncle, it is in your home that Marquis Dorsainville finds his happiness and the end of his sufferings.

DORIMOND: I am ready to die of joy. Madam, what excuses I must make to you! Sir, would you refuse Cenia to Clerval's love?

CENIA: Father, you have read my heart; am I worthy of your kindness?

DORSAINVILLE: Could I condemn such just feelings? You owe to Clerval your fortune, your station, your father. (*to Dorimond*) Sir, by giving him my daughter, I still do not repay everything I owe him.

CLERVAL: Cenia . . . madam . . . Uncle, by making me happy, will you leave my brother the dreadful misfortune of your disfavor?

DORIMOND: I will give him enough to live in high society, his native element, but I will not see him. Come then, let's all live together, and may death alone separate us.

ORPHISE: May you enjoy, sir, the happiness that you spread over everyone around you. If excessive kindness is sometimes deceived, it is still the chiefest of virtues.

Exeunt.

END.

NOTES

1. The original plan was to produce a bilingual edition. Because the French texts of the plays are to be published separately, the textual apparatus has been removed from the present volume.

2. A. Joannidès, *La Comédie-Française de 1680 à 1900, Dictionnaire général des pièces et des auteurs* (1901; reprint Geneva: Slatkine, 1970).

3. On the salons, see Carolyn C. Lougee, *Le Paradis des Femmes: Women, Salons, and Social Stratification in Seventeenth-Century France* (Princeton: Princeton UP, 1976); Dorothy A. L. Backer, *Precious Women* (New York: Basic Books, 1974); Evelyn Gordon Bodek, "Salonières and Bluestockings: Educated Obsolescence and Germinating Feminism" in *Feminist Studies* (1976), 197–99.

4. The sole biography of this author is by Fernand Baldensperger, "Françoise Pascal, fille lyonnaise" in his *Etudes d'histoire littéraire* (Paris: Droz, 1939) 1–31.

5. *Le Vieillard amoureux ou l'heureuse feinte* (Lyons: Antoine Offray, 1664) 3. All translations of French quotations are my own.

6. Sophie-Wilma Deierkauf-Holsboer, *Le Théâtre de l'Hôtel de Bourgogne* (Paris: Nizet, 1968–70) 2:109–10.

7. Baldensperger 18.

8. The names of the characters are typical of comedies of the period, and some are particularly appropriate to the character, such as Philon (the lover). The text does not specify where the action is set, but Pascal probably had her native city in mind.

9. The identity of the dedicatee remains a mystery. This is unusual for Pascal, who normally dedicated her compositions to well-known individuals, whose names she would have no reason to hide. The dedication is for the entire volume of *Diverses Poésies*, not for this play specifically.

10. Parnassus is the symbol of poetic inspiration. This speech provides the first hint of Philon's madness, one of his symptoms being that he seems to believe literally in the gods of classical mythology and in their ability to communicate with him.

11. Philon is here presumably inspired by a medieval genre, the blason. When describing female beauty, writers of blasons generally began with the hair and treated the other parts of the body in descending order. Philon's failure to follow this, or any, order prompts Cliton's critique at v. 117.

12. In this scene and again in the scenes with Cliton, Philon mingles aspects of the Christian hell, populated by demons and frightening spirits, with the underworld of mythology, in which Pluto and Proserpina presided over the abode of both blissful and tormented shades. While such confusion was not unusual in the poetry of the time, the assimilation of Pluto's residence to a human palace filled with pages, lackeys, and doormen is clearly parodic.

13. This is the only break in the linking of scenes. Presumably, Cleandre has reentered stealthily before this point and has waited for everyone to leave before approaching Amaranthe's house.

14. This characterization of the three Fates as holding humans in chains is an obvious parody on the part of the author. As Cliton may or may not know, the Fates were said to weave a thread representing each human life, and the breaking of that thread meant death.

15. This is one of the speediest resolutions in the history of comedy. We are left with the impression that the departure of Philon removes the obstacles to all three marriages, although logically this could not be the case. When the play is performed, however, the audience has neither the time nor the inclination to ask for more precise explanations.

16. See Bruce A. Morrissette, *The Life and Works of Marie-Catherine Desjardins (Madame de Villedieu) (1632–1683)* Washington University Studies, New Series 17 (St. Louis, 1947); Micheline Cuénin, *Roman et société sous Louis XIV: Madame de Villedieu (Marie-Catherine Desjardins (1640–1683)* (Lille: Université de Lille and Paris: Honoré Champion, 1979) 25–176.

17. Quoted in Pierre Mélèse, *Le Théâtre et le public à Paris sous Louis XIV 1659–1715* (Paris: Droz, 1934) 131.

18. This synopsis is taken from Henry Carrington Lancaster, *A History of French Dramatic Literature in the Seventeenth Century* (Baltimore: Johns Hopkins, 1929–43) 2:545–46.

19. Tallemant des Réaux, *Historiettes*, ed. Antoine Adam, Bibliothèque de la Pléiade (Paris: Gallimard, 1961) 2:908.

20. Morrissette 76.

21. *Le Registre de La Grange 1659–1685*, ed. Bert Edward Young and Grace Philputt Young (Paris: Droz, 1947) 1:76.

22. Hugues de Lionne (1611–71) was an eminent statesman and diplomat who negotiated a number of important treaties for the French crown. The spelling of proper names (Lione/Lionne) was inconsistent during that period.

23. This and subsequent references to early morning are to assure the audience that the unity of time will be observed. Moncade's disgrace and return to favor will occur in the course of a single day.

24. Lindamira is presumably reading from a book of verse. It is unlikely that the poem is a missive from Moncade or some other admirer.

25. In French tragedy it is common to find a character who, having long concealed a consuming passion, can restrain himself no longer and announces his feelings with an explosive force that sets the plot in motion. Normally, the secret passion is love; here, most unusually, it is self-doubt.

26. The playwright could not possibly have intended this passage to suggest homosexual tendencies in the king. Given Louis' violent distaste for such behavior, the play could never have been staged at court, had anyone interpreted the king's language in that way. The passage, which seems somewhat overblown, perhaps reflects Louis' desire for universal control and adulation.

27. At the end of the preceding act Moncade had resolved to seek the king and try to justify himself.

28. In this and his next speech Moncade presents a series of maxims derived from ancient philosophy, especially the Stoics. Their use here is ironic because the listener, Elvira, has no patience with such old-fashioned ideas.

29. This surprising statement is required in order to preserve the unity of place. However, given Elvira's habit of paying Lindamira unwanted visits in her room (see vv. 370–72), her concern may well be warranted.

30. This soliloquy, filled with apostrophes to emotions and moral abstractions, is clearly in the mold of Corneille, as is the insistence on the link between heroic love and nobility of soul.

31. This love letter contains all the clichés of the gallant style, as Elvira is quick to point out.

32. The only full biography of this author is Alexandre Calame, *Anne de La Roche-Guilhen, romancière huguenote* (Geneva: Droz, 1972). On the play, see also Spire Pitou, "A Forgotten Play: La Roche-Guilhen's *Rare en tout* (1677)," *Modern Language Notes* 72 (1957), 357–60. Her name is often spelled La Roche-Guilhem, but, as Calame has shown, the correct form of her name has a final "n."

33. On French opera in England, see André Tissier, "Robert Cambert à Londres," *Revue musicale* 9 (1927), 101–22; W. H. Grattan Flood, "Cambert et Grabu à Londres," *Revue musicale* 9 (1928), 351–61; Edward J. Dent, *Foundations of English Opera* (New York: Da Capo, 1965), especially 107–08; W. J. Lawrence, "Foreign Singers and Musicians at the Court of Charles II," *Musical Quarterly* (1923), 217–25; Pierre Danchin, "The Foundation of the Royal Academy of Music in 1674 and Pierre Perrin's *Ariane,*" *Theatre Survey* 25 (1984), 55–67.

34. Eleanore Boswell, *The Restoration Court Stage (1660–1702)* (Cambridge: Harvard UP, 1932) 122–23; cf. 112–13.

35. Isabella Bennet, Duchess of Grafton (1667–1723), was daughter and heiress of the Earl of Arlington. In 1672 she was married to Henry Fitzroy (1663–90), natural son of King Charles II. In 1675 Henry acquired the title of first Duke of Grafton. Isabella, who was only ten years old at the time of this play, was still living in her parents' home. Her official marriage to the Duke, who was to have a distinguished military career, did not come until 1679. Isabella, in addition to being the King's daughter-in-law, was also sister-in-law to Lady Sussex, the close friend of the author's protectress, the Duchess de Mazarin.

36. The allegorical prologue with nymphs personifying major rivers was a common feature of court ballets and early French operas. Lully and Quinault's *Alceste* (1674), a work referred to later in this play, began with a similar prologue, featuring as its solo characters the nymphs of the Seine, the Marne, and the Tuileries Palace, plus the goddess Glory.

37. Bellona was the classical goddess of war; here she may represent Louis XIV.

38. Either the personification of the sea, or else the Greek sea god Oceanus, eldest of the Titans.

39. Thetis, a sea goddess, was also the mother of Achilles.

40. The allusion to the presence of the king in the audience was an important feature in French court ballets and operas, as well as in the English masque tradition.

41. Even though a 100-line soliloquy would have been frowned upon by theorists of French classicism, La Roche-Guilhen had few other options for her exposition. Only three members of her cast could take speaking roles; the singers confined themselves exclusively to song and pantomime.

42. Apparently the Nymph remained onstage throughout Act I, although her presence would be largely ignored until the following interlude.

43. The Marais was the theatre district of Paris, as well as the site of many fashionable residences.

44. The amusing neologism in the French ("Tarquiniser") refers to the rape of Lucretia by Sextus Tarquinius, son of the last king of Rome. La Treille's learning is more extensive than what we normally find in the valets of comedy.

45. This may be a thinly veiled allusion to the author's protectress, the Duchess de Mazarin. Hortense Mancini (1646–99), niece of Cardinal Mazarin, had been courted by Charles II during his years of exile in Paris. When she came to live in London in 1675, she accepted a pension from the monarch and a lodging in St. James' Palace, but declined to become his mistress. Her sister, the Duchess de Bouillon, had received the dedication of La Roche-Guilhen's novel *Arioviste* two years earlier and would later be the dedicatee of *Arria and Paetus*.

46. According to the obituary notice for Robert Cambert in the *Mercure* of April 1677, many of the singers he recruited did indeed come from Gascony.

47. This exchange of views about love provides a humorous echo of the main plot.

48. Michel Lambert (1610–96) had been music master at the court of Louis XIV since 1661. He published over twenty collections of airs and was esteemed as the finest singing teacher in Paris. Lully was his son-in-law.

49. It is hard to tell whether this is an allusion to a specific play. There was no shortage of plays, either in England or in France, that featured the anger of women betrayed by their lovers.

50. A clear reference to Lully's *Alceste*, where the barking of the dog Cerberus was represented musically by a wordless quartet of male voices (IV.4). Lully's contemporaries criticized this effect as too undignified for serious opera, and it was cut from subsequent performances and from published scores.

51. It is surprising that La Roche-Guilhen did not specify at least the titles of the English airs used in the performance. The pieces may have been supplied by the young Henry Purcell, or by court composer John Bannister, both of whom wrote much music for the playhouses.

52. Either Isabelle begins a new song here, or else she performs the second verse of the previous song.

53. Matachins were grotesque dancers armed with swords and bucklers.

54. It is possible that Climene enters Isabelle's house at this point and that both ladies come out a few moments later, either to the doorway or onto a balcony, to overhear All-Wondrous' soliloquy.

55. These marriages have been arranged with great haste, since only twenty-two lines have elapsed between Isabelle's exit and Finette's entrance.

56. Eris, the goddess of discord, was often depicted with snakes instead of hair.

57. In this hyperbolic flattery of the British court, Cupid announces that London has replaced Cythera (island in the Aegean Sea, now called Cerigo, site in ancient times of a magnificent temple to Aphrodite) as the abode of love.

58. This is a typical final celebration for comedy-ballets and operas with a happy ending. The contrast between the followers of Cupid and those of Bacchus, followed by a reconciliation, was also found in earlier comedy-

ballets, most notably the original version of Molière's *George Dandin* (1668).

59. The only full biography is Eugène Asse, *Une Nièce du grand Corneille, Mlle Bernard* (Paris: Revue Biblio-Iconographique, 1900). See also Eugène Cassin, "Catherine Bernard," *Revue de Rouen et de Normandie* (1845), 228–31; Catherine Plusquellec, "Qui était Catherine Bernard?" *Revue d'histoire littéraire de la France* 85 (1985), 667–69.

60. Abbé Trublet made this accusation in the *Mercure* of 1757; Voltaire included it in his *Siècle de Louis XIV*, "Catalogue des écrivains français" (published 1751).

61. Asse 38, from *Mercure galant* of December 1690.

62. Justin (Marcus Julianus Justinus), *The Abridgment of the Histories of Trogus Pompeius*, tr. Arthur Goldyng (London: Thomas Marshe, 1564), fol. 117r (28.3), with my own emendation. In the Latin edition which I consulted, *Ex Trogi Pompeii Historia, Libri* 44 (London: Bynneman, 1572), her name is spelled Laodomia (p. 250).

63. Catherine Bernard probably did not know the work of the Greek military historian Polyaenus, who calls our heroine Deidamia and describes her as a warrior maiden who succeeded in capturing a rebellious city and dictating a peace treaty in which the Epirots would acknowledge her hereditary rights. In this account, a group of Epirot malcontents hired Milo, a man already known to be guilty of parricide, to assassinate her. This he did while she was in the temple of Diana Hegemone. See *Stratagems of War*, tr. R. Shepherd (Chicago: Ares Publishers, 1974) 353 (8.52).

64. René Louis de Voyer de Paulmy, Marquis d'Argenson, *Notices sur les Oeuvres de théâtre*, ed. H. Lagrave, in *Studies on Voltaire and the Eighteenth Century* Nos. 42–43 (1966), 1:315, 324–25.

65. With the exception of the two sisters, Gelon and Milo, all the characters are fictional. Their names, drawn from classical history or mythology, may have been deliberately chosen because they were already familiar from earlier French plays. There is no dedication since the play was not published until long after the author's death. Bernard dedicated her second tragedy, *Brutus,* to the Duchess de Bourbon, daughter of Louis XIV and Mme de Montespan.

66. This verse signals that the unity of time will be observed: the action occurs on the day arranged for Attale's return and victory celebration, on which occasion he is to set the date of his wedding to Laodamia.

67. These characters, mentioned only once in the play, are fictional. The name Cineas, which is found in Justin XVIII.2, refers there to a minister of King Pyrrhus of Epirus, a brilliant orator and alleged pupil of Demosthenes.

68. This public demonstration on behalf of Gelon is the first of multiple interventions by the common people and the soldiers, who, though unseen, play a significant role in the action.

69. As often happens in the last act of French tragedies, time is speeded up. Hardly enough time has elapsed since Gelon's exit (at v. 1276) for so much action to occur.

70. This seems an inadequate reason for the wounded queen to enter the temple, but Bernard, in the one passage where she tries to be faithful to history, felt it necessary to have her heroine die there.

71. Bernard altered and speeded up the death of Milo, who, according to Justin, went mad and died painfully from self-inflicted wounds after twelve days. She thus achieves a clearer impression of poetic justice, as well as observing the unity of time. The lynching of a wicked advisor may have been inspired by the death of Narcisse in Racine's *Britannicus*.

72. The fullest study of her life and works is Charles Michau, "Le Théâtre de Mlle Barbier," *Mémoires de la Société d'Agriculture, Sciences, Belles-lettres et Arts d'Orléans* 75 (1906), 117–38. See also Henry Carrington Lancaster, *Sunset: A History of Parisian Drama in the Last Years of Louis XIV, 1701–1715* (Baltimore: Johns Hopkins, 1945), 69–70.

73. The *privilège* (royal permission needed for publication) for the 1745 edition of her collected plays, dated 19 July 1743, and registered 23 July 1743, reads in part: "I, Marie-Anne Barbier, acknowledge giving up to M. Briasson the privilège which I obtained for my mother's works, in conformity with the agreements made between us." I am at a loss to understand this statement, unless we are dealing with a serious typographical error. If we accept 1745 as the date of her death, why would she delegate such a negotiation to anyone else? Did she have a daughter? If so, would the girl be named Marie-Anne Barbier, exactly like her mother (unless, perhaps, she was illegitimate)? If Barbier had married at some point in her life, why

insist on the name "Mademoiselle Barbier" for the privilège and the title page? Moreover, even after her death, she was invariably referred to as Mademoiselle Barbier.

74. Perhaps the most grotesque indignity was Voltaire's charge, in the preface to his tragedy *La Mort de César* (1736), that Barbier wrote her play of the same name (1709) in collaboration with Fontenelle, whom she probably never even met. Voltaire, who took a violent dislike to any author, living or dead, who treated the same subjects as he did, was presumably not even trying to be objective. He also criticized Barbier for weakening the plot by adding a love interest. The brothers Parfaict claimed, likewise with no foundation, that Abbé Pellegrin, with whom she collaborated on two of her opera libretti, was the real author of her spoken plays. No subsequent scholars have taken these charges seriously.

75. Martial, *Epigrams*, tr. Walter C. A. Ker (Cambridge and London: Harvard UP and William Heineman, 1968) 39.

76. Cassius Dio, *Dio's Roman History*, tr. Earnest Cary (Cambridge and London: Harvard UP and William Heineman, 1961–69) 7:407–09.

77. Pliny the Younger, *Letters and Panegyricus*, tr. Betty Radice (Cambridge and London: Harvard UP and William Heineman, 1969) 1: 221 (letter to Maecilius Nepos).

78. Marie-Anne Mancini, Duchess de Bouillon (1646–1714), niece of Mazarin, became in her later years a patroness of letters.

79. The story of Arria was indeed well-known, since earlier writers, both in France and elsewhere, had often cited her as a model of female heroism. Barbier does not seem to have known Gabriel Gilbert's earlier tragedy on the same subject, *Arie et Petus, ou les amours de Neron* (1660). The two plays have several similarities, especially the emperor's love for the heroine and his willingness to get rid of his current wife in order to marry her, and a stormy meeting for the female leads in which the empress fails to understand the heroine's nobility of character. But these are far outweighed by the differences between the tragedies, including, to cite just the most obvious, Gilbert's choice of Nero as the emperor, and the fact that the latter is already married to his passionate, but not politically astute, second wife, Poppaea.

80. Edme Boursault (1638–1701), best remembered today for his enmity to Molière and Boileau, was a highly respected playwright, several of whose

comedies remained in the repertory for many generations. Corneille was his mentor and lifelong friend.

81. Madeleine de Scudéry (1607–1701) was an extremely influential novelist and salon hostess. Henriette de Coligny, Countess de La Suze (1618–73) published several volumes of poetry. Mme Deshoulières, born Antoinette du Ligier de La Garde (1634–94), was highly esteemed as a poet and was an ardent champion of the Moderns; she also wrote a tragedy. Her daughter, Antoinette-Thérèse Deshoulières (1662–1718), also wrote poetry; although less celebrated than her mother, she won the poetry prize of the French Academy in 1688.

82. Messalina was executed in 48; Agrippina became empress the following year.

83. Agrippina was Claudius' niece. The emperor was obliged to change the laws, since marriage between uncle and niece was traditionally considered incestuous.

84. Germanicus was brother of Claudius, nephew of Tiberius, and father of Caligula and Agrippina. A dashing and popular military commander, he died in Syria in 19. It was widely suspected that the governor of Syria had poisoned him.

85. This is the first in a series of references to divine justice, a cliché in French classical drama, serving to indicate that the virtuous characters are part of a cosmic moral order. But, as Arria observes in the second act, the intervention of the gods to punish human villainy is often long delayed.

86. In all editions Agrippina enters, not with her own confidante, Julia, but with her rival's confidante, Flavia. Since this is manifestly absurd, and since there would be no reason for the confidante, if she were present, not to remain at v. 616, I have eliminated the name altogether.

87. This is an aesthetic blunder on Barbier's part, since Arria will have the same prophetic vision, expressed more vividly, as she is dying (vv. 1602–06). It is generally believed that Agrippina poisoned Claudius.

88. The fasces (bundles of rods and axes) were the visible symbols of authority, borne by lictors who attended Roman kings; following the expulsion of the kings, the fasces were retained by the consuls.

89. Given that her dying father ordered her to marry Paetus, and that their love is mutual, it is hard to see why Arria should have waited until

this moment to agree to the marriage. Her fear of seeming immodest if she runs away with a man who is not yet her husband may be a deliberate echo of Aricie in Racine's *Phèdre*.

90. Nero, mentioned here for the only time in the play, was born in 37. Agrippina arranged for him to marry Claudius' daughter Octavia, and later for Claudius to adopt him. He did in fact murder his mother in 59. The story of the astrologers' prediction and Agrippina's reaction to it is derived from Tacitus, *Annals* XIV.9.

91. This port at the mouth of the Tiber had been annexed to Rome during the period of the kings.

92. This line, placed in the mouth of one of Paetus' enemies, shows the lengths to which Barbier was prepared to go in rehabilitating her hero.

93. Consuls wore a purple border around their garments; they donned a full purple toga (originally one of the trappings of royalty) only on festival days or when celebrating a triumph.

94. When the Roman Empire was established, many of the offices from the republican period, including the senate, were retained, although with greatly reduced power.

95. Caligula, who died in 41, was Claudius' nephew and immediate predecessor.

96. Cassius Chaerea and Gaius Sabinus were the principal assassins of Caligula. Claudius, who knew that they had also plotted his own death, ordered their execution.

97. Augustus had divorced his wife Scribonia in order to marry Livia, the grandmother of Claudius.

98. Presumably, the confidante, who fails to guess Arria's intentions, returns to her apartment, rather than remaining outside to keep watch. She does not reappear in the play.

99. Although this cry of despair and remorse makes an effective ending to the play, the spectators are supposed to remember that Claudius did not die until many years later, in 54.

100. The most extensive biography is Georges Noël, *Une "Primitive" oubliée de l'école des "coeurs sensibles": Madame de Grafigny (1695–1758)* (Paris: Plon, 1913). See also the edition of Graffigny's complete correspondence, of which

three volumes have so far appeared: *Correspondance,* ed. English Showalter, Jr. et al. (Oxford: Voltaire Foundation and Taylor Institution, 1985–).

101. The play received ecstatic reviews. Baron Grimm actually declared, "There is no man of talent and merit in France who would not be delighted to be the author of this play" (letter of 15 July 1754) (*Correspondance littéraire* [Paris: Furne et Ladrange, 1829] 1:176–80). Rousseau in the *Lettre à M. d'Alembert sur son article Genève* praises both Graffigny and her play, even though he claims in principle that women are incapable of being good writers (ed. Michel Launay [Paris: Garnier-Flammarion, 1967] 114). Lessing, in his *Hamburgische Dramaturgie,* praises the style and characterization (letter 20 [7 July 1767]), while criticizing Luise Gottsched's overly prolix German translation. In letter 53 of the same collection (3 November 1767) he argues against the accusation that *Cenia* was really the work of a man and defends against Rousseau the principle that women can achieve literary distinction. For a sampling of contemporary tributes, see Noël 240–50. Among the other letters and pamphlets that followed the play's Paris premiere, an anonymous *Lettre à Madame *** sur Cénie, Comédie en Prose et en cinq Actes* praises Graffigny for forging a new language of sentiment, "Never, madam, has anyone created the language of the heart or varied it with so much elegance and purity" (5). The story that Diderot considered *Cenia* as the single most important precursor of the *drame* is apparently apocryphal.

102. Noël iii–vi, 377.

103. According to Félix Gaiffe, *Le Drame en France au XVIIIe siècle* (Paris: Armand Colin, 1910), Diderot is the undisputed inventor of the new genre. Gustave Lanson, *Nivelle de La Chaussée et la comédie larmoyante* (1903; reprint New York: Burt Franklin, 1971) thinks that title belongs to La Chaussée. He contemptuously dismisses *Cenia* in just one sentence, "a play analogous to *La Gouvernante* in its subject matter, which caused the earlier play to be forgotten but was not nearly so good" (276).

104. This discussion is especially indebted to Lanson, *Nivelle de La Chaussée* 232–65.

105. The name Cénie (here anglicized as Cenia) was apparently invented by Mme de Graffigny, as an anagram of the word "nièce." The niece in question was Minette de Ligniville, who had come to live with her early in 1749. The wealthy financier and *philosophe* Helvétius, one of the regular visitors to the Graffigny salon, fell in love with Minette. After more

than two years of complications and delays, largely stemming from family opposition, they were wed on August 14, 1751. It was widely believed at the time that Cenia's situation and character were directly modeled after those of the future Mme Helvétius.

106. Louis de Bourbon-Condé, Count de Clermont (1709–71) did indeed distinguish himself in a number of campaigns during the War of the Austrian Succession (although in the following decade he would be responsible for several disastrous defeats in the Seven Years' War). The Count was extremely interested in literature and got himself elected to the French Academy in 1754. He also gave Graffigny considerable assistance in negotiating with the Comédie-Française.

107. During the second half of the eighteenth century the rehabilitation, even glorification, of the businessman was to become a commonplace in French drama. Dorimond does not make clear how he could have retained his rights as a nobleman while engaging in commerce, since the aristocracy were forbidden to participate in profit-making activities.

108. The edicts against dueling, first promulgated by Cardinal Richelieu a century earlier, were still in effect. The victor in a duel risked arrest unless he immediately fled the country, and in many cases his property would be confiscated, as well. As a convenient dramatic device for separating men from their wives and children for many years and then allowing for tearful reunions, the duel was often employed by authors of *drames*.

109. This speech may reflect the author's personal experience. In 1740, following the death of her protectress, Mme de Richelieu, Graffigny found herself penniless and without a home, only to discover that the convent of the Filles Sainte-Elisabeth was unwilling to shelter her for more than a few months as a charity case.

110. This unusually extended discussion of woman's lot allows the author to air some of her personal views and grievances.

111. There is a hint of the standard device known as the call of blood: Orphise feels a special attachment to Cenia long before she learns that the girl is her daughter.

112. Cenia's pity for Clerval but not for herself is clearly a transposition, in a non-tragic register, of the convention that mingled stoicism with passionate love in the personality of the ideal dramatic heroine.

113. Dorimond's fortune must be enormous for Mericourt to involve himself in such a scheme (if the motivation indicated here is indeed the determining one): the old man has already promised him a quarter of it, and Mericourt could not expect to inherit more than three-quarters of it even if he married Cenia, unless he could somehow manage to have Clerval disinherited.

114. Clerval seems to forget that Cenia has never made any commitment to him and has not yet revealed her love for him.

115. This discussion of prejudice, with hints of natural law, stamps Clerval as a *philosophe*.

116. An interesting example of dramatic irony: Cenia's wish to seek her father is immediately followed by his arrival. Of course, the suspense in such a play depends on the author's skill in keeping two crucial characters (here, Orphise and Dorsainville) from meeting until the last possible moment.